THE FACEBOOK OF THE DEAD

Also by Valerie Laws
from Red Squirrel Press

Crime:
The Rotting Spot
(Bruce and Bennett Mystery 1, 2009)
The Operator
(Bruce and Bennett Mystery 11, 2014)

Poetry:
All That Lives
(poetry of sex, death and pathology. 2011)

Other books by Valerie Laws include
Lydia Bennet's Blog
Quantum Sheep
Moonbathing
Changing Age, Changing Minds
Hadaway
Star Trek—the Poems

Poet, crime novelist, performer, playwright,
Writer-in-Residence at science institutes,
sci-art installation specialist, mathematician,
Valerie Laws has had thirteen books published.
www.valerielaws.com

THE FACEBOOK of the Dead

Poems

VALERIE LAWS

RED SQUIRREL PRESS

First published in the UK in 2014 by Red Squirrel Press
www.redsquirrelpress.com

Red Squirrel Press is distributed by Central Books Ltd.
and represented by Inpress Books Ltd.
www.inpressbooks.co.uk

Designed and typeset by Gerry Cambridge
gerry.cambridge@btinternet.com

Cover image: Cursive hieroglyphs from the Papyrus of Ani,
an example of the Egyptian *Book of the Dead*

A CIP record is available from The British Library.

ISBN: 978 1 906700 966

Printed by Martins the Printers
www.martins-the-printers.co.uk

Acknowledgments

The following poems won awards and/or were previously published in books, magazines, anthologies or online:

'Water's Bright Words (A Quantum Haiku)' was commissioned by BBC 2 TV for their documentary *Why Poetry Matters* presented by Griff Rhys Jones, filmed and activated at Hackney Lido by me, Griff, and volunteers in the pool with the words on inflated beach balls. It was also performed live at Royal Festival Hall, London. (Video is on YouTube or my site valerielaws.com.) It was published in *Maintenant 6* (Dada anthology, Three Rooms Press, New York City, 2012).

'Acute Mountain Sickness: Everest' was featured on BBC Radio 4's *World at One*, and won 2nd Prize in the 2014 Hippocrates NHS Awards for Poetry and Medicine (and like all such prizewinners below, was published in the corresponding winners' anthology).

'Pestering an Eye Research Neuroscientist' won a Commended Prize in the 2014 Hippocrates Awards.

'Hitting the road with Frida Kahlo' won 3rd Prize in the 2013 Cardiff International Poetry Competition and was published in *New Welsh Review*.

'Keepers' was published in *Poetry Review*.

'1981: Kraftwerk? Ja, Danke' and 'God is a DJ' were published in the *Double Bill* anthology, ed. Andy Jackson (Red Squirrel Press 2014).

'Best Selling: Father and Son Hunting Package Deals' was published in the anthology *For Rhino in a Shrinking World* ed. Harry Owen (The Poets' Printery, South Africa 2013, all proceeds to rhino conservation). It was read aloud by Harry at the Global March for Lions, Grahamstown, SA, a protest against canned hunting.

‘At a stroke: collateral circulation’ won Commended Prize in the 2013 Hippocrates Awards (NHS).

‘Arab Spring, America’s Fall’ was published in *The Robin Hood Book: Verses Versus Austerity*, ed. Alan Morrison and Angela Topping (Caparison 2012) and quoted in the *Morning Star* review.

‘Mrs Bennet’s Burden’ was published in *Advice on Proposals*, poems inspired by Jane Austen, ed. Angela Topping (Like This Press, 2014).

‘Chainsaw Massacre’ was published in *Sweet Breast and Acid Tongue*, poems inspired by William Shakespeare, ed. Angela Topping (Like This Press, 2014). It was also published in *Not on our Green Belt*, ed. Lindsey Holland (North West Poets 2013) and originally in *Quantum Sheep* (Peterloo).

‘Scent for a Suffragette’ was commissioned for the Penning Perfumes project and published in the anthology ed. Claire Trevien. It was a response to Lush scent *The smell of weather turning*.

‘Retirement speech of a Swarovski Crystal from Stella McCartney’s “Lucky Spot”’ was published in *The Ofi Press Magazine* (Mexico City) in English and Spanish.

‘A Question for Neuroscientists’ won a Commended Prize in 2012 NHS Hippocrates Awards.

‘Plants Mirror Minds (a Quantum Haiku)’ was commissioned for my ongoing Residency at Dilston Physic Garden, Northumberland, which grows mind-altering medicinal plants. The quantum haiku is activated on water, each word carved on wooden ‘leaves’. Also commissioned was ‘Remembering Love: a Scent Spell’ which had a perfume which aids memory created for it by Dr Nicolette Perry.

'Debridement I–II' were published in my anti-ageism book *Changing Age, Changing Minds* (IAH, University of Newcastle, 2011).

'Apoptosis: Cell Suicide I–II' is a version of the sequence created for Wellcome Trust-funded project *This Fatal Subject*, animated on film by Barney Quinton and Susan Aldworth (featuring her artwork), shown in exhibitions in Gordon Museum and in Old Operating Theatre Museum, London.

Published online, as part of activist and/or literary projects:

'The Sex Life of Slugs' in *Against Rape* (http://peonymoon.wordpress.com/) and formerly in the joint collection *For Crying Out Loud* (Iron Press).

'Free! All-you-can-read Buffet' in *Writers for Libraries* (http://writersforlibraries.wordpress.com).

'Baking Scones for Eminem' in *The Great British Bard-Off* (http://greatbritishbardoff.blogspot.co.uk/2012/09/baking-scones-for-eminem-by-valerie-laws.html).

'Boundless Heart' and four other Selkie songs were written for my play *The Selkie*, commissioned for Cloud Nine, which premiered at Sage Gateshead and toured. Music by The Keelers who performed the songs on stage along with Katie Doherty as The Selkie herself.

'Lowering the Teaune' was written for Archers fan Val McDermid who always thought of Caroline Bone spelled this way and always wanted Caroline and Shula to get together!

Many of the 'Pathology' poems result from my funded Residencies at Gordon Museum of Pathology, London: Anatomy Dept, Kings College London: Institute for Ageing and Health (also access to Institute of Neuroscience), Newcastle University: Leeds Hospitals for TONIC via Char March. For many more pathology-related poems on the science of dying, see my previous collection *All That Lives.*

My thanks to all who assisted in these projects and as ever, to my publisher Sheila Wakefield, Founder and Managing Editor of Red Squirrel Press.

Contents

Hitting the Road with Frida Kahlo / 13
The Facebook of the Dead / 14
Baking Scones for Eminem / 16
Speed Dating for Tortoises / 17
When Satan was My Boyfriend / 18
Mrs Bennet's Burden / 19
Ophelia's Sista / 20
1981: Kraftwerk? Ja, Danke / 21
God is a DJ / 23
Retirement Speech of a Swarovski Crystal / 24
Our Lady of the Mascaras / 25
Phone Sex / 26
Lowering the Teaune / 28
Song from The Selkie: Boundless Heart / 29
Scent for a Suffragette / 30
Water's Bright Words: a Quantum Haiku / 32
Epithalamion / 33
Will She be Stuffed? / 37
Keepers / 38
My Pet Dead Bat / 40
Acute Mountain Sickness: Everest / 41
At a Stroke: Collateral Circulation / 43
Apoptosis: Cell Suicide I / 44
Apoptosis: Cell Suicide II / 45
A Question for Neuroscientists / 46
Pestering an Eye Research Neuroscientist / 48
To a Friend undergoing ECT / 50
A Comfortable Fiction / 51
Deathbed Writing Workshop:
I: Debridement / 52
II: Sharing the Work / 53
Murder Should Out / 54

Skinbound Baby / 56
Conjoined Parasitic Head / 57
Plants Mirror Minds : A Quantum Haiku / 58
Remembering Love: A Scent Spell / 59
Free! All-You-Can-Read-Buffet / 63
'Best Selling: Father and Son Hunting Package Deals' / 64
The Sex Life of Slugs / 66
Chainsaw Massacre / 67
Arab Spring, America's Fall / 68

For my son Robin and my daughter Lydia,
with love

Hitting the Road with Frida Kahlo

The sound of my thirteen bones breaking
Rings through my limbs, the world slows
Down, slooowwwws right down, the noise I'm
Making a deep bass mooing. The dashboard
Travelling in towards my knees crawls
Like a glacier, my feet, leg, ribs, arm
Already smashed. This point on this road
Will always be where this happened. I know
That when the car stops spinning, everything
Will have changed. Time after time I live it
Through the years, the impact, see the sunburst
Explode through glass, crazed splinters fly
Like photons of light, tiny needles still
Rebounding out of my face six weeks on.

This time, as my car slip-slides over the A19,
Frida's there, her bones splitting, body pierced
By the javelin hand-rail of her bus as mine will be
By surgeons, flesh and metal forced to mesh.
Her dark eyes hold my green. Her brown hand
Holds my white right hand, the one without
The bones poked through the wrist. We learn
The weakness of steel, the persistence of pain,
The strength of skin and scar, the euphoria
Of living to paint, to write, to love. Crushed
And buckled bus, trolley and cars stop dead,
Write-offs. I clamber out, broken bones grating,
Scrunching like brown sugar, fall down
To lie on the icy road, beginning my new life
Looking up at a sky as blue as hers in Mexico.

The Facebook of the Dead

(For my friend LH)

In life we leave the dead behind. On Facebook
They gallop along with us, like racehorses
Whose jockeys have been jettisoned. Like you,
Your life cut short but not your timeline, though
Your relationship status, life events, favourite
Films and books will never change again.

We go out without you on your birthday then
Write on your wall to tell you about it as if
You can read our words on some virtual
Laptop though you can't reply. We tag you
As if you can feel it, feel us thinking of you,
Remembering that night, yes that one, LOL!
One posts to tell you he's saved your number
On a new phone, as if you can see his message
But he can't text you—it's complicated.

We tell you where you are. Resting in peace,
You 'Rip', but with us in spirit, here beside us,
No, watching from above; sleeping with the angels
But no, you're giving them merry hell up there, I mean
What are you like! We gift you the greed of our grief
As boys compete to be your bezzie mate, the worst hurt;
Girls line up to be your widow, claim the most kisses.

Scrolling down the papyrus of your page I travel
Back in time through the confused, incredulous
Comments as your updated status spread: dead.
Many saw it on Facebook first, I at second hand
Seeing her face drain white as she looked at her phone
As if charging it with her blood, a transfusion too late.

Go back far enough, down, down, suddenly it's your voice
Speaking, your last comments which you didn't know would
Be your last. A bit crack, a bit banter, irony, witty put-downs,
RIP Richard Griffiths, plans for the future, all four days of it.

Your cheeky profile pic pops up among my friends, weighing
On my heart each time I catch your eye, and if I could,
I'd unfriend Death for you, report him for abuse, the troll
Who poked you, who is 'following' us all, block him for good.

Note: 'Rip': as well as a misspelling of RIP, rip is a Tyneside word for a lively, mischievous lad.

Baking Scones for Eminem

Someone should be. Someone should be
Walking through the door with a heavy tray,
Steam rising from scones like puffball clouds
Golden and swollen, light as fluff, jam
Glowing ruby, warm as mother's blood,
Primrose-cool butter waiting calmly
To spread and melt. And Marshall, he
Should be slouching on a suburb sofa
Which has seen better days and sticky
Fingers, and he should spring erect
At the scent of new baking as flour, fat,
Sugar make their music, and she
Will say, casually swiping his feet
In their box-fresh fuck-off trainers
Off the coffee table with a hand
Trained by years of nose-wiping,
'Now now, Marshall!' as she lets
The tray land like a spacecraft
Bringing peace to earth. Not me,
Even though my heavenly scones
Could save him, free him to sing
Of something more than money
And how crap his childhood was.
I've been there, done that
With the mothering, the Be-Ro
And the Stork. Still doing it. Still
Having different ideas about muscular
Younger men on sofas, even Slim
With his antimacassar of tattoos,
Though butter and jam could still be
Involved. Not me, then.

But someone should be.

Speed Dating for Tortoises

Introduced while unconscious, chilly and withdrawn,
Though both are unattached; an unpromising start
For a romance to bring them out of their shells.
Over tea and lemon drizzle in the cold lounge
Both families meet to matchmake, and rehome
Him, recently widowed, with her, alone and celibate.
We speculate, is his prospective lady straight, and
Definitely female? Is her plastron dished or flat? Hard
To remember what it looked like last November.

They are fifty-odd, still horny teens in tortoise-years,
Dreaming Greek sun still straddles their checkerboard
Backs, speed-dating their reptilian blood to arousal.
The tock-tock of shells meeting is a memory timing
Their sleep. We agree their first date will wait for spring.
Waking with a stranger after four month's sleep could be
A shock resulting in the slowest-ever walk of shame.

Leaving amid shavings of snow, I wonder if
He and I were hibernating all along in separate icy
Boxes, only dreaming our shared summer: if love
Had not survived the winter, but was already
An empty shell waiting to be discovered.

When Satan was My Boyfriend

Yes, I had a crush on Satan. Well, every girl
Loves a bad boy in her teens. I'd sit in school
Scrawling on my books in pseudo-Tudor swirls
With more serif than sense, 'Satan lives!'
Between boyband cuties, the devil was my date,
Strutting, sneering, the ultimate rebel, getting
In God's face until that uptight buzzkill Dad
Grounded him for good for his bad attitude.
Lucifer Lightbearer with rock star looks,
Muscles and charisma, no respect, rising
From the fire still full of hell... what more
Could a girl desire? Who'd want an angel,
Singing songs of praise (that dreary TV show)
For ever, end of? What kind of egomaniac creates
A cosmos, just to hear Himself hymned? Milton
Tried to justify the wrong guy: William Blake
Was my devil's advocate, Satan's 'Paradise Lost' PR.

In time I found paradise in more earthly arms,
The Pandemonium of adolescence left behind
With Satan. But our world outdid him long ago with sins
More diabolical by far than his refusal to sing hymns,
My fallen star, my Jimmy Dean with wings.

Mrs Bennet's Burden

My nerves are married to his indifference. So handsome
He was once, and I a beauty, but we have rubbed each other
Against the grain, worn away our early bloom. Girl after girl,
A row of bonnets burdening his budget. Is he punishing
My womb's refusal to house his son? If he even cares
That much. His library is his cozy refuge from my terror,
From his daughters' need of him, and it is his for life.
I watch him at table daily for signs of apoplexy, dropsy,
Fever, for the end of him will end our lives at Longbourn.
Out in the cold, five wombs now for sale or hire become
Five warm young bodies, I their desperate pander, dignity
Beyond my purse. He loves to teaze me, dangle bachelors
Like trinkets in my face, shame me with his mockery of my
Husband-hunting ways, my restless suspense, waiting
To lose my home with losing him, to starve in the ditch perhaps
As Lucases and Longs drive by, smugly blind. Anyone,
Any men, who'll take my girls will do, if they can give that
Precious gift, a roof. I had such hopes of lovely Jane, Lizzy's
Eyes, Lydia's boldness, Kitty's youth, Mary's biddability,
Hopes that dwindle with each grey hair on his complacent head.
If I could wish for more than home and sustenance,
It would be that my daughters spare me the grief of seeing them
Unable to respect their partner in life, for I know how it hurts.
But alone, I cannot afford that luxury for my lovely girls.

Note & Attribution: '...the grief of seeing you unable to respect your partner in life' is said by Mr Bennet to Lizzy, in Pride and Prejudice *by Jane Austen. It could just as easily have been said by his long-suffering wife.*

Ophelia's Sista

So her boyfriend goes mad, starts vacillating—
Seeing his dead dad's ghost, exacerbating
His mother issues. Reach for the tissues,
Woe is him, no longer nice, still dim.
Dumps our sis, goodbye wedded bliss;
Listen, Hamlet. To make an omelette,
Eggs get broken, soliloquies get spoken.
Get over it, move on. Your daddy's gone,
And so's our dad: that was Hamlet's bad,
Dishing out death for eavesdropping. Stopping
Our father's heart was just the start
Of the Elsinore blood-letting, the insanity getting
Into our Feels, who decides to join the eels,
Head for the water. Not Polonius' only daughter,
Not she, for a start there's me.
I'm not one to lie around in ponds,
Letting things drift, there's steel under my shift,
Not sticklebacks. It's not that our brother lacks
Get up and go, but Laertes is gung ho,
Lots of sword-waving, almost as raving
As Prince Danish Bacon. When in drink taken
He'll switch from bone idle to full-on suicidal.
No, *I'll* kick Hamlet's arras, though I'm but a lass,
Egg them all on to do each other in, then bin
The corrupt aristocracy, set up a democracy.
This is one monarchy best forgotten, yes,
The system in Denmark is well and truly rotten.

We'll have one last outburst of domestic violence
For the one percent—for the rest, no more silence.

1981: Kraftwerk? Ja, danke.

Kraftwerk at Newcastle City Hall. They are the future,
Like robots singing love songs to machines. They
Are the anti-matter to more earthly stars—it's all
About them, not being about them. We get it. So cool
To be cold. Teutonic, perfect, disciplined, yet something
Joyful, yearning, troubled filters through the synthesised
Sound, as if computers have souls. I wear flying suits. I
Am the future too, borrow farmer friends' overalls at first
Until boutiques catch up with me. We dance like robots,
Our faces blank, our actions repetitive as our music. Decadent
Yet mechanical, our nightclubs are Roman orgies re-created
On Saturn. We long to see the band, part of me still expects
Heavy metal's love me, fuck me, stage-front writhing
But they are at the back lined up like showroom dummies,
Their neon name-boards taking centre stage. They play.
The music's perfect, nothing distorted but the band themselves.
Each stands beside his replica; eight androids. Strobe lights
  flicker,
Making real men fake and models seem to move. Just once,
With tiny instruments on palms they venture to the front, play
Pocket Calculator. Then into the pause before applause a yell,
Human, joyful, yearning from our ranks: 'I love you, Florian!'

All four freeze, almost shyly scuttle back behind their consoles
As the crowd laughs warmly, a wave of love like radioactivity
Pursuing them off stage. I picture them sitting still, recharging,
Waiting for daylight, can't bear to imagine fags, porn mags,
Cans of lager, fart jokes in that tour bus. In my near future
On an autobahn in Sunderland I'm left part-metal with a robot
  walk.
Now decades on the technology to fix me, make me pain-free,
  perfect

As a machine still waits off stage. The tweeting android in my
palm
Tells me Kraftwerk, three of them replicants, will be playing at
Tate Modern, but not, I hope, to the gallery. They are still
the future.

God is a DJ

(Amin van Buuren, A State Of Trance @ Privilege, Ibiza, July 2013)

No longer secret but still a cult, we faithful mass together
In a dark cathedral of ice, fire, lasers, glitter, acrobats
Instead of architecture. We dance with our arms reaching
Beyond the lofty roof, in heaven but still aspiring higher,
Our hands pulled up by music, in a State of Trance.
Thousands of us, blissful, euphoric, lifted above ourselves,
Full of love for each other and for Armin. Even his name
Almost a prayer, our smiling deity raises his own arms wide
In benediction. We feel right through us the soaring, building
Heartbeat of House, the waiting, waiting for the tune to break—
The ecstasy of release, the glorious electronic chords,
The flowing, intertwining riffs, the voices pure, angelic.

We are happy.

This is the blessing of religion, without the thou shalt nots,
The hate, the torture, oppression, hypocrisy, war.
Yet this is what was driven underground when ravers met
In empty factories gifted, ironically, by Thatcher the antichrist.
Persecuted by the law, they spread the Word through holy texts,
Driven to party at the extremes of the M25. Pleasure's a threat
To governments. But why? Why do they all adopt the dark side
Of religion, instead of this pure joy? Tonight if god is love,
God is a DJ, one of many, and we are one, the Privileged,
Our fingers stretched to touch Ibiza's stars, feel them tingle
Like frosty glitter against our skin. Our faces upturned
To receive the host's communion, chanting our responses
We are grateful not humble, all of us raised up, equally high.

Note: 'God is a DJ': trance track from the album Sunday 8PM *by Faithless, 1998.*

Retirement Speech of a Swarovski Crystal From Stella McCartney's 'Lucky Spot'

(Seen on a poster: 'Sale of retired Swarovski crystals')

It's not easy, always having to shine. Breathing
Light in, out, simultaneously like playing
A didgeridoo with circular breath, it's wearying.
Quivering like a dewdrop in a lupin leaf, but
Never allowed to evaporate, is limiting.
I have always wanted to follow the light I give,
Upwards and away, rising rain, to pause
High up, a tiny spherical rainbow, tasting
The indigo deliciousness of falling. But no.
Threaded on wire to give the illusion of a horse
I can't see, nor feel its muscled leap, held fast
Yet having to be bright at all times, never a dull
Moment, oh, the strain of it. From the minute
I was ground, my faces cut by many blades
Powered by beck and burn, forcing waterlight
Into my pores, I have beamed constantly. I am
My own tear, which never brims or drops.

Now retired, put out to glass, sold off, I may
Have to settle for some part-time sparkling.
But I still dream of flight, of flaming to earth
A many-coloured meteorite.

'Lucky Spot' was exhibited at Belsay Hall, Northumberland

Our Lady of the Mascaras

At the retreat house window, light floods in
Like a blessing, pinging the sacred heart
Of my crimson Marc Jacobs compact mirror.
Applying mascara, I'm hoping for a *False*
Lash Effect. True blondes are tried
And found wanting in the eyelash area.
It's mortifying. I lay on the strokes, heavy
Black around the blue, *maximising impact.*
Suddenly outside I see a nun, spare, short, brittle,
Outlined in a habit sooty-black as Maybelline
And I wonder if she's a *fan of spectacular lashes*
In her *inky shade of Endless Black*. Whether
She ever goes outside without her slap on.

Phone Sex

Phone sex, phone sex,
Better than being alone sex,
Let your fingers do the walking,
While you trade some dirty talking
And for the hottest telephone date
Set your mobile to vibrate.

It's cheap, it's fun, it's comfortable;
You can hear him shout, 'God almighty!'
When you say you're wearing body paint
Though it's really a flannelette nightie.

You can surprise your special guy
If you know when he's going to phone;
Start without him, then when he rings let fly,
Pour out every moan and groan.

He'll love it; though last time I did that
I heard a strange voice say, 'Amazing!
We don't normally get cold call customers
So thrilled about our double glazing!'

If the kids or your grandma walk in
When you're making the phone lines hum,
You might have trouble talking
As it's hard to converse in mid-come.

You can hastily hide your sex toy
Or pretend it's for curling your hair
But it's harder to switch off your sex noise
When you've made all the street car alarms blare.

Phone sex, phone sex,
Better than being alone sex,
Let your fingers do the walking,
While you trade some dirty talking
And for the hottest telephone date
Set your mobile to vibrate.

Lowering the Teaune

(For Val)

The good folk of Ambridge all sit by the pheaune
In the hope of a call from Caroline Beaune.
This cool English rose with the cut-crystal vowels
Can cause a commotion in those rural bowels.
But who is there fitting to sit on the threaune
By the side of that empress, Ms Caroline Beaune?
As she straddles her mare with thighs that are teauned
She reflects whether any deserve to be Beauned.
Jazza is limp, and Ed Grundy is Dross,
Eddie's horny hat is both tacky and gross.
Bert thinks the clitoris is some kind of spud,
While Mike boasts the less interesting kind of hard wood.
So is she doomed to spend nights all aleaune
With only the sound of the vibrator's dreaune?
Tom's leeks are the only things long, firm and big,
While Neil spends his life with his arm up a pig.
Robert Snell's love is virtual, Kenton's neurotic,
Clive's shotgun foreplay is simply psychotic.
Oh will she dry up like some old virgin creaune
With Harvey Nicks knickers as dry as a beaune?
There's the ladies—but every one's straight as a ruler.
Hang on though: can she really be sure about Shula?
In no time her jodhpurs are off and she's preaune
And her clipped elocution makes the Archer lass meaune.
Their riding crops twine in a surge of sensation,
While Alistair the vet provides cheap lubrication.
At last Borsetshire has a pair who are Sapphic,
And dinners grow cold as their acts pornographic
Are broadcast to Britain, both whinnying and greauning,
'Cause we all want to hear Ms Caroline Beauning.

Song from The Selkie: *Boundless Heart*

Oh the sea has a cold and boundless heart,
Its pulse beats on the sand.
You feel its tides within your blood
While you cling to the life on land.

The sea has strong and winding arms
Which hold all earth embraced.
Though you walk dryshod she's inside you;
That's why tears have a salty taste.

The sea has ever changing beauty,
Always there when you need her to be.
She asks nothing of you in word or duty,
You can love her and still be free.

Like a mother seal she gave us life
Then left us to stay or follow.
She kills without hate, gives birth without love,
Sees her children die without sorrow.

For the sea has a cold and boundless heart
Which holds us all with ease,
Without needing or testing or playing a part,
Without caring to hurt or please.

For we long to give love and our human hearts burn
To be loved by child, parent or lover.
The sea you can love with no need of return
From this immortal, unknowable mother.

Scent for a Suffragette

(Green, white, & violet were their colours)

Violet, a glimpse, a glimmer of soft blue-purple, musk-warm
breath of cool moist petals swamped by

Green. Lush tangling hedgebank grass, wood sorrel's
juicy stems,
lavish moss with coiling hooks and fists, clean
medicinal chlorophyll. Sudden spike of

White mint, the Polo I sucked before eating cold tongue
in Nana's kitchen, to feel the chill
on my heated throat. Camphor, too,

White Vick, in her scullery medicine cabinet I stood on a chair
to tidy, over and over, inhaling

Green disinfectant, TCP for wounds, the talcum powder tin
dusted with Ashes of

Violet. They are here below the brambly grasses now,
a dim haze beneath the astringent

Green like Izal toilet paper, austere and glossy; and an eau de
cologne stick to write cool words on feverish foreheads,

White wax like a lipstick candle. And still, musky, lying low,
quietly sensual, deep deep down among the

Green and the spotless

White but the mostly

Green   is

Violet,   sweetening the pale stem of my wrist, warming my pulse.

Written in response to Lush's scent 'The Smell of Weather Turning'.

Water's Bright Words

A Quantum Haiku

(Eleven words sprayed onto beach balls, moved by/ in water, can be randomly rearranged to form almost 40 million poems. Commissioned for BBC2 TV poetry documentary, also activated live at Royal Festival Hall, London.)

Wings dance the air waves.
Beneath, silver sparks—fish,
Water's bright words!

Some of the poems generated at Hackney Lido:

The air, waves, fish:
Bright wings beneath.
Words dance, water's sparks
Silver.

Water's fish sparks
Silver wings,
The air dance waves
Beneath bright words.

Beneath water's bright waves,
Wings. Fish sparks the air;
Dance, silver words!

Silver sparks, water's dance,
Words beneath bright wings
Fish the air waves.

Epithalamion

A sonnet for the civil partnership ceremony of D & C, who I introduced.

When first I joined by email their two names
I hardly dared to hope I'd make a match
To strike a spark, ignite eternal flames,
Yet love flared up as if I'd clicked 'Attach'.
Two lovely men then newly flying solo,
Ready for adventure, free as air:
It seemed they'd travel further with a co-
Pilot, have more fun being single as a pair.
With dual purpose then I thought to bring them
Together, as lovers or as mates.
Now they are both! The joining of two 'wing men'
Has brought them here, the happiest of states.
We wish them lifelong love, a clear blue sky
As they take off—for it takes two wings to fly.

Poems of Pathology, Anatomy, and Dealing with Death

Will She be Stuffed?

'Will she be stuffed? And in a glass case?'
We are driving my son to the Co-op Chapel
Of Rest to view his Great-Grandmother. He
Is five. A logical question; he has seen birds
So displayed, and Nana is his first human death.
Disappointing to find a cold and empty face
Surrounded by nylon frills when she could have
Been sitting under a dome, at home, her best hat
Skewered into her perm, posed to give him lemon
Curd and Tunnocks Teacakes. Or near the end,
Sipping pre-dinner Harvey's Bristol in the carehome
With her mates, a cheeky custom she began. At 91,
She had more friends than a teenager and fell out
With them as often. Umbrage, huffs, 'taking the pip',
Though his question's more likely to have given her
The giggles. No, let her be immovable and magnificent
In her flat, with a soundtrack of her voice routing
Door-knocking Jehovah's Witnesses with narrations
Of her almost-century of life in every detail, dialogue
Included, until they fled all along their Watchtowers.

Shyly, interested, he touches her ungiving skin.
Then, death dealt with, waits for me to do the same
As his sister-to-be rolls over in the dome of my belly.

Keepers

(2012 doll 're-borner', 1859 post-mortem photographer.)

I am putting in his eyes,
I am painting in her eyes.
'Adorable Arctic Blue', optical grade
Acrylic, guaranteed not to fade.
Inked onto dead, closed lids,
Her soulless pupils gaze into my lens
I hand-root his lashes, micro-root his brows,
Her lashes, I'll draw later; and a white dot
For the spark of life, onto the ambrotype plate.
The soft fine mohair swirling on his scalp
Is inserted over many hours. Perfection takes time.
The exposure takes time. My subjects
Never fidget, but gravity tugs them out of true,
The earth impatient for them. Even ice
Can't keep time still. Every 'Forever Nursery'
Reborn baby, I care for as my own.

Nine days dead, this child.
My lamp begins to warm and wake her. Gagging,
My nostrils plugged with menthol, I recreate her
Living likeness, preserve her mother's motherhood,
Proof of the child, the future, she once had.
Packing plastic beads into limbs and torso, I weight
Each newborn to sag just right in the crook of my arm.
I brace her dead weight upright, the iron frame
Hidden by the frock her mama was keeping for best.
I strive for that perfect reborn, for absolute realism,
Use 'Genesis' heat-set paints in stippled layers
For moist lips, milk spots, tastebuds, the flush of sleep.
Her image blooms upon the plate; I add a faint rose tint

To cheeks last flushed with fever. A special order, this,
From a photo of a baby grown or gone to heaven.
Last, I slip into his breast the flutter of a beating heart
(Batteries included), send him to his new Mummy,
Forever young, *forever safe*.

My Pet Dead Bat

My father gave me a dead bat he found
On the golf course. Tiny, fragile, dry
As a black bee, its fur soot-soft, its face
A puckered fist, it lay on my palm as if already
Preserved. Its wings were webs, its claws
Burr hooks. Hummingbird-sized,
Seeming hollow, fleshless, it lay in state
On the dining room dresser. So clean,
So perfect, wholesome as bone.

A few days later, something foul salted
The air, something I shrank and ran from,
Knew in my bones. So hard to believe
It came from that dainty husk, so sweetly dead.

Acute Mountain Sickness: Everest

They race their own death to the summit. Slow suicide,
Fast climbing. It's all about the maths, the brain
Calculating on the abacus of its cells what to jettison,
What to take. As blood climbs to the brain's summit,
The Sherpa corpuscles' haemoglobin is too lightly loaded
With oxygen, but it's in short supply up there. In cylinders
It takes too much oxygen to carry in that freeze-dried air.
In the mountain's 'Death Zone' it's all about O_2,
All else is sacrificed, like safety, ice-blackened toes, clear
Thinking, even concern for those who stop, drop by the path
Unable to stand, go on, go back. Fatally they rest; the body
Dies first, frozen to the core, while still the voice can moan
Appeals to those who pass, until that too is silenced
By the bone-scouring wind that polished Mallory's bare back
To ivory over decades. Those passing by keep moving, but
Their digestion stops. Sugar fails to reach their neurones.
Starved of their spark, but still ionic pumping, they 'idle',
Cling to the face of hope that food will come again, that air
Will fill the lungs which now fill up with water as the brain
With fluid, oedematous, soggy, swollen, carrying the sea inside.
Perhaps this Mountain Sickness is just the body homesick
For sea-level where we first breathed air and still belong. But
Chilled, muddled minds hold fast to one desire, to 'get there',
'Reach the top', yes it's all about the maths, what to give up,
What to risk losing to feel like a winner for a brief moment
Before the rush to descend, back to air with warmth, with life,
To where they wouldn't stumble past a dying man or woman
Ignoring their last words until the mountain seals their mouths.

So climbers, all dying, pass them in procession through the years
Lying in plain sight, long dead, their bright weatherproofs

Fluttering in the blizzards. Some have become waymarkers,
Warnings: David,Green Boots, Frances, Hannelore; all life
In them, even rot, stopped.

At a Stroke: Collateral Circulation

The brain hangs like fruit in a netting of blood
Veining the folds of our deepest dreams,
Clasping our memories in hot wire mesh,
Pegged by deep vessels way down in the cortex.

So a new flush of blood can flood over the desert
Of cells lately stricken by drought and disaster,
Lifesaving relief, if the stroke's over fast,
Though one link of the net may be broken or blocked.

But he's bleeding out, so the bleached reef
Of brain cells spreads on, no relief,
Cut off from his heart which labours
And stops, unfed and unfeeding; his belly
Ballooning with blood, useless plenty,
As the aneurysm opens its fist like a bomb.

So the cortex, penumbra, and brainstem are felled
Like forest trees scorched by wildfire and drought,
And with them the sight of his dying wife's face,
Dances at the Empress, that RAF beetroot
That dyed his piss purple, the taste of caught crab,
And that annoying bloke off the telly who cooks.

The brain's cupboard candles against sudden power cuts
Can hold darkness at bay, but this time they blew

Out

Apoptosis: Cell Suicide I

This poem will partly self-destruct through apoptosis (programmed cell death) just as each of our cells is told each day whether to live and divide or die for the good of the body.

Your life is built on a death-wish.
From our conception, every cell has a default hope,
Longing to collapse like a winter deckchair
Burst its skin and stir itself to slush like a spade-sliced
    jellyfish,
Relax into salty consommé, let those coded instructions
    it carries
Float away, dissolve undone.
But the guilt-trip call, the signal to stay alive
Never stops coming. Says, Don't give in to your jones
For Mr Bones! Hold on, don't jump, come down from that
    ledge,
Keep living! Do it for the team!
Keep giving! Work, feed, breathe, give birth,
Tear yourself in two—DIVIDE
To multiply. Labour, all you myriad cells,
We need each brick in the body's living walls.
One day at a time, you can do it!
Don't give in!
Not yet, wait!

Not yet, wait!

Not yet, wait!

Apoptosis: Cell Suicide II

Your life is built on a death wish.
    our concept   , cell de a t h,
        to self-destruct, collapse like a winter deckchair
Burst its skin and stir itself to slush like a spade-sliced
    jellyfish,
Relax into salty consommé, let those coded instructions
    it carries
Float away, dissolve undone.

            the guilt-trip call, the signal to stay alive
            stops coming. S o give in to your jones
For Mr Bones!   jump   down from that ledge,
                                    Do it for the team!

Tear yourself in two—DI   E!
W eed   the body's living walls.
                        do it!

   give in!
No   w   !

No   w   !

No   w   !

A Question for Neuroscientists

Where does a memory sit, when it's at leisure?
Where does it cool its heels, await our pleasure?
For whenever we are shown the busy brain,
We see the thoughts and memories entertain
Us, but always like honey bees in a hive,
Entering and leaving, keeping themselves alive
In restless motion, either coming in and out,
Or from lobe to lobe, bustling round about.
In through the senses' portals in endless flow,
Or out through speech or action, what we know
Flickers from cell to cell like summer lightning,
The dendrite forests darkening and brightening
As something being stored, or being recalled,
Is passed round like a parcel: never stalled?
Never at rest? Or are there hours or days
When a memory's not moving? When it stays
Still, drowsing like a sleepy drone,
Not being thought on, just being left alone.
So where's its home? Its niche? Its nest?
The place it hangs out when it needs a rest?
In the nucleus at a neurone's heart?
In many neurones? In what part
Of cell or lobe or brain does it reside
While waiting for the call to come onside?
And in what shape or form is it recorded,
Until it comes forth, smiling and applauded,
Twinkling, a galaxy of stars, each spark
Peppering our consciousness through dark
Times and good: soothing, aiding or warning,
Awake or in dreams, to make us smile at morning.
If thought, like light, can be particle, or wave,
What is memory's photon, how is it saved?

To recall them is to move them, so which cell keeps
Each of my honeyed memories, while it sleeps?

Pestering an Eye Research Neuroscientist

I asked, do eyes themselves have expression?
Do they speak? Surely love at first sight
Is both the beloved's image entering our
Eyes, and what we see come from theirs,
The subtle signals of pupil and lid, language
Hid from conscious sight, but understood.
Hard, though, for science to explain it, hard
To reproduce it in laboratories. But we know
When another's eye sees us, knows us, with what
Emotion it dims or lights up, moistens or narrows.

We can measure what goes into the eye, the effect
Of light which strikes it like a spear and penetrates
Deep to the occiput through and through.
Its charge ignites the brain with colour that sears
Us, seems true: though the electrons of what's before us
Absorb the wavelengths of the colours we *don't* see,
Leaving behind the shades we do, as autumn leaves
Glow red and gold when green has drained away
Leaving a display of redundant colour, a final show,
Tints which were always there now brought to bloom.

But can the eye mirror the brain, when the brain
Is failing? Can an ailing brain express itself
In the eye? When the proteins clog the axons
Deep within, do they also clothe the cornea
In a horny skin? I asked because I'd seen
The eyes of my mother afflicted with dementia
Become opaque, narrow, the whites stained
Like parchment. Was this a true observation?
Was her eye expressing her clouded brain,
Whose plaques and tangles reached for the light?

Or was I looking into them with my too partial sight?
And why do our eyes spring open, as breathing stops,
As if avid for a last gasp of light, before the dead

leaf

drops?

To a Friend Undergoing ECT

As you lie beached on the table,
Lightning will stab the right side
Of your brain. Your thoughts,
Stranded on neural floes,will
Stretch out teetering hands
Across widening straits of chaos.

May you be like a dolphin, sleeping
With half of your mind, the right side
Which zig-zags with electric storms.
May the left side of your brain explode
With dreams like freed pigeons from crees,
Swirling like music, like breath through
Water. Afterwards may your dolphin self,
Awake, swim sunken remembered streets
Recollecting each perfect image like a shell
Dropped and now found again, whole,
The familiar shape sandblasted clean as pearl.

A Comfortable Fiction

Comfortable is how hospitals describe you
When you've, say, paraglided into a cliff, breaking
Every bone except those little ones in your ears.
Comfortable is a parabolic curve. Picture it, a U,

Where the two open ends opposite at the lip
Touch the maximum value representing most
Comfortable. One end represents 'Dead', the other
'Fine.' Both ways, you are truly comfortable. Equally
Between these extremes, yet furthest away in value,
Comfortable-quotient zero, the base of the U touches
Cruelly conscious agony and long-term damage.
Comfortable, perversely, is what hospitals call *that*.

Comfortable is you, contemplating no privacy, no
Autonomy, no sleep, no future plan, no end of pain.
Comfortable is you contemplating bedpans, bed-baths,
Bed-arrest, slow drug trolleys and other people's
Choice of daytime TV injected into your eyeballs.
Comfortable. A comfortable fiction for everyone
But you, to make them feel more comfortable.

And as for 'satisfactory'...

Deathbed Writing Workshop

I: Debridement

Her notes say 'debridement': stripping away dead tissue
From an infected wound. And this high bed is the antithesis
Of a bridal couch. It holds her as if digesting her, absorbing
Her flesh through sucking tubes, leaving her light
As a dry fly's
Husk. While its loud cheyne-stokes snorting drowns out
Her fluttering breaths, her brain debrides her from within,
Peeling away the wife, mother, daughter, friend, she was,
As her experiences, passions, are nibbled away by
Dementia's maggot.

I am here to give a writing workshop for this woman whose
pale eyes
Are unseeing slits, whose mouth hangs open, soft and
toothless.
I sit a long time by her huge and greedy bed as she dies
by inches,
Feeling the peace that emanates from her. She is teaching me
already
About acceptance, the strength that comes beyond what
we call
Dignity. Her face is radiant, calm, relaxed. She mutters
Random phrases, timed to a rhythm as if conversing. I begin
To respond, ask quiet questions, between her phrases,
antiphonally.
And she begins to answer.

'Do you have a garden?' '*Yes, I have a garden.*'
'What kind of garden?' '*It's just a casual garden.*'

In that toxic box, nothing thrives but flesh-eating bacteria;
No flowers, no sky, no rain, no sound of nature,
No colour, no scents, no fruit, no music, all,
Ironically, banished in the name of sterility.

Between us, we conjure up her garden, write poetry,
As words emerge from her like earthworms after rain.

II: Sharing the Work

A week later, she's still there but silent.
She's past responding, says the nurse
Who looks at the poem. 'She said all that?'
We agree you can somehow tell
She is a lovely person. I read her the poem.
She does not move. Then I say I'll have to go,
And her face tenses slowly, her lips move,
And clearly, she mouths, 'Thank you.'

Another week on, she's on morphine, but
She opens her eyes, closes her mouth, as
I play birdsong on CD. Robins and blackbirds
Fill the room, pecking up maggots and microbes,
Turning them into song, debriding the dead air
She has to die in. We sit a while in the bird-washed
Room, then I say goodbye, and leave.

A few days later, she is dead. The poem
Stands on the windowsill in place of a view

Murder Should Out

Where is the angel like a pendulous dugong
Heavy with rain and rage that will bloom
Over the land, brood over the rows
Of houses and drives, paved and gravelled
Gardens and call them, all the buried women
To rise, spit the soil out of their mouths? All
The women who 'went away with a man', who
'Just went out and never came back', who
'Didn't love us any more darling, let's not
Mention her name again', who
Never even visited or sent a postcard, who
Disappeared but never really left. Let us have
A resurrection of the patio women, who
Have borne the weight of stone, of earth,
Have sprouted seedlings out of their wombs,
Whose bones are still there.

Still.

Whose children have run lightly over them,
Tripped and fallen to lie on top of them,
Mouth above dead mouth, crying 'Mummy!'
To the distant memory of the bad woman
Who abandoned them and does not care, he says.
Let the women unfurl like ferns, pale bones jutting
Like autumn crocus, let them stand, let them point
The finger at each man who robbed them
Of life, of being mourned, fondly remembered.
Let his jaw drop like a corpse's, let him freeze
Like the winter ground he put her in, be known
For what he is. Let the women rise up, a skeletal
Forest of branching coral, years and years

And years of perfect murders, to accuse the men who
Took everything but the blame from women who
Stayed unseen, underground, beneath contempt.
Let the angel bring them back to light, conjure up
The patio women's glorious resurrection.

Skinbound Baby

(Foetal specimen with ichthyosis)

He grew, fighting against his skin
Which split like a caterpillar's, but
Would not be shed, refused to give
Or stretch. Scaled, yet he's no fish,
Nor sinuously reptilian. Swaddled
In too-tight bands of stiffened hide,
Deep slashes expose his flesh.
His eyes are blebs of blood
Pushed through his horny mask.
His skin cells were too eager,
Could not stop piling up faster
Than their siblings could die
To form these ragged bandages
Which hold him rigid. His mouth,
An overfilled rubber ring, bulges
As if blurting pain. He was born
Trussed in himself, hide-bound,
Hooped, coopered like a barrel.
Now his kind can escape the womb,
The specimen jar, the prison
Of their skin, by incessant
Moisturising, softening, Vitamin A.

Too late for this little Buddha, born
To the agony of raw nerves, delivered
From breath by self-asphyxiation.

Conjoined Parastic Head

(Foetal specimen, pathology museum)

A leather ball with a face on each side
Trying to push through the skin
As if straining to break out, break away
In opposite directions. They shared intent,
A brain, two minds crammed in one space;
Can never part, nor see each other's face.

Plants Mirror Minds

A Quantum Haiku

Nine words carved on wooden leaves floating freely on the water, moved by wind and weather, can be randomly rearranged to form 362,880 combinations. Commissioned by Dilston Physic Garden, Northumberland, to celebrate the way plants evolved chemicals which mimic/mirror our brain chemistry. We grow and nurture them as they feed and heal us, although we can each destroy the other. We use them for medication and the spiritual or hedonistic effects of the substances they create in self-defence.

Starting poem:

Plants mirror minds,
Healing, harming powers
Growing green thoughts.

Some poems generated:

Minds, plants' powers
Growing green mirror thoughts,
Harming, healing.

Growing thoughts, plants'
Harming powers. Green minds
Mirror healing.

Healing green mirror,
Harming thoughts. Minds
Growing plants' powers.

Remembering Love: A Scent Spell

(A perfume based on rosemary, which can enter the bloodstream enhancing memory and cognitive function, was created for this poem at Dilston Physic Garden.)

Breathe me, let me in to your blood.
In a rush clear as water I'll bring
All of it back to you. Remember
All the hands you held, that didn't
Pull away until you let them go.
The scent of skin, of linen sun-stroked,
The feel, the heat, against your cheek.
The sound of summer rain, the storm
Before the calm, earth drinking its fill.
And you, drunk on memory, rushing
To recall in perfect clarity all those
Moments, all those kinds of love.

Poems of Politics, Activism and Protest

Free! All-you-can-read Buffet

As a child, my mother owned half a book;
She and my father grew up hungry for words
And learning. Poverty breeds inherited greed:
Although they bought me books, my endless need
For them, devouring them in gulps, they couldn't slake.
'She's read it by we get home from the shops!'
Enter the library. An all-you-can-eat free meal. I'd take
All my family's tickets, stagger out behind a tower
Of tomes a week, scoff them swiftly in the street,
In bed, in bath, in class under the desk…gorging
From Blyton to Christie and beyond to new worlds,
Lives, voices. At university, first in the family
To go (a dream denied till then by poverty)
When not in the bar, I'd roam the stacks, celebrate
End of term feasting on non-compulsory books.
Lying in summer grass with Gide and Gitanes, wine
And Waugh as *Brideshead Revisited* met the Toon,
I filled up on words to fuel the books I'd write.

'Best Selling: Father and Son Hunting Package Deals'

The world is big and wide, son.
It's ours to rule and ride, son.
Come hunting the Big Five, son,
It's all about male pride.

Game animals are grand, son,
And you must understand, son,
They are ours, as is the land, son,
It's all about God's plan.

The elephant, the lion, son,
The buffalo and leopard, son,
The rare and savage rhino, son;
Stalking them is hard.

So beautiful they are, son,
Most dangerous by far, son.
Come hunting with your Pa, son,
For nights beneath the stars.

I promise you it's fun, son,
With servants and two guns, son,
We'll bag them every one, son,
Until the job is done.

They'll snap us with our Five, son,
Propped up as if alive, son,
Then carve steaks with their knives, son,
For us to feast upon.

And when you eat your fill, son,
Of meat and see blood spill, son,
And when you've learned to kill, son,
You've learned a manly skill.

We'll fly back home to Mom, son,
With washing to be done, son,
And trophies to be shown, son,
The skins, the horns, the bone.

It's a kind of conservation, son,
These beasts need preservation, son,
So we shoot them on reservations, son,
So you can take your son.

The Sex Life of Slugs

Slugs make a civilised business of mating.
Each one both male and female,
They come together side by side.
A fat white rope joins them,
An umbilicus through which
They exchange genetic material.
Both lay eggs, a pearly caviar.

Slugs do not have, take, or posess:
They build bridges between two equals,
Share their twin-sexed selves.

If only we could share so easily
The male and female in us with our lovers.
The penetrating and the child-bearing
Keep pulling us apart.

Meanwhile, after dark, slugs stroll
The pavements, fearless of rape.

Chainsaw Massacre

After Shakespeare's sonnet 73

This time of year when I would hope to see
Green buds on boughs that shake against the cold,
I hear the growling chainsaw gnaw each tree
To a stump, brought low for growing too high, too old,
Or daring to touch the net of wires which hang
Connecting each house to a stark dead pole.
'Bare ruined choirs where late the sweet birds sang'?
Bare, ruined indeed, this street without a soul.
No room for trees, now rows of sleek cars stand
Glittering where once there spread full leafy shade.
Sycamore, chestnut, beech, are on too grand
A scale; polluted air for clean's a dirty trade.
But perching on wires, the birds still sing as sweet,
While our silent voices thread between their feet.

Arab Spring, America's Fall

Green as a dollar bill, Liberty's wading ashore, but
Hasn't quite set foot on Manhattan. Her blank eyes
Reflect the spaces where the twin towers aren't.
Two days ago, bright sun sparked freak October snow
In Central Park, when marathon runners occupied the city.
The barriers unloaded from NYPD trucks freed them
To move unhindered through the congregating watchers.
Genial officers wished cyclists, joggers, skaters a nice day.
Like today. As I hold aloft the torch of my hand to snare
A yellow cab, Liberty behind me, she and I can see
A bus full of cops head for Wall Street, sent to serve
And protect the bankers who bankroll the one percent.

For the Arab Spring has become America's Fall,
Less welcome now it's over here. Those silenced
By fear of being 'enemies of freedom, commies'
For questioning the American Dream's no-show,
Their foreclosed mortgages, massive medical bills,
Now hear each other, spread the word online,
Bypass the media singing the government's tune.
The police, distracted by those sirens, are confused
By protesters who are respectable, even renowned.
Those who occupy, brave pepper spray and worse,
Know that liberty is a marathon, not a sprint. It hurts.
It walks on water, but hasn't quite landed here
On Manhattan, or in England, or anywhere.

The Book Of Beastly Creatures

The Book Of Beastly Creatures

Hex Arcana: Volume I

2020

The Book Of Beastly Creatures
Hex Arcana: Volume I

Stories by Lawrie Brewster, Thomas Staunton, & Sarah Daly

Illustrations by James Olley

Game Rules by Lawrie Brewster, Kieran Wyse, Victoria Mackie, & Liam Mitchell

Layout by Todd Sanders - locusgraphic.com

www.hexmedia.tv

FIRST EDITION - 2020

Printed in the United Kingdom
ISBN: 978-1-913663-06-3

Table of Contents

Foreword	Lawrie Brewster	7
And It Walked Into The Sea	Thomas Staunton	13
The Woman In White	Lawrie Brewster	27
The Black Hare	Lawrie Brewster	35
The Spider Mother Of Hoia Baciu	Sarah Daly	47
The Carnival Returns	Thomas Staunton	57
The Siren Of Silver Falls	Sarah Daly	65
Tooth	Thomas Staunton	75
The Curse Of Pinnilekk	Sarah Daly	89
The Reunion	Thomas Staunton	101
Black Santa	Lawrie Brewster	111
The Mould	Thomas Staunton	121
Dig For Fire	Thomas Staunton	131
The Bog	Thomas Staunton	141
The Owlman	Lawrie Brewster	151
Baldurrock	Sarah Daly	159
Mom & Pop	Lawrie Brewster	175
The Below	Thomas Staunton	187
The Immortal Princess	Lawrie Brewster	199
Game Rules		243
Acknowledgements		279

Foreword

BY

LAWRIE BREWSTER

And so, upon these dark cobbled streets, across the mists and shadows of time and space, we meet at last; you, the reader and supporter of Hex Studios' first-ever publishing endeavour, and us, the humble authors of these monstrous tales.

The Book of Beastly Creatures is the first in a series of original short story compilations, inspired by our deepest affection for ancient creatures, infernal demons and cosmological terrors.

It is a book comprising the works of three authors: myself, Lawrie Brewster, director of 'The Devil's Machine', 'The Unkindness of Ravens' and 'Lord of Tears', noted screenwriter and collaborator, Sarah Daly, and finally, Tom. Who is Tom, or should I say, Thomas Staunton? Tom is an excellent horror filmmaker in his own right, contributing two segments to our anthology feature film 'For We Are Many'. It is also worth noting that Tom makes a fabulous sausage casserole!

Enough about us, what hideous wonders does this tome contain, I hear you ask?

Our anthology begins with 'And It Walked Into The Sea', a tale of a hideous automaton with frozen fish fingers for limbs! Okay, not exactly... In fact, our first tale by Thomas Staunton writhes with Lovecraftian inspiration as an intrepid curiosity seeker descends a mysterious staircase towards a terrifying date with destiny.

Next up are 'The Woman in White' and 'The Black Hare', two tales of my own which began as written pieces known as 'creepypasta', before being adapted into a more traditional short story format. The Woman in White, with inspiration from M. R. James' classic supernatural story 'Martin's Close', sees a visitor to an obscure Scottish island pursued by an entity whose benign appearance conceals a terrifying truth. As for 'The Black Hare', well, this is a story that features an iconic character reminiscent of 'The Owlman', the ancient and terrible entity that features in my films 'Lord of Tears' and 'The Black Gloves'. The Black Hare is based on an unsettling childhood account of an entity that haunted a small mining town on the same date each year, coinciding with a spate of tragic disappearances.

Set in a famously spooky real-life Romanian forest, 'The Spider Mother of Hoia Baciu' tells the story of an over-protective mother, who just happens to have eight legs and hundreds of eyes! When her young are threatened, she descends from the tree-tops to ensnare unwary prey. Written by Sarah Daly, this unsettling account brings a degree of pedigree to our volume (Sarah Daly has written for Hollywood stars such as Gary Oldman and Anne Hathaway). Here, she provides a sober warning for what may befall you if you should stray too far into the forest.

With bright lights and cheerful music, the circus comes to town in Thomas Staunton's 'The Carnival Returns', though not perhaps with the ringmaster we hoped for, as a small town finds itself entrapped by an ancient, malevolent puppet-master and his legion of devout followers.

Sarah Daly strikes again with 'The Siren of Silver Falls', a tale which takes inspiration from ancient folk-tales to explore the timeless, boundless fury of a vengeful spirit with an insatiable appetite for children.

Somewhat following the gastronomic theme, we come to 'Tooth' written by Thomas Staunton, which envisages what might happen to eighteenth-century occultists should they endanger the lives of children in their pursuit of unholy powers.

'The Curse of Pinnilekk' emerges from the sand to reveal a spine-tingling body horror with ancient inspirations. Sarah Daly spins this hideous tale which may forever spoil your trips to the beach. What is revealed beneath the golden sand will linger with you as it has for me since I first read this masterful tale.

Next, you will attend 'The Reunion' by Thomas Staunton, which envisages a doomed gathering of old school friends that turns sour after the arrival of an unexpected guest. The real horror of this story lies in its gut-wrenching twist, however.

We all know the jolly soul that is Santa Claus, chuckling kindly in his red tunic, eyes twinkling at us from passing Coca-Cola trucks. But, what if there was another Santa Claus, one whose suit was not a cheery red, but instead, a hopeless black? A Santa who demanded more visceral treats on Christmas Eve than the usual cookies and carrots for Rudolph? Well, you're about to meet him in this twisted, festive fable.

As someone who grew up with a fear of filmic creatures such as 'The Blob' or the living mush that comprised 'The Stuff', I must say it was with some trepidation that I read Thomas Staunton's 'The Mould', where an unwitting tradesman gets more than he bargained for.

The two tales which follow are also written by Thomas Staunton, entitled 'Dig for Fire' and 'The Bog', each of which describe ancient and demonic entities which come to life on the page. 'Dig for Fire' features a whispering tormentor who might lure you to the garden with a pickaxe in hand and the darkest of intentions. While 'The Bog', based on an ancient Celtic legend, features a tale in which a pickaxe might be quite useful as a defensive weapon against this hideous, cackling entity.

'The Owlman' finally makes an appearance in this 'meta' story about one especially over-eager Owlman fan who goes to extraordinary lengths to secure a meeting with his idol, the ancient one, the Lord of Tears... the Owlman.

Next up is a very different offering featuring the dreaded Owlman, entitled 'Baldurrock', written by Sarah Daly. Set in the mansion which features in our films 'Lord of Tears' and 'The Black Gloves', this gothic tale plays out against a bleak, post-apocalyptic background where a group of survivors seek refuge, unaware of the horror that lurks within the ancient walls.

Then comes a tale of parental terror like no other. 'Mom & Pop', written by myself, is a chilling tale of one man's struggle to overcome a troubled childhood in which his imaginary friends, under the guise of picture-perfect parents 'Mom & Pop', eventually sought to destroy him. Years later, in an attempt to unravel the painful mystery of his uncanny childhood, he returns to his former home to confront his demons once and for all.

Our penultimate tale, 'The Below' by Thomas Staunton, inspired by the legends of his own hometown, provides an explosive, cosmological contribution to the collection. This story's wildly original monster evokes as much awe as it might terror.

My final story, 'The Immortal Princess', is, in fact, a novella, which provides a comprehensive and chilling account of the legendary automaton of that name and its notorious curse, a subject which inspired my feature film 'The Devil's Machine'.

Our tale recounts the experiences of Alexander Mackintosh, the famed inventor of the most advanced automaton ever known, produced during the reign of Prussia's King Frederick the Great in the latter half of the eighteenth century. Our story charts his trials and tribulations, and those of the man who would become his nemesis, a legendary military man known as 'The General' who commissioned the clockwork doll to resemble his daughter Talia.

And there you have it, my friends. This first volume in the Hex Arcana hurtles thus to its bloody conclusion. With its eighteen creepy tales of monsters, demons, ghosts and gods, I hope that you will each find the perfect creature to haunt your nightmares.

Hex Studios is known for the production of horror movies, and we look forward to producing many more, but our great love for storytelling in all its forms means that we hope to publish many more volumes of our tales, and in doing so, to support the future of print media as well.

It is with great affection that I thank you all for purchasing our book, and I humbly hope that you all enjoy reading it as much as we enjoyed producing it.

Darkest Regards,
Lawrie Brewster

And It Walked Into The Sea

BY

Thomas Staunton

Greetings from Porthaven, where dreams come true!

Harry flipped the battered postcard.

"I've never heard of Porthaven."

"That's exactly how they like it."

Harry was on Berwick pier with a total stranger, a young, high-cheeked man by the name of Sydney. Hats held firmly, they shuffled along the promenade, bracing against the autumn wind.

"Did you see her there?" asked Harry. He saw his wife's delicate features flash before his eyes. She was smiling.

"Aye, of course. You always notice a stranger in town."

"Who sent her the postcard?"

"I don't know, but I have my suspicions. Look, I'm not doing you any favours by telling you the hows or whys of any of this. You need to be careful. My village is not like other villages. It has a history."

Harry looked into Sydney's eyes. The man was frightened.

"Is that why you left?"

Sydney lit a cigarette.

"Don't go down to the beach after midnight, and don't ask me why, because you won't take me seriously. Just don't do it."

Harry flipped the postcard back around and studied the watercolour of Porthaven, a quaint seaside village of white-washed houses with terracotta roofs, hugged by a little cove.

"Why are you helping me?"

"I'm not, believe me. Don't trust them, Mr Redman." Sydney turned up the collar of his trench coat and walked away.

Harry sat in his car looking out across the murky, grey sea to the other side of the bay where a string of coastal towns twinkled in the dusk. He pulled a photograph from his coat pocket, a picture of his wife and young son picnicking under a weeping willow. The tears started to fall, but he quickly wiped them away. There was no time for that. Pocketing the photograph, he inspected the postcard one last time. On the back, in neat handwriting, it read:

We answer all prayers. Come alone.

○

Harry saw the bonfire before he saw Porthaven. Beyond the sea wall, the tower of flame spewed a plume of white smoke into the black sky. He pulled into a lay-by overlooking the village and watched the drama unfold. The heat kissed his cheeks, even all the way up here. On the beach below, shadows danced, circling the fire, and then erupted into a cacophony of joyous cheering. Harry closed his fist and took a deep breath. Someone down there had answers.

Harry parked outside the little Porthaven inn and went for a walk through the village, which he quickly found to be deserted. All the houses were clustered either side of a narrow, winding cul-de-sac. Smoked fish and plucked chickens hung over doorways, and on the windowsills sat wooden blocks with sea creatures engraved into them. Oyster baskets and fishing rods lay scattered on the cobblestones. Halfway down the main street, he came to a long, steep wynd that snaked down to the beach, lit by flickering, green lanterns.

Harry stepped onto the sand and into a party. The whole village was here; a mass of drinkers, revellers, and dancers. Some sat at tables in a large, white marquee while others huddled around their own little fires dotted about the beach. He saw children frolicking on the peripheries and parents reprimanding them half-heartedly, teenagers kissing in the dark, giggling and chattering, and all the while, the bonfire blazed behind a massive dune, its intense heat making the night sky shimmer. Harry cupped his brow and saw a thin, old woman in a mottled gown standing by the fire. She was already looking at him.

"Hello, stranger!"

Startled, Harry turned to address the greeting. A middle-aged man in a creased linen suit ambled towards him, his tobacco-stained hair blowing wispily behind him and his arm extended for a handshake. He clasped Harry's hand warmly.

"I see you've stumbled on our little party. I'm Gordon Hensley, the unofficial Mayor of Porthaven. For now, anyway!" He laughed uproariously. "And who might you be, young sir?"

"You'll have to forgive me, Mr Hensley. I think my business would be best attended to tomorrow when the festivities are over."

Mr Hensley wrapped his arm around Harry's shoulder and guided him towards the marquee.

"Nonsense! There is no better time to discuss business than at a party. Ha! We can put the world to rights over a drink!"

Harry was a little uncomfortable with this over-familiarity until it became clear that Mr Hensley was entirely drunk. They zig-zagged gracelessly into the crowded marquee and sat down at a bench. Mr Hensley snagged a passing teenager and pulled him down onto his lap. The boy smirked.

"Two enormous red wines for two important businessmen please, Tonto!"

The boy left for the bar in a fit of giggles. Harry cleared his throat and thought for a moment. He wasn't exactly sure how to broach the subject, now that he was here. He tried to judge Mr Hensley's present drunken mood, but there really was no way of telling how the man would react to his questions.

"My name is Harry Redman. I think my wife may have visited your village a few weeks back."

Mr Hensley sat up at once. He tried to compose himself, but his head began to bob slowly from side to side.

"Mr Redman, you have my deepest, deepest sympathies. The sea can be such a cruel place..."

Harry was taken aback.

"How do you know about that?"

Mr Hensley grabbed his wine and dismissed the teenager sharply.

"It's my business to know, Mr Redman. I am a politician, and news from both sides of the estuary comes to me. Tragic events, Mr Redman! We sea-folk see more tragedy than most."

"Do you know why she came here?"

Mr Hensley chugged his wine back in a single slurp.

"Aye, sadly, I do. She was looking for help. Help to find your boy. She must have tried every house in the village. We felt the greatest sympathy for her, but we couldn't help, unfortunately."

Harry braced himself for that morbid, sinking feeling he had grown so accustomed to. It was becoming too much to bear; the questions, the anger, the grief. William had passed away in the summer of 1951 after finally succumbing to the polio he had contracted when he was just a toddler. Agnes was inconsolable. She became a ghost, haunting her own house, searching endlessly for William, even calling for him in her sleep. Until, one morning that summer, she walked out of the house and never came back. Harry had such a vivid recollection of that cold steel table, the shorn fragment of the summer dress with the sunflowers... He shook his head and downed his wine.

"How long did she stay?"

"Not long, just one night. We did tell all this to the police, for all the good it did. I'm surprised you didn't come sooner, actually. I hope you don't mind me saying."

The police had no leads, not even a cause of death. All they had was a tattered, bloody dress. Now it seemed that officers on either side of the estuary were not in communication with each other. He didn't know whether to see it as sloppy or suspicious. His mind was a fog. The postcard was sitting in his inside coat pocket, waiting to be produced at just the right moment. Someone had invited her here, well-intentioned or not, and she had paid for it.

A stout fisherman hurried over to Mr Hensley. He looked at Harry with piercing scrutiny and then bent low to whisper in Hensley's ear.

"Mr Redman, we need to leave the beach. We're expecting a mighty gust, ha!"

A signal was given. On cue, the fires were quenched. Then, one by one, the villagers trailed up the wynd, back to their homes. Mr Hensley escorted

Harry to the inn, lighting a cigarette as he stumbled across the cobbles. As they passed, the houses lit up like lanterns, and music and laughter filtered out into the night.

Mr Hensley took a drag from his cigarette and chuckled through a cloud of smoke.

"I wouldn't expect to get any sleep tonight, Mr. Redman. They'll be at it till sunrise."

"What exactly are you celebrating?"

"Oh, it's our 400th anniversary! True, we don't get the tourists anymore, but we're very proud of our wee village all the same. They used to come in their droves for our fish suppers!"

A metallic screech rang out from the far end of the street. Two men in storm jackets dragged a massive black gate across the cobblestones. They brought it up to the threshold of the wynd and secured it to the wall with a heavy *clunk*.

Mr Hensley smiled a little sheepishly.

"We don't like the wee ones venturing down to the beach at this time of the night."

Harry remembered Sydney, the man on the pier. *Don't go down to the beach after midnight.* Suddenly, the similarities between Mr Hensley and Sydney became apparent; the cheekbones, the sandy hair and twinkling green eyes. Harry suspected that he was talking to Sydney's father.

"Come see me in the afternoon. I shall hopefully be of more use to you then."

"Thank you, Mr Hensley."

Harry was trying to remain wary, but Mr. Hensley had been nothing but kind so far, and charming in his own drunken way.

"Now, I think this is as good a time as any to say goodnight, ha!"

Mr Hensley bumbled his way down the street and disappeared into the shadows.

Harry lit a cigarette and sat on the front steps of the inn. Far in the distance, a strange, reverberating yawn bellowed out from across the sea—an alien sound so disturbing and unnatural that Harry fell backwards and dropped his cigarette. He ran into the inn and shut the door.

○

Harry saw Agnes and William sitting under the weeping willow. They gorged on pies, cakes, and fat, juicy strawberries. Their mouths were tiny and puckered, and when they opened, he saw that they had serrated teeth within, like piranhas', gnashing hungrily.

BANG! A clap of thunder, a bolt of lightning, and the weeping willow split in half.

BANG BANG BANG BANG!

Tap Tap Tap Tap...

Harry rolled over in his bed and saw a figure at the window. He rubbed the sleep out of his eyes, got out of bed and pulled back the drapes. It was an old woman, the same one who had met his gaze at the bonfire. She was dressed in a heavy black raincoat, her hair frazzled from the moist morning air.

Harry nudged open the window.

"Can I help you?"

"Mrs Shaw, how do you do?" She stepped closer and handed him a folded piece of paper.

"Do you see that islet across the estuary?"

Harry looked over her head and saw a faint patch of land in the middle of the sea.

"That's St. John's. Take a boat out to it. Do it now and do it quietly."

Harry unfolded the paper. At first, he had no idea what he was looking at, but then he realised it was a crude drawing of the islet, with a trail leading from a harbour to the centre.

"Row out to the islet and follow the trail."

"What's out there?"

"Answers. Take this and go. Now!"

She passed him up a small lantern, donned her hood and walked briskly away down the cobblestones. Harry stood there in the early morning silence, trying to work out what it all meant.

○

It was midday when Harry reached the islet. The sky was a steely grey as he hauled the boat onto the sand. With aching arms, he unfolded the map and scrutinised it. St. John's had three paths, with tributaries branching out to what looked like landmarks, or maybe buildings. His route was marked in bold red ink. He traced his way across the paper with his finger and tapped at a large black cross on the north-west side of the islet.

It was a dreary, windswept land of ruined buildings, shrouded in wild vegetation. The place had been uninhabited for a long time. He plodded forward, deeper and deeper into the centre. He was glad of the old woman's map, rudimentary though it was. The place was a warren of trails, and without it, he would undoubtedly have lost his way.

Finally, he arrived at his destination. Standing before him was a round structure, ten or twelve meters high, with thick walls of solid stone and a tall metal door to one side. For the first time, Harry wasn't entirely sure what he was doing here, or what he might find at the end of all of this. His grief had cast a wicked spell, imbuing him with a tenacity that sent him further and further into the deep. He pulled open the metal door, held the lantern high and stepped inside.

The building was a dark, empty husk, save for a howling wind. Harry studied the map as if to extract some psychic guidance. Panning the lantern across the room, he saw a spiral staircase descending underground, and clasped his throat. The phantom choke of claustrophobia was looming. Approaching the stairs, he peered over the rail and looked down into the dark. *This is ridiculous. I should turn back.* But then, he saw it; a postcard lying on the second step. The terracotta roofs had smudged into the white of the tiny houses, the blue sky now turned a murky brown.

G eet ngs fr m P rth ven, wh re dreams c me tr e!

With a pounding heart and his fist clasped tightly around the lantern handle, he descended the staircase.

Harry reached the last step, stopped, and held his breath. All around him was the hollow sound of dripping water. Was he in a cave? He passed his lantern around the room. If this was a basement, it had long been abandoned to nature. The walls were smothered in green algae, and the air was thick with the smell of fish and seawater.

Something twinkled in the lamplight. How did Harry ever miss it? In an enormous pile lay a vast array of shimmering adornments: gold bracelets, silver lockets, pendants, gems, and necklaces. He stepped further into the cave, manoeuvred the lamplight behind a pillar, and saw hundreds of

Porthaven postcards scattered across the ground, all smudged, faded and torn. Words and thoughts failed him in that horrifying moment. None of it made sense.

Something floated across a puddle of oily water. On closer inspection, he could see that it was a tattered swatch of summer dress, patterned with sunflowers. It couldn't be. IT COULDN'T BE!

Tears running down his face, he went to retrieve it and stepped on something spongy. He let out a yelp. The floor was littered with bones.

Harry stumbled backwards, turned on his heel and ran for the stairs. He had only set foot on the first step when a terrible rumbling yawn filled the chamber. Wrapping his free arm around the railing, he directed the lantern to where the sound was coming from.

In the darkest recesses of the basement, a massive hole had been torn out of the masonry, and something moved within. Harry watched in horror as a monstrous beast came slithering out in a deluge of gushing seawater. The tentacles came first, then its flat, round body followed. As it passed through the lamplight, its skin turned from brilliant silver to pale, translucent pink and back again, in a shimmering kaleidoscope of nauseating colours. There were no eyes—no face at all that he could see—only mouths, hundreds of puckered holes dotted in rows across its underside, like teats on a sow. All the mouths opened wide, and rows of tiny, serrated teeth gnashed mechanically, up and down, up and down. Harry fell back onto the stairs and smashed his lantern, plunging him into darkness. He froze in sheer panic as a tentacle coiled around his shoe and flung it away in one swift pull. He was certain then that he would die. In his heart, he knew that this had been Agnes's fate, and now it would be his. The creature drew closer, closer, until finally, as if shocked with electricity, Harry's brain kicked into action, and he bolted.

o

Mr Hensley's rotund fisherman friend was leaning against his boat when Harry climbed down onto the beach. Elated to see another human, he sprinted across the dirt and fell to his knees in the swash.

The fisherman looked on with his arms folded, thoroughly unmoved. He glared at Harry for a brief moment and then lunged at him.

They rolled around in the lapping water, each desperately struggling for dominance. Harry managed to get on top of the man, but he soon grabbed him by his shirt and threw him onto his back. Before Harry had a chance to catch his breath, the fisherman was upon him. With chilling ease, he pulled a long knife from his belt and thrust it forward. Harry was quick to react. He grabbed the fisherman's hand and pushed it deep into the wet sand. The fisherman relinquished the knife and quickly repositioned himself. With a meaty fist, he punched Harry hard in the face, but Harry stayed firm in his fury and took the blow. Flustered, the fisherman leaned sideways to retrieve the knife, and in that moment of imbalance, Harry shoved with all his might, toppling the man with a heavy thud. He grabbed the fisherman by his collar and head-butted him so ferociously that a jet of blood blasted out of the man's nose. Harry grabbed the knife and plunged it deep into the fisherman's belly. The blood flowed fast to meet the foam.

○

The sky was heavy with dark clouds and angry streaks of crimson as Harry pushed the little boat out to sea. Exhausted, he tumbled into it and started to row towards the mainland, helped now by the tide. His mind wandered to Agnes. In her grief, she had thought that Porthaven could somehow be the answer to her prayers, to her wish to see William again. Did she get her wish? Perhaps he would never know. She was gone. Someone in that godforsaken village had lured her here and into the lair of that vile beast. Harry looked to his bloody hands and began to weep. He wailed his sadness and his fury at the darkening skies, cursing the gods for his ill fortune.

He steered the boat towards the far end of the cove, out of sight of the twinkling lights of Porthaven. It was time to find real answers. No more wishes.

Close behind him, a thunderous roar filled the estuary, and he rowed faster.

○

Tap tap tap. The street was empty, the lanterns snuffed, and Harry stood in the darkness outside Mrs Shaw's house.

Tap tap tap.

Pressing his ear to the door, he heard the soft patter of slippers. Mrs Shaw opened the door and let out a yelp. Harry stepped out of the shadows and into the sitting room, the light glancing off his blade.

"Mr Redman, you've... returned!" Harry shut the door and eased his way towards her, resolutely mute.

"Did... did you find what you were looking for?"

"You seem shocked to see me."

Mrs Shaw agonised over her next words. "I'm... relieved, that's all. Are you well?"

Harry stepped closer again.

"Well, no, I can see that you're not, but the rest of the village would be so delighted to see you back, perhaps we could let them know!"

Harry said nothing. He was distracted by the sight of two enormous stacks of paper piled up on a bureau in the corner of the room. He picked up a bundle from the first stack and inspected them.

Certificate of Death - Thomas Haden - Age: 5 years old
Certificate of Death - Rachel Gibbs - Age: 7 years old

Harry wondered if he would see William's name in there. Indignant, he toppled the second stack: hundreds of Porthaven postcards, all of them filled out and ready to be sent to the bereaved of the world.

Fishing, he thought.

By the time Harry turned back around, Mrs Shaw had run from the house and down the street.

"Gordon! Goooooordon!" she cried.

Harry locked the door behind her. As he stood in the stillness of the sitting room, waiting for the inevitable, he realised that he was no longer afraid.

Before long, there came the sound of marching feet. A line of flickering torches congregated outside the house.

"Mr Redman," said Mr Hensley, "you can burn inside the house, or you can come out here, and we'll hang you. You decide which is preferable."

Harry thought of Agnes, of William.

"Burn it down. Perhaps I'll take you all with me."

As he said his last words, he heard a familiar, beastly roar. His heart sank into the pit of his stomach. Outside the house, the torches swished and crashed into each other. The mob scattered up and down the street, shouting and screaming. He heard the slamming of doors, one by one. He was alone again, in the silence.

He stared out the window and waited. After what felt like an eternity, a heavenly white light appeared, shining through the window with brilliant intensity. Harry was mesmerised. Two figures; one tall and one small, walked past the window, silhouetted against the light. Harry felt a strange feeling of familiarity. He couldn't help himself. He rushed to the door and opened it wide.

A woman and a little boy were walking down the village street. They turned at the wynd, heading down to the beach below. Harry chased after them. He ran down the hill and onto the sand where they both stood, hand in hand, smiling at him; Agnes, with her kind, hazel eyes, and William, with his freckled cheeks. He was home. He walked towards them, his face streaming with tears, and embraced them both tightly.

Little William took an enormous bite out of Harry's neck and pulled a mouthful of flesh clean away. Agnes devoured his face, her teeth gnashing up and down, up and down. Locked together, they pulled him into the cold, dark water. The mesmerising veil had been lifted. Agnes and William were gone, and Harry felt the soft, wet hug of a tentacle wrapping around his chest as he sank below the waves.

In his last moments, before the black, he saw the first sparks of a dawning bonfire.

The Woman In White

by

Lawrie Brewster

It's been almost a week since I first arrived on the Isle of Jura, just one of over two hundred small islands scattered off the west coast of Scotland. Jura is a lonely rock, a windswept place dominated by volcanic rocks and bleak hills, and the most cut off of all the Scottish isles.

On Jura's northernmost tip is a tiny village which the locals call 'Sithean', and it is from that desolate place that I cannot escape. I am not, however, imprisoned by the people that live here. In fact, they have sent for a doctor from the mainland to remove me. They are concerned by my refusal to leave my car, and, after days of supplying me with food and water through a small gap in the window, they have finally succumbed to their impatience.

I don't expect them to understand the... circumstances that find me imprisoned here. I am confined against my will by someone or something so terrible and otherworldly that I might welcome death over the prospect of it finding me. I am so fearful of the consequences of what will happen when they pull me from my car that I've taken the precaution of writing this testimony, which, if you're reading this now, was indeed my last.

My name is Alexander, and I am a recently-widowed high school history teacher from Edinburgh, Scotland. My wife, whom I loved dearly, passed away after succumbing to a long illness. In the aftermath of that tragedy, I sought to re-establish old friendships with my former schoolmates. They were quite amused at the fact that I had become a teacher, and were mostly married, pre-occupied with children and family life.

In many ways, this accentuated my feeling of loneliness, and so it was with some perverse relief that I found one old friend, Simon, who had experienced a life-changing tragedy of his own. His wife had left him, and, overwrought with grief, he'd thrown himself into his work, expending that terrible energy with frequent travel across the Scottish isles. It was his job to monitor fish stocks and the general health of sea creatures so that he could file environmental reports to the government.

He visited me in Edinburgh, where we had a wonderful time regaling the tales of our youth before he left for his tour of the islands. A week after he departed, I received a message that carried with it a strange sense of unease.

"Alexander, I invite you to join me on the Isle of Jura, where I've secured us lodgings. It is a beautiful place, and I would be especially grateful if you would come because I need some help leaving the island."

The tone of the message was strange, and I wondered why he would suggest that he needed help to leave? I learned that the island was visited twice a week by a small ship that brought supplies from the mainland, and while there was no indication of threat in his message, surely he could telephone the authorities should the worst-case scenario arise?

Yet, amidst the drudgery of teaching and grief, this message was a welcome diversion, even better that it was also an invitation to adventure. I packed my belongings, and within twenty-four hours, I was standing at the bow of the *Seahorse* as it penetrated the icy winds of the Atlantic to arrive at the harbour outside Sithean.

Simon was there to greet me, dressed for the blustering sea winds in a thick coat, hood and scarf, while I arrived in the same threadbare suit I usually wore to work. At first glance, he looked alright, his broad features resplendent with a welcoming grin, and yet, I couldn't miss the dark shadows under his eyes.

As any good friend should, I marched Simon, with the aid of his directions, towards the village tavern. There, I checked in my belongings and ordered us a full bottle of malt whisky, which, accompanied by the bar's roaring fire, did much to restore my friend's spirits.

Soon, we laughed and joked as we had during his visit to Edinburgh, and I decided not to mention the strange aspect of his letter. I would leave that for tomorrow.

That first night, I slept well and, to my delight, as the sun rose the next day, I observed that the weather had dramatically transformed from the wintry chill of the evening before to a bright summer's day.

The ship would not return for two days, which gave Simon and me plenty of time to discuss his situation. Meanwhile, the historian in me was rather keen to explore the island for its famous ruin, an early Christian chapel which stood atop an imposing cliff overlooking the sea.

Fortunately, I had packed a pair of hiking boots, and so, after a hearty breakfast, we ventured for a hike through the rugged hills of the island. It was a gruelling walk, but the beautiful weather aided us greatly, and after a few hours, we caught sight of the distant ruin. Up until then, Simon had been in good form, amiable and cheerful even, so I hadn't yet broached the subject of his strange message.

This was about to change, for reasons that would haunt me for the rest of my life. I cannot begin to describe the inexplicable dread that fills me as I write about what happened next, and I'm sure I will lose you along the way to feelings of doubt, scepticism or even ridicule. Just know that as you read these words, I may already be dead on account of what has happened here.

Do not laugh at it, do not laugh at me and do not come to this place.

As we traversed the gravel path that ran along the base of the hill, I looked up towards the ruins which almost glittered under the afternoon sun. They were beautiful, but the hill was about three hundred feet high, and I was already exhausted.

Simon, whose face betrayed a peculiar anxiety, seemed relieved by my hesitation. He suggested that we keep along the path instead, which would eventually return us to the village, while offering us some spectacular views of the ruin from afar.

I consented to this, upon which Simon laughed with relief, and we carried on. As we walked, I glanced up from time to time to admire the ruin, and it was during one such glimpse that I caught sight of a pretty woman at the top of the hill, waving at us.

Although at some distance, I could discern that she was a beautiful young woman with a cheerful expression, with long locks of curly blonde hair and a white cotton dress that came to her feet. She waved her arm in a wide, sweeping motion while calling out for our attention.

The wind was picking up, obscuring her words, but her familiar expression clearly implied that she must already be acquainted with Simon. If I were a young man, I might even have been jealous, for she was a radiant creature.

I tapped his shoulder and said, "Simon, you have an admirer up there!"

As I reached to point up to her, I was surprised to find Simon still walking, refusing to stop. His body was tensed and his breathing quick.

"Don't look at her... keep walking."

I was perturbed by this, as it seemed incredibly rude to ignore her. She persisted in waving, still cheerfully cooing for his attention. I was a little angry then, as the gentleman in me wondered if she was perhaps some naïve girl he'd previously exploited.

Stopping in my tracks, I called out to Simon. With careful intention, he turned to avoid looking at the ruin and grabbed my shoulder, practically dragging me back with him along the trail.

I almost stumbled, and as I did, I turned one last time to the girl on the hill, shrugging apologetically on behalf of my callous friend. I think she registered this in some way, as her attention was now fixed upon myself as she continued to wave.

The hour's walk back to the village was tense as Simon refused to answer my questions concerning the woman we'd left behind. Surely a troubled love affair was not the cause of his strange message?

Simon's sense of calm returned once we made it back to the fiery hearth of the tavern bar, and eventually, a few whiskies loosened his tongue. Fidgeting with his glass, Simon looked at me, a flash of urgency shimmering in his eyes.

"Alex... was she looking at me?"

I nodded, and then I recalled how her attention had eventually fixed itself on me. I didn't tell him, unsure of what any of this meant.

As the evening wore on, his strange mood worsened as he became drunk. It was quite distressing to see Simon like this, reminiscent as it was of my own dark days following the loss of my wife. I decided then to confront him about his strange message, but first I needed a moment alone to collect myself for this intervention. I say this, but I believe that his state of anxiety was provoking something of its kind in me also.

I just needed a moment to myself.

Simon gave me the keys to his rental car, which was parked just outside the tavern.

It was dark outside, and that beautiful day had descended into the rage of a summer storm, the type that produced vicious bolts of lightning and rain pellets so hard that they might crack the window panes. I would brave it all for a moment to catch my breath in solitude, so I dashed out of the tavern and slipped into Simon's car.

So terrific was the storm, that in the few seconds it took me to run to the car, I was already soaked to the bone. The weather took a different form from the comfort and privacy of the car. The sharpness of the rain felt subdued here, and I could feel something like a sense of calm return to me as I planned how I might tackle the serious discussion ahead.

The windscreen was swamped with rain, obscuring my view of the street. In a village such as this, there are no street-lamps, so the only light was that emanating from the windows of people's homes, which served to silhouette rather than reveal that which stood in its path.

And something did stand in its path...

I pressed my face to the windscreen as an uncanny dread engulfed me. There, in the middle of the night, in the middle of the road, in the midst of a storm, was a person standing perfectly still some twenty feet ahead.

I could see virtually nothing except a sliver of their shape, a rim of light that came and went with a familiar movement; the wide, sweeping motion of an arm waving.

Then, it shuffled forward, closer and closer towards the light to reveal itself. The beautiful girl from before, now soaked with rain, yet seemingly oblivious to the storm, waved at me. Her expression, completely unchanged from before, still exuded the amiable familiarity one might encounter on bumping into a casual acquaintance in the street.

As she moved ever closer, I could see her lips moving as she appeared to speak in casual conversation. It looked as if she were asking simple things like, 'how are you?' and 'it's been a long time,' though again, I stress, I could not hear a word.

She kept coming until she reached the driver's side of the car where I was sitting. It was locked already as she pressed her face to the glass. Her expression remained constant, friendly with a hint of confusion, as she gestured for me to open the car door.

She seemed to exist out of all time and place, but there she remained, in the pouring rain, tapping her fingers at the window, smiling and speaking soundlessly. How can I describe the way that she stared at me? Why, despite her amiable appearance, was I so terrified?

It felt as if she were from another place, a void of sorts, and that in that place, she could see only one thing in the darkness... and that thing was prey... that thing was me.

Smiling as she traced her fingers across the window, she gracefully reached for the back door. Was it locked? In petrified silence, I choked in horror as I heard the *clunk* of the door opening. With a speed that one can manage only when driven by absolute terror, I rushed to pull back the door.

In the struggle, the terrific sound of the storm filled the car and my senses were overwhelmed by the sight of the woman in white as the lightning illuminated her, revealing for a moment what lay behind that beautiful mask of fake humanity.

With every door locked, she still continued to tap at the windows, to coo at me with alluring looks and soundless phrases, for me to 'please open the door'. But in that flash of lightning I had seen the truth, and so fearful was I that I might see it again, that I hid my head under my coat, and pressed my fingers into my ears.

When morning came, the innkeeper told me that Simon was gone. Finally, the meaning of his message had become clear. I learned that he'd boarded the *Seahorse* that day and returned to the mainland. As the day wore on, concerned locals tried to lure me out of the car, but she is out there, somewhere, waiting for the moment when I will be forced out of this precarious safety.

As I write these final words, I can already see the doctor heading my way with a group of men. They think they're going to save me... but the woman behind them has other plans.

The Black Hare

BY

Lawrie Brewster

When I was twelve years old, back in the early nineties, our family moved from the beautiful countryside to a former mining town, a blue-collar place where people fought hard just to survive. Industry had long since left, and those inhabitants that remained were among the poorest in the country. The rich, green, natural landscape of my youth was gone, replaced with a world of concrete apartment blocks and long-abandoned cars. The town's most distinguishing feature was the old pit tower of its once-lucrative mine. The rusting structure loomed over the town, its red paint cracked with age, its iron frame bent and twisted, on the verge of collapse.

To make matters worse, my father found a job as a teacher at the local school, the school I would attend. The other kids teased me and kept their distance, so I forged a friendship with the school caretaker, a kindly old man who'd seen much in his time. It was this friendship that would save me from what was to come.

One day, four months after we'd moved into town, I was wandering the green-tiled corridors of my school, alone as usual, but something was different. The kids, who were always so boisterous and quick to pick on me, instead ignored me completely. They were subdued, distant. I would have welcomed this relief had the same oppressive atmosphere not filled the classrooms, enshrouding even the teachers in a cloud of dread.

I learned that someone had nailed a scroll to the ancient street lamp that adorned our town square. The notice had struck a nerve among the locals, who considered it a joke made in poor taste. Resembling an antique circus poster, it read:

Come, ye children, to the town square at noon tomorrow for a day of frivolity and delight with the Black Hare!

A consensus had spread among the parents that the scroll was a prank. The question of why it should be so concerning to the locals burned in my mind. What did it matter? What did it mean?

As I made my way home, just yards from the entrance to our apartment building, something grabbed my arm. I twisted to break free, before recognising that the anxious man staring at me was my friend, the school caretaker.

"Play it safe," he whispered, his face pale as death. "Leave school early and go to the town square at noon tomorrow."

He wouldn't let me go until I nodded my agreement, but he would explain nothing of what I might expect.

That night, I struggled to sleep. My brain conjured a stream of nightmares, each more horrific than the last, and yet, terrible though they were, they would not compete with what awaited me the next day.

By morning, a different mood had taken hold at school. My classmates expressed scepticism about the scroll at the town square. I felt jealous that their parents had spoken to them about the legend of the Black Hare while mine had not.

I thought of the school caretaker and the promise I had made him, yet once at school and among my classmates, it felt absurd to leave on the orders of some unknown prankster. Still, as noon approached, I noticed that some kids were missing, and wondered if they had left to attend the meeting.

I prevaricated for some time and then followed them. I would not arrive by midday, but if I was late, would it matter? When I reached the town square, there were a dozen kids hanging around the ornate lamp. They were laughing, eating snacks and playing, with no sign of the mysterious entertainer and its day of 'frivolity and delight.'

At twelve-thirty, I gave up waiting and started walking back to school. I was just a few streets away from the town square when I heard the music.

It sounded like an old carnival tune played through a music box; a jaunty, twisted melody that was at the same time familiar and unfamiliar. The sound didn't carry on the wind, but instead seemed to play in my head. I winced as the intensity of the music grew, producing a tinnitus effect that sickened me, clouding my vision and hearing. From the town square, I heard muffled sounds of laughter turn to screams, then silence.

I stayed rooted to the spot in terror for a few moments before survival instincts kicked in and I fled, hiding out of sight behind some bins. I could hear footsteps running towards me and gritted my teeth, terrified that some insane assailant might charge straight into me, but the sound passed by and carried on towards the other end of the street. Peering out from my hiding place, I saw a child running in terror. For years, I have fought the memory of what happened next, and I still pray that one day I might forget it.

The running child stopped at a junction and looked left to right, fear etched on his face, as a huge black figure sped towards him. The speed of the thing defied explanation, with its long bounding strides and arms stretched outwards beyond all human proportion. It scooped the child up in an instant and vanished out of sight.

Once I was certain the thing had gone, I left my hiding place and returned to the town square. To my surprise, the other kids were unharmed.

None of them would tell me what had happened, but their eyes told me that I didn't want to know. Those that stayed in the square hadn't been hurt, but of course, I had not stayed, which explained the uncertain looks they gave me.

Then, disaster struck.

A terrific rumble shook the buildings of the town square. We turned in unison to see the pit tower collapse and tumble down the hill, carried by an enormous landslide. Coal... earth... dust... careering in an avalanche of devastation that tore straight through the school. The force of the collapse sent a wall of soot and dust thundering towards us, engulfing the town in darkness. Amidst the screams, shouts, and blaring car alarms, I saw a figure bounding towards me in the mist. Its thin arms stretched outwards, followed by a piercing shriek like that of a broken toy;

"Time to come with meeeeeeeeee!"

I ran and ran until I fell unconscious some miles out of town. When the police found me, I was taken home and put to bed, exhausted but unhurt. I soon learned the full magnitude of the tragedy that had beset the town. The school had collapsed under the landslide, killing eleven and injuring dozens more. The survivors were being treated for inhalation of poisons released from the collapsed mine, and yet no harm had come to those children who remained at the town square.

Later that evening, I received an unexpected visitor. My friend, the school caretaker, came to call on me, relieved that I had survived. After dispensing with his gift of boiled sweets, he leaned in close and whispered;

"Did you go?"

Afraid and ashamed, I admitted to the truth and shook my head.

The old man's smile disappeared, replaced with a fatalistic expression. He leaned even closer, checking first that my parents would not overhear. I will never forget his words.

"The Black Hare will know, and he will come for you. You must survive until midnight."

When the old man left, I can say that I had never felt more alone in my life. My parents would never believe me, and I was too ill to make a stand or to escape.

I looked at my bedroom clock. The red LED lights flashed 9:46 pm, still hours to go until midnight. My bedroom was small, with a wardrobe at the foot of my bed and a large window beside it. The second-floor window gave me an excellent view of the street below and the moonlit sky. In the distance, I could see a ring of emergency vehicles buzzing around the ruins of the school.

Time passed at an agonising pace, causing me to flinch in terror at every sound or shadow. It was even worse when my parents went to bed, and I was truly alone. I staggered to the wardrobe and checked once more that its doors were latched shut, then looked under the bed, and stared out into the street. All seemed quiet while the LED light of my alarm clock flashed its countdown towards midnight.

The time was 11:26 pm. In thirty-four minutes, I would be safe.

At 11:27 pm, the sound of something rattling inside the wardrobe caught my attention. *Rattle-rattle, rattle-rattle.*

I drew the bed sheets around me and peered through a tiny gap. My blood chilled as I observed that the latch on the wardrobe had released itself.

It occurred to me that the rattling sound was not a rattle, but a tittering, which now emanated from the dark space between the wardrobe doors.

The doors creaked open, and in the terrible blackness, I could just make out the shapes of my clothes on the hangers and my childhood stuffed toys. I held my breath, too afraid to make a sound. The familiar shapes of my possessions would have given me comfort had I not recognised that one of the stuffed toys was not my own. The thing had long limbs and rabbit-like ears, with eyes that twinkled in the dark. I glanced at my alarm clock as the dread inside me grew to hysteria. 11:46 pm flashed in the darkness—still fourteen minutes left—and it had found me.

I turned to the wardrobe, where the stuffed toy remained. It hadn't moved, but what little comfort I felt at this was to be short-lived.

Titter titter...

The cruel laugh was much louder this time, but it seemed stifled, muffled by something, muffled by the glass!

Sick with dread, I looked towards the window, and there it was, silhouetted by the moon, staring straight at me. The enormous head was flat and round; a large, black disc that filled the window frame. Two tall ears shot out from the top of its head, and its eyes were diamond-shaped, comprised of complex patterns and intertwining lines, a hideous kaleidoscope. Its body seemed hewn together, constructed of black-painted wood and decorated with colourful polka-dots. It looked like something a child would make, yet it felt alien and ancient, an evil depiction of pure insanity.

Its head bobbed towards me, face tapping against the windowpane before shrieking like the twisted strings of a broken violin;

"Let me in, gentle friend, and we shall play while the grown-ups are asleep."

I turned away in horror, but as my eyes glanced past the wardrobe, I could see that the stuffed toy was no longer there. The clock flashed 11:54 pm.

I shouted in defiance at the monster at the window and its expression changed from fake delight to hungry rage.

My spirits plunged when I caught sight of the window latch. While I was distracted, something had opened it. The Black Hare could detect my terror, and its huge pupils flashed towards the latch before returning to meet mine.

Its great claw swung to haul up the window. I threw the full weight of my body against it. The wood cracked under the pressure, and inch by inch, the window opened.

With mounting excitement, it sang;

"Time to come with me now, time to come with meeeeeee!!!"

With every ounce of strength I had left, I forced the window down, splintering the frame and shattering the glass. Long arms reached for me through the broken window, the monster's razor-sharp claws tearing at my legs as I crawled towards the bedroom door. It grabbed hold of my ankle, dragging me across the shattered glass on the floor towards its gibbering mouth. In its malevolent eyes, I could see no mercy, only violent triumph. With my strength gone, I was powerless to prevent it from pulling me out the second-floor window to my death.

Beep Beep Beep blared from my alarm clock. Midnight had come. The Black Hare vanished, its plan thwarted with less than a second to go. I collapsed onto the floor, exhausted and bleeding. I can remember hearing the mad commotion of my parents as they burst into the bedroom. I awoke in an ambulance headed straight to the hospital. The rest remained a blur until my recovery one week later.

A sane person might struggle to understand why I continue to live in this town, but the tragedy of what happened united the townspeople, and my family. It filled us with a determination to forge new friendships and to rebuild what was lost. In the months afterwards, I made lifelong friends among those who had once bullied me, while a year later, my friend and guardian, the old school caretaker, passed away.

Even on his dying day, he dared not explain the full story of The Black Hare. As months passed into years, me and the other children who had seen it came to doubt our own memories. The release of poisonous gases from the collapsed mine could have caused hallucinations, shaped by the controversy of the scroll and our fear of 'The Black Hare' legend.

Entering adulthood, I followed in my father's footsteps and became a teacher. My passion was for history. As well as teaching the subject, I took charge of the town's local historical society.

As I trawled through the mountain of records collected over the years, I discovered a box of historical photographs depicting the townspeople. There was one picture taken each year from 1905 to 1913, always on the 23rd of

September, the date of the Harvest Celebration. The last picture, dated 1913, showed two rows of children in front of the old school building. This picture was different. Something about it disturbed me, and I realised that it was their faces. These children were not smiling, they were afraid.

At first, I thought it was a smudge on the paper; the strange, dark shape on the far left of the photo. I used a magnifying glass to discern what it might be. As the shape came into focus, a pitiless sense of despair engulfed me, for I could now see that behind the children stood a nightmarish figure with long limbs and protruding ears.

Could the Black Hare be real?

Only the oldest inhabitants of our town would know anything about the local legend, and they were the least likely to talk about it. The story of the Black Hare was something that the town had wanted to bury, but perhaps the discovery of this photograph might persuade some to share what they knew.

For months, I struggled to get any information, until a shocking discovery led me to a breakthrough. I learned by accident that one of the earliest chairmen of our historical society was still alive, committed many years ago to a nursing home some miles from town. With no surviving relatives, most had assumed he had long-since passed away, having suffered from dementia for years. At 105 years old, he would have been a young child at the time the photograph was taken, and despite his condition, he remained my best chance of learning more.

I am not proud of what I did next.

Upon visiting the elderly man, I found him in no fit state to speak, either because of his resistance to my questioning or the severity of his illness. This did not prevent me from making a discreet search through his personal effects, and among them, I discovered letters and notes which tell a story never heard until now.

I will let you judge for yourself from these extracts I have copied.

It began on the 1st of March, 1912, when the townspeople awoke to discover an ornately-written scroll nailed to a post in the town square. It advised the mothers and fathers of the town to bring their children to the square the following morning, promising 'a day of frivolity and delight with The Black Hare.' The next day, curious parents arrived with their children to discover the so-called Black Hare awaiting them with a startling and uncanny visage.

It stood seven-feet-tall and its 'body' was painted black with yellow polka-dots, its collar adorned with a red and green bow-tie. The figure appeared to be of wooden construction, and yet, it moved of its own accord, presumably with the aid of an actor hidden inside.

The Black Hare danced for the children with a peculiar and unnerving gait, its stretched limbs swinging and extending beyond their perceived length. It spoke and sang with a voice that possessed an unsettling, high-pitched quality.

The strange entertainer bemused the mothers and fathers, refusing any reward for its performance, before vanishing as mysteriously as it had arrived. Not long after the town returned to its ordinary routine, the first tragedy occurred; a child vanished without a trace. As the months rolled by, others would disappear, all of them children.

As the first anniversary of the strange visit approached, a mother of one of the missing children shared a startling revelation; all the children who had vanished had ignored the scroll's call to meet the Black Hare. Fear spread through the town, so that when a second scroll appeared, almost all of the children heeded its message.

Again, they played together, but now the children were afraid. The high-pitched voice no longer sang pretty songs or told sweet stories. Instead, it whispered of sinister acts, of dark and terrible deeds that the terrified children dared not repeat to us for fear of their lives.

A group of townspeople whose children were missing attempted to confront the Black Hare that day. Upon their arrival, it took off suddenly with unnatural speed, its great legs striding through the dense fields that surrounded the town, to the shock and horror of all who witnessed it. One month later, the sole child who could not attend that day, due to being bedridden with illness, vanished, never to be seen again.

Determined to seek revenge, the townspeople planned for its return on the third anniversary, keeping watch over the town square for the allotted time that the scroll should appear. They hoped to catch the Black Hare and reveal the murderer inside, but it was not to be.

The Great War saw the men of our town drafted into service, with the women and children forced to work at the munitions factories. No scroll ever appeared again, and so terrible were the horrors of war that the events of the Black Hare were eventually consigned to legend.

I pray that the Black Hare never again returns to feast on the misery of our children or to rain further destruction upon our community.

These notes leave me even more uncertain and afraid than before, and I know that I will always question what truly occurred in my childhood. As I pass the empty desks in the classroom, I am thankful for each day that spares my students from crossing paths with the Black Hare. If a creature with such an irrepressible appetite for children does exist, then it can only be a matter of time before it returns.

I am writing to you now because I feel that time might be coming. This morning, I discovered, in that same empty classroom, an object covered in dust, hidden in shadow... a stuffed toy with eyes that twinkle in the dark.

The Spider Mother Of Hoia Baciu

by

Sarah Daly

The road that leads to Hoia Baciu forest is little more than a dirt track, a narrow gravel spine laid to accommodate the few rare souls who find themselves upon it. You won't find it on any maps or see it signposted from the nearby city of Cluj-Napoca. If you were to ask a local for directions to Hoia Baciu, your request would likely be met with hostility, spewed forth in a stream of Romanian swearing that you'll be lucky not to understand.

The track leads to a humbler trail still, wide enough only for walkers and cyclists, that runs directly into the heart of the forest, where it stops dead. From this point, those who venture on must weave through a maze of twisted trees that protrude at peculiar angles from the earth, their trunks choosing to hug the forest floor before curving upwards in a spiral pattern, for some reason as yet undiscovered.

It was in the midst of this unnatural phenomenon that James Elliot found himself. It started with one of those viral articles with a headline like; 'Would you live in a haunted forest for £30,000 a year?' For James, it was an easy 'yes'. He applied, never expecting anything to come of it, but just two weeks later, he found himself on a plane to Romania, a country he'd never even visited, to begin a whole new chapter of his life. It was exactly the escape he had been looking for—alone in the middle of nowhere, thousands of miles from everything and everyone he knew. He could be someone new here. He could forget everything that had happened and start again. How ironic, he thought, to come to what was supposedly the world's most haunted forest to escape his own ghosts.

The job was simple, the lodgings even more so. His new home was a small log cabin, hardly more than a shed, with a wood burner for warmth and a vast library of books to keep him occupied on the long winter nights. It was all he needed. The solitude, the peace, the quiet—it was everything he had hoped it would be. Still, in the middle of the night, he would wake up screaming, drenched in sweat, his heart beating thunderously in his chest. He might be better able here to push her out of his thoughts when awake, but he had no such control over his unconscious mind. The nightmares were as bad as ever. It was always the same thing; a vivid, brutal re-enactment of the crash. The truck. The blinding light. The sickening crunch. Her limbs contorted at odd angles. Her eyes; wide open and staring at nothing. Every night since the accident it had been the same. Seven months now. He wondered if he would ever stop seeing her like that. He wondered if he deserved to.

It was because of the dream that he doubted what he heard that night. It was 3 am and he'd woken with a jolt, his heart beating like a battle drum in his ears, his sheets soaked in sweat. He thought it was an animal at first, a fox maybe. Whatever it was, it was in pain. He hadn't encountered one yet, but he knew that there were brown bears in the forest. It could be that the poor thing was being attacked, ripped apart by the vicious claws of the predator. This was the story he told himself, but the guttural wails he heard were unlike any animal he had ever heard. It sounded almost like a woman, screaming her agonies into the wind, yet, the cries weren't quite human either. He considered venturing out into the night to check. If, after all, there was a woman in distress, in need of help, then it was his duty to help her, but some primal, instinctive part of him told him to stay inside with the door locked fast and forget what he had heard.

In the grey light of morning, he dismissed the fears of the night before. He was letting the stories and superstitions get to him. No doubt it had been some animal native to these parts that he was not familiar with. It had only been a couple of months, and there was plenty still to learn about Hoia Baciu. It was unlikely that he would ever learn all there was to know about the place, but each day, he grew more familiar with it, finding a strange affinity with the forest; its tangled branches, twisted in on themselves, its defiance of time and progress, the way it wore its darkness like a protective shroud. He could sense its contempt for those few curious travellers who ventured into its depths. Yet, he never felt shunned by the forest. He felt that he was part of it, just another gnarled elm, refusing to grow as it should.

His main responsibility as caretaker was to make sure that the woods were kept clean, and any bonfires put out. He had also been tasked with doing a survey of the forest's vast stock of trees, marking any that were dead or dying. It was an epic undertaking, and one that would keep him occupied for many months. This suited him fine. On that particular day, he was headed to the eastern edge of the forest, an area that he had not yet explored. It was from the east that the troubling wails of the night before had come, and so he chose to go that way, in defiance of his earlier fears, or so he told himself. In truth, he hoped he might stumble across the corpse of the creature who had made those dreadful sounds, so that he could set aside his mind's imaginings and put some reasonable explanation in their stead.

The day was quiet, as they all were, since there were no birds in Hoia Baciu. It's amazing just how quiet a place becomes without bird song, how deeply wrong it feels to hear nothing but the soft crunch of your own footsteps. As James walked, he stopped occasionally to mark any condemned trees with a red 'X' across the trunk. He was examining a diseased elm when another tree caught his attention. It was certainly in trouble, but the parasite that infected it wasn't like any other he'd seen. The entire trunk was coated in a translucent slime. It gave off a greyish shimmer, and within it were black vein-like strata that swam beneath the viscous surface of the substance, seemingly alive, but perhaps just floating, driven to motion by whatever minute currents moved within the mass. James leaned in close to inspect the infestation, reaching out to touch it, when a drop of liquid fell from above, landing on the bare skin of his neck. He jolted upright, reflexively wiping it off, then looked up. In the branches above him hung a nightmarish mass, a slimy conglomeration of tumours maybe six feet wide and twice as long. In terms of its scale, it bore little relation to anything James had encountered in all his years as a ranger, but, if he set the size of the thing aside, he had to admit that it looked for all the world like a collection of egg sacs. The thing was abhorrent. Still, a natural curiosity drove him to overcome his repulsion and examine the abomination more closely.

Climbing the tree was not an option, as the slick and slippery coating made it impossible, but the tree next to it was unaffected, and would get him close enough to cut down one of the egg sacs with his branch-cutters. The diagonal angle of the tree's trunk made climbing it easy. He lay across a thick branch, his legs wrapped around it for stability, and reached out with the cutters, trapping the 'stem' of one of the sacs in its blades. He snapped the blades shut and the thing fell with a damp thud to the forest floor. He dropped the branch cutters after it, and was preparing to climb down when a scuttling sound distracted him, a sound that was hard to describe but somehow hideously familiar. It was the sound of bones cracking underwater, of a swarm of flies trapped inside a jar, violently trying to escape by propelling themselves against the glass, a cacophony of scuttling, squirming somethings.

The thing was distressed by the loss of one of its number—more than that—it was enraged. As he watched, something moved within one of the sacs, its shadow just visible behind the semi-transparent outer membrane. The thing inside wasn't entirely opaque. It had flesh of some kind, not yet fully-formed, and within that flesh, bones that formed long limbs. Too many limbs. As he stared at the vile creature, awestruck and horrified, an all-too-familiar form pressed against the surface of the sac. It was a face... a humanoid face.

In his shock and terror, he loosed his grip and fell from the tree, landing face down in the dirt. Suddenly, he was there again, in the driver's seat, as the truck exploded into the side of them, as the airbag bloomed in slow motion, breaking his nose and two of his ribs, as he saw her broken body through the smoke and the mangled metal, and knew that nothing would ever be the same again.

He came-to with a cry of anguish and found himself staring at the sac he had separated from the cluster. It had become opaque, so he could no longer see the creature inside, but he knew by the gentle squirming and twitching of the sac that, whatever it was, it was still alive.

He held a bag of ice to his cheek, red and swollen from the fall, and never took his eyes off the thing which sat on the wooden table beside him, pulsing ever so slightly in a heartbeat rhythm. Sooner or later, if it didn't die, it would be born. He had to know what kind of life the egg harboured but couldn't bring himself to simply slice the sac open. Even if the thing was ugly, repulsive, alien, it wasn't his place to decide whether it should live or die. He must wait.

When it was time to sleep, he left it wrapped in a blanket by the fire, guessing that it would need warmth to incubate, warmth he had deprived it of by excising it from its siblings. He lay in bed, just a few feet away, since all the cabin's amenities were conveniently located in a single room, and let his mind wander. What could the strange sac contain? Had he stumbled upon some new species out here in this desolate wilderness? He hoped not. The last thing he wanted was to draw attention to himself, to risk his new-found idyll being swarmed by scientists and press. As his mind ran through the various scenarios, each less favourable than the last, he began to drift off, and when he did, for once, he dreamed a different dream. This one was much worse.

He was trapped inside a giant egg sac, suspended in the jelly substance which filled his nose, his mouth, his lungs! He tried to scream but found it soundless, absorbed by the thick, milky fluid. He felt something brush against the back of his leg, something cold. He turned, in the cruel slow motion afforded by the mucus, to face whatever thing he shared the vile womb with. He saw the dark hair first, twisting and coiling in long tendrils. The body then came into view, its corpse-white skin, its too-long limbs fractured into improbable positions, the bones within crushed and disjointed. It spun round, a twisted ballerina in a music box, to reveal the glassy eyes of his wife, staring into nothing, her mouth locked in an eternal scream. She was on top of him now, pressed against him in the confines of the sac. Her hair wrapped around him, attaching itself to him, pulling his face close to hers as he thrashed and kicked, desperate to disentangle himself from the heinous spectre of the woman he had once loved, who he loved still. As her gaping black mouth drew nearer, he heard that terrible scuttling; the sound of insect wings, of thousands of tiny feet pitter-pattering into a crescendo. He managed to turn away, and began to tear at the walls of his fleshy prison. As he slashed at the walls, the sound got louder and louder until he couldn't bear it any more and then... he woke.

But the sound didn't stop with the nightmare. There it was, still, quieter than it was in the dream, but closer and more immediate. Something was scuttling on the roof above him. Something big.

He reached under the bed for his gun. He kept it close in case he ever found himself face to face with one of the forest's bears in the dead of night. They were strong enough to break down a door apparently, if they were hungry enough. But this was no bear. Bears didn't scuttle.

The clattering stopped suddenly, leaving a deafening silence in its wake. Then, a scream, like the ones he'd heard the night before, but so utterly chilling at close range that he instinctively backed into the corner of the room and put his hands over his ears. It was a visceral wail of purest agony, deepest rage! He looked to the egg sac, still gently pulsing on the table, and knew. Whatever it was that was on his roof, this was its baby.

That was when the pounding began—powerful, persistent battering on the cabin roof. The wooden beams cracked and creaked under the pressure. It was only a matter of time before they would give way and the creature would be in there with him; the man who had stolen her offspring. He decided then that, rather than be a sitting duck, confined within the cabin with some unknown beast, he would instead go out to meet it. He would offer it its child back, unharmed, and hope that that would be enough to satisfy it, that it would scuttle back into the forest and leave him be. He scooped the sac up in his arms and walked out into the pitch-black night.

At first, all he saw were the eyes, glowing silver in the blackness, dozens of them. As his own eyes grew accustomed to the dark, the body of the creature began to take shape, grey and glistening. It looked, at first, like a woman lying on her back, suspended in mid air. The torso was certainly that of a human woman, despite the unnatural colour and sheen, but, attached to it were a collection of limbs altogether inhuman—eight of them—long, spindly and pointed at the ends into cruel spikes. He gasped at the utter horror of the sight. Alerted to his presence, the spider woman snapped her long neck round to look at him. It was, by its very nature, hideously contorted, the head being connected to the body with its back parallel to the ground, so, to look at him, the chimera had to bend its neck backwards. The face that hovered there, upside-down, had the rough shape of a human face, but was covered almost completely with those shiny silver-black eyes, and beneath them, two enormous fangs. The thing hissed... a deep, rattling hiss that made its violent intentions clear. James slowly, gently, bent down, and placed the egg sac softly on the ground by his feet, then stepped back, his hands up, signalling his own intent. Although the thing on the roof was hideous beyond measure, there was a tragedy to it too, a piteousness to its condition. It reminded him of... no, he couldn't bear to see her in this abomination, this monster! She was beautiful, she was love, she was goodness, she was nothing like this vile mutation, but still, somehow he found that he was crying not with fear, but with a profound sense of pity, of grief, of guilt.

"I'm sorry," he said, his voice quivering, "I didn't know what I was doing."

For a moment, it seemed the thing had understood. It fell silent. It stood perfectly still. Then, in a whip-fast movement, it flipped onto its 'back' and leapt down off the roof, scuttling along on its eight legs at a terrifying speed towards him, screaming in several frequencies at once. The creature knocked James onto his back before he even had a chance to run, and plunged its vicious fangs into the prone flesh of his neck.

The venom paralysed him instantly. He could only watch as the creature set to work on him, binding him from the feet up with a rope-thick web. She made quick work of him. Within a minute, he was bound to his neck, and frozen with terror as she began wrapping his head in the sticky cord. He could barely breathe as it was. He would surely suffocate inside the web. All went dark. For a while, he listened with increasing panic to the muffled sounds of his shallow breathing as it grew shallower still. Then, he passed out.

When he woke some hours later, still encased within the cocoon but no longer paralysed, he found, to his surprise, that he was glad to be alive. For such a long time he'd longed for the courage to end it all. Since the crash, he'd felt that he had no right to live, and running away had not changed anything. He was the driver, after all. It should have been him. Still, here he was, in this nightmare, fighting to live as he clawed his way out of the spider woman's web, thrashing and tearing with all his strength. He didn't want to die like this, at the hands of some monster. He didn't want to die at all.

As dawn broke, he managed to free himself. He found himself in a cavern, its floor littered with bones, animal and human. Freezing cold, aching and shaken, he stumbled out of the cave and into the rose-coloured day. He began his journey back to the cabin, passing on his way the tree which had once harboured the spider's eggs. All that remained of the vile cluster was a thick pool of grey sludge, and a scattering of empty sacs. Somewhere in the woods, the spider babies scuttled, seeking their meal of flesh.

The forest was not haunted, it was a hunting ground, and James no longer felt like being prey. He returned one final time to the cabin, packed his meagre belongings, and headed for that humble dirt track out of Hoia Baciu. It was time to go home.

The Carnival Returns

by

Thomas Staunton

On and on they came through clouds of foul dust, headlights swallowing the night for just a moment and then back again to black. The convoy coiled around the Little Basin road, then over the river that bisects the village, before thundering down into the valley. The trucks were heading west out of town, and I sat at my window, praying that they wouldn't stop. *Keep going, you sonofabitch!* But it was not to be. The great beast turned off the road just outside of town and parked up in an open field, its various vehicles arranged in a half moon. I closed the curtain, fell back onto my chair, and nursed the scarred, itching skin of my hands. My greatest nightmare had returned. The *Step Right Up* Carnival was here to feed.

When this story began, I was just a young boy, a sick child, often bedridden and confined to my house. With no friends to speak of, I occupied myself with my own adventures. In the end, the outside world felt entirely out of reach. It moved ever forward while I remained still.

How differently I had felt when, one summer morning, a week after my 13th birthday, I looked out my bedroom window to the field adjoining our house and saw a hubbub of activity. Crabby, chain-smoking roustabouts marched to and fro, raising the carnival from the ground up. First to go up were the rides, then the tents, then the game stalls, and finally the ticket kiosk at the cow gate. I didn't move from my window for the whole day. That evening, when the work was done, the lights finally came on, a misty glow of reds, whites and blues. I sat in wonder at the beauty of it all, my bedroom shimmering like a moonlit pool. As the first patrons arrived at the carnival, I felt a tingle of the kind of anxious excitement that only a child can understand, an intense longing to explore this strange, new world. I had to go.

"Max, stop this! You're still too sick! I'll be back on Tuesday, and we can talk about going next time."

My father left the house with a slam of the door, and just like every time before, I watched his car pull away, off to another town that I would never see. Next time? When would that be? Another year from now?

After Mom died, he took a second job travelling the county selling bibles, and I hardly ever saw him. Tonight, I had a new babysitter, a disinterested teenager who spent all her time calling friends on the phone.

"Your dad says you've got to take these," she said, throwing the little pillbox at me.

I bashed my pillows into a believable, boy-like shape. I thought it could work. I doubted that the babysitter would even bother checking. Getting back up to my bedroom would be the tricky part, but that was a problem for later. I looked out my bedroom window and saw the sign:

STEP RIGHT UP!

I was smiling so hard that it hurt my face. This was it. I was going.

o

Night was approaching fast as I arrived at the kiosk. Townsfolk tumbled out of the carnival in a constant stream, laughing and smiling, their arms filled with food and stuffed animal prizes.

"Doors will be closing soon, little lad. Best hurry up."

The old carny sat on a little camping chair, shrouded in darkness except for the glowing embers of his pipe.

"Go on in, no charge."

He took a long pull from his pipe and puffed out a silky plume of sweet-smelling smoke. I smiled politely, nodded a thank you, and walked in.

The main thoroughfare, now almost empty, had become a mudslide impressed with thousands of footprints. It hardly mattered. I was so mesmerised by the colourful signs and stands: hook-a-duck, water guns, air rifles, dodgems. Behind the stalls, the whirling lights of the merry-go-round caught my eye. I couldn't stop smiling. I stomped through the mud towards it.

"We're closed, come back tomorrow."

The tall carny shut the little gate to the merry-go-round and stretched a thick chain across it. That's when it started.

The lights across the carnival started to dim as stallholders packed up their wares, and one by one, the rides ground to a halt. A chilly night breeze blew across the thoroughfare. I felt myself starting to cry, a deep anguish welling up and up and up. This was supposed to be my moment, my first taste of freedom. Heaven was just out of reach.

"Young man! Young man!"

Out of the misty dark, an exotic-looking woman in a fiery, red dress approached, her neck and wrists adorned with gaudy, jangling jewellery. I remember her eyes the most, a piercing emerald green. I was captivated.

"Don't cry, little man. Tomorrow is another day. Come, let me read your palm! Perhaps your night has just begun!"

°

The caravan was warm and scented with a musky incense. The seats were upholstered in red velvet, with pretty cushions and silks scattered here and there. An oil lamp sat atop a wooden table, and behind that, little gems and trinkets twinkled behind the glass doors of a large cabinet. The fortune-teller beckoned me to sit.

"Your palm, dear." Her finger ran along the centre line of my hand. "Ah, hmm. The line breaks here, do you see? That is a great and powerful change. Always good. Always good."

A dark shape was reflected in the glass of the cabinet. Something was behind me.

"Pay attention to my reading, boy. Do you see the branch here?"

I wasn't listening anymore. I could sense the shadow looming over my shoulder, and then all was dark.

o

I awoke in a pool of sweat, a wave of unbearable heat beating down on me. With some effort, I willed one of my eyes to open and took my first glimpse at the room that haunts me to this day. It was a small, domed chamber, hewn out of grey rock. I seemed to be underground.

I tried to open my other eye, but couldn't. I went to move my legs, but nothing happened. I felt no bindings or rope of any kind. I was paralysed.

A deep, sluggish voice came from somewhere in the chamber.

"Ah! Dessert! A delicious, pink candy!"

A chorus of voices followed.

"CANDY! CANDY! CANDY! CANDY!"

A scrawny set of legs walked over to my limp body. The tall man threw me onto his back and hauled me deeper into the chamber. The cavernous room was full of naked people, carnival folk, all chanting and moaning in perfect unison. I shut my eye and screamed inside my head.

"Let us see him," said the deep, sluggish voice.

"LET US SEE HIM," said the room.

I was thrown onto the ground like a sack of corn and rolled onto my side. Unbeknownst to my captors, my index finger was twitching.

There was silence for an unbearable amount of time. I heard footsteps coming and going, and then heavy breathing. I had to look. I had to know what was to come. I opened my one working eye, just enough.

What I saw was a monster; a giant, translucent blob suspended from hundreds of pink and slippery tendrils that splayed out in all directions, penetrating the grey rock. Deep inside the transparent jelly, floating in suspension, was an elderly man, dying or dead, haloed by the effervescent fizz of his dissolving flesh.

I felt a twinge in my legs.

The blob stirred. Two little globules circumnavigated its surface and converged to form the lips of a hideous mouth.

"I'm ready," said the wet mouth.

Without ceremony, I was lifted into the air and thrown at the blob. Its mouth closed over me, sealing me in. With no air in my lungs, I started to drown.

My knee jerked forward, a panicked reflex. Outside the blob, the room was muttering.

"He moves!" they said.

The liquid started to burn like acid, and with that, I was kicked into life, my arms windmilling violently. The blob let out a loud, watery hoot, and the voices in the chamber grew louder.

"He moves! Get him!" they said.

I punched the membrane of the blob, hoping that it would break. Nothing. Too thick. I tried another blow, but I couldn't break through. My fist-shaped imprints soon faded and disappeared. The acid seeped into my eyes, and I swallowed the foul liquid. This couldn't be it; an invalid my whole, too-short life and then this awful, alien death?

Shaping my fingers into a bony dagger, I stabbed the membrane. The blob let out a painful wail. With all my strength, I thrust again and again, and finally pierced it. The liquid poured through the hole, the tear growing larger and larger until the blob suddenly split open like a ruptured water balloon, and I tumbled out onto the floor.

Gasping for air, I coughed and sputtered and wretched out the liquid. My skin still burned furiously, but I knew that there was no time left. I had to escape.

I wiped my bleary, stinging eyes and tried to see around the chamber. The room was littered with the writhing bodies of the carnival folk. They wailed and moaned and then went limp, like fishes left to flounder on the shore. The blob hung from its tendrils, deflated and broken.

I saw the entrance to a tunnel on the other side of the chamber and crawled upwards towards a wooden trapdoor. I pushed it open with what little strength I had left, and found myself in the fortune-teller's caravan. Her body lay flat and motionless on the ground. I stepped over it and made to leave.

"We will return, sweet child," said the fortune-teller, the gurgling, inhuman voice of the blob speaking through her. "We will return."

I ran down the thoroughfare, stepping over bodies as I fled. They called after me, all with that same voice, the voice of their master.

"We will return, mark our words! We always have our feed! Always!"

○

Now I am an old man, sick and weak and still nursing these burns, but I have lived and loved despite their efforts.

Across the fields, they prepare to feast again. This time, I am ready to die, and I intend to take them with me. Tonight, we will all burn.

The Siren Of Silver Falls

BY

Sarah Daly

Every town has its legends, tall tales and campfire stories passed down through the ages to scare children into obedience. My town is no different, except that our legend is true. I know because I saw it, I saw *her* with my own eyes.

Silver Falls, Indiana first appears on the map with the name 'Tranquille' around 1697, when it was settled by the French, who held it for almost a hundred years. The notoriously bloody Battle of Tranquille in 1793 saw the French defeated by the Americans, who took over the town and changed its name to Crimson Falls. The new moniker referred to the waterfall on the town's northern limits, which, supposedly, flowed red with the blood of battle for three days and nights. Just fifty years ago, they shed this unsavoury title and opted instead for the more palatable 'Silver Falls'.

Few records remain of the details of The Battle of Tranquille, but one particularly gruesome story has endured, no doubt embellished over the centuries, but, nonetheless, true. The tale describes the tragic fate of a Tranquille resident by the name of Marie-Fleur Deschamps. Marie-Fleur was a mother of two children, Michel and Alizé, who she raised alone following the death of her husband Alain from typhoid. She was well-known in the town for her beautiful singing voice, which would echo through Tranquille's narrow streets as she sang her children to sleep. On the night of the 'battle' which was, in truth, a massacre, Marie-Fleur and the children lay asleep in their beds, unaware of the invaders skulking those same streets, driven by a lust for violence and conquest.

Marie-Fleur awoke to the sound of her children screaming; first both, then, a single voice alone. Half-awake still, but moved by a rising terror, she threw open the door to her children's room, and the sight that confronted her there drew the air from her lungs. Michel lay dead in his bed, his throat slashed. The man who had killed him stood over Alizé, a sword raised aloft, ready to strike her. Marie-Fleur threw herself between the man and her precious child just as the sword came down. The force of it was so great that it split the woman in two. As it is described, her head first peeled open like the petals of a flower, drawing apart her neck and chest. The left side of her slid downwards, then dropped like a felled tree. According to the man's account, the right side remained standing for what felt like an impossible amount of time, the right eye staring at him, wild with a mother's rage, until she finally hit the floor.

That was the beginning of it—a brutal, unforgivable act of violence against a defenceless woman and her children. Then came the legend.

I first heard about the so-called 'Siren of Silver Falls' when I was eleven years old. My best friend at the time, Seb, was obsessed with monsters and aliens, and all things unexplained. He'd heard the story from his granddad, who claimed to have seen her one time, back in the fifties. He'd never been back to the falls since. According to the legend, Marie-Fleur had stuck around after her death, seeking revenge for what had happened to her and her children. She wanted to make the new inhabitants of Crimson Falls pay for their brutality by taking their children, just as they had taken hers. Even as the decades and centuries passed, still her song could be heard echoing through the town, luring the children from their beds and into her eternal embrace. That was the worst part—her embrace. She didn't just kill the children... she absorbed them. As she held the poor things in her arms, her body would split in two down the middle, just as it had at the moment of her death, and the two halves would envelop the child, encasing them inside her flesh like a Russian nesting doll. Trapped inside the monster, they would suffocate, and their bodies would decay within her cursed shell, giving her the nourishment to sustain her assault on the town.

Of course, Seb wanted to witness this hideous creature for himself, and he wanted me to come with him. I was fearless then, and keen for the adventure, so I agreed. This was, without a doubt, the worst decision of my life.

It was October 18th, 1993, the 200th anniversary of the Battle of Tranquille, and so, the perfect time to mount a search for the siren. We set out in the late afternoon, planning to make camp at the waterfall for the night, giddy with excitement for the quest ahead. Seb had told his parents that he was sleeping over at mine. I'd told my parents nothing, since they rarely noticed if I was there or not, unless there was some chore that needed doing. It sounds tragic, but for the most part, I enjoyed the independence that their indifference afforded me. I was pretty much free to do as I pleased.

As dusk descended, we lit a fire. It took us a long time to get it going, since we didn't really know what we were doing, but it was worth it. We felt like outlaws, like adventurers, like men. We stayed up late into the night, each doing our best to seem tough, to act like we weren't terrified to be out there in the dark. Every little sound sent cold, sharp shocks of fear down my spine. Every shadow was a creature skulking in the blackness, hungry for our young flesh.

We ate a balanced dinner of Twinkies and Reese's Pieces, then settled in for the night. I never thought I'd manage to get any sleep out there, but, as frightened as I was, I was even more exhausted, and so I drifted off pretty quickly.

I woke a couple of hours later to see Seb sitting up in his sleeping bag, peering into the darkness.

"What is it?"

"Shh," he put a finger to his lips. I was suddenly wide awake. Something was wrong.

"Don't you hear it?" he whispered.

I listened out for whatever sound had him so transfixed. At first, I heard nothing. I wondered if perhaps he was dreaming, or imagining things. Then, I heard it. It was so faint and so gentle that you could easily have mistaken it for a breeze blowing through the trees, or the soft streaming wash of the waterfall, but this was not a natural sound—it had a melody—the sweetest, most soothing tune you can imagine. The voice was lilting and pure, and getting louder. I looked to Seb in terror. It had to be her. It was real! The stories were real! Seb did not share my concern. He was mesmerised, utterly in the thrall of the siren's song. I begged him not to go, but he took off walking into the woods, following the sweet voice. With every fibre of my being I wanted to run the other way, to go home and forget all about that awful night, but I knew I had to follow him, to make sure he would be all right.

With nothing to guide me but the sound of her voice, I stumbled blindly through the trees, snagging my clothes and skin on the jagged branches that grabbed at me like skeletal fingers. I couldn't see Seb. I could barely see anything at all. The town wasn't far, but the comforting glow of its lights were lost in the thick canopy of trees. After what felt like hours spent like this, fumbling through the darkness, all went quiet. She stopped singing, and my heart went cold. I knew what it meant. She had him.

"Seb!" I shouted, terrified to draw attention to myself, but more frightened for my friend. No response. I started to run. I suppose you never know how you'll react in a crisis until one comes along. Back then, I was the sort of person who ran towards danger. I'm not that person any more.

I arrived at a clearing. A low fog lay on the ground, a thick, silvery soup that devoured me up to my knees, swirling and heaving as if it were alive. It gave the clearing the appearance of a bleak and murky lake. As I looked across the blue-grey mass of it, I saw two figures standing in the centre of the clearing, moving toward each other through the fog, as if floating. One of them was Seb, the other was a pale woman with long, dark hair. She was beautiful. She was smiling. She was the most terrifying thing I had ever seen in my life.

She held out her arms to embrace Seb, and he went to her, in some kind of trance. I could feel her power, her pull. Although it seemed like madness to submit to her like that, knowing what she was, knowing what she was capable of, I understood why he'd done it. She was utterly alluring in every sense, the perfect embodiment of womanhood and motherhood at once. To be near her was to be hers. I knew that there was nothing I could do to prevent what was about to happen, still I stood there at the edge of the clearing, watching, hoping beyond hope that I was wrong and that everything would be all right. Then, it started. The two sides of her face began to curl away from each other, like ferns unfurling. Next, her torso split down the middle, her dress tearing apart, revealing the naked flesh beneath, the dreadful hollowness within. All the while, as the body separated, the arms held Seb tightly. He was struggling now, the horror of it rousing him from his trance. He knew what was about to happen. She was pulling him closer, forcing him into the space between the two halves of her. I stared in abject terror at the hideous metamorphosis. She was like some carnivorous plant, and he an unwitting insect stumbling into her trap, but there was nothing natural about the act, the way her flesh rearranged itself around him, her two halves becoming whole again from the bottom up, as fleshy tendrils stretched across the gulf, combining hungrily. Before long, Seb was encased within the creature. I could hear his muffled cries as Marie-Fleur became whole around him. Her body at first was swollen and distended, like a snake bulging with the bulk of some poor prey, slowly being digested inside it. Then, as Seb's body was broken down within her, she returned to her normal, slender shape, and was beautiful once more. It was as if he had never existed.

She turned to me and smiled. She knew that I had been there, watching, all that time. She didn't want to take me, to kill me as she'd killed Seb. She wanted me to be the witness to her atrocity. She wanted me to tell the story. This was her vengeance, and it would never stop. She would never stop taking the children of Silver Falls, as it had taken her children from her.

I ran. I ran through the woods, through the darkness and into the dawn. It feels sometimes that I have never stopped running since that day.

Of course, no one believed me. Everyone had their explanation. I had dreamed it. I'd somehow imagined the story, a fantasy to block out what had really happened. I'd lost my mind out there in the dark. The only person who gave my account any credence was Seb's grandfather, the one who'd told him about the siren in the first place, but, sadly, he died that same winter. I was left all alone to defend myself against the town's insatiable hunger for answers, but the only one I could give them was not what they wanted to hear. Seb's mother was the worst of all of them. I felt sorry for her, of course, and guilty that I hadn't been able to protect her son, but she hounded me, day and night. She would wait at the school gates, primed with a hundred questions, becoming more desperate, more unhinged by the day. I had hoped that my parents might actually start to pay attention, since something had really happened to me and it was obvious that I needed someone in my corner, but they were just as disinterested as ever. People don't change. So, I kept my head down as best I could, and got through the next few years with an escape plan always at the forefront of my thoughts. I would leave that cursed town at the earliest possible opportunity and go live in the city. Any city. Somewhere without forests, without waterfalls, without history. Somewhere where everything was new.

I stayed true to my plan. At 16, I gathered what few belongings I had, and a thousand dollars I'd managed to save working part-time at the hardware store, and took a bus out of town. I didn't tell anyone I was leaving. There were no sad goodbyes. I just got on the bus and never looked back.

First, it was Chicago, then Atlanta, Washington, New York. I could never find a place that felt new, that felt fresh. Wherever I went, I took Silver Falls with me, and the monsters that lurked there. I've been in San Francisco for six months now and it's the most amazing city—friendly, exciting, buzzing, beautiful—but still I can't just be here and be happy. I hoped that if I found the perfect place, then I could leave the past behind and move on, but now I see that it isn't true. Running will never work. I have to somehow reclaim that half of me that I left in a foggy field in Silver Falls all those years ago. I have to go back.

So, here I am, twenty years later, back where it all began. Nothing much has changed, except that the place feels even more left behind now than it did when I was a kid. It has the feel of a place that's been dying for a long, long time but stubbornly refuses to just let go. I head down Main Street towards what used to be my parent's house and wonder if it still is. I've sent them a Christmas card every year with my latest address and phone number, but either they haven't been getting them or... well, they just don't care.

I hang back a little, out of sight but with a good view of the house, and I wait. Before long, I see a woman at the window. My mother. The years have not been kind to her, but time rarely is, I suppose. She was a stranger to me before. Now she is a ghost. I don't bother going in, since I already know exactly how that would go, and that's not what I came here for.

I keep walking, past the tired little houses, past the abandoned play-park, past the graveyard. I wonder how many of the graves, like Seb's, have no bodies in them. The October wind starts to bite as I reach the outskirts of the town. It's not far now. We never were that far from town, from safety.

The leaves crunch beneath my feet as I make my way through the woods to the waterfall. The place has been neglected. Trees felled by storms criss-cross the path, their massive root systems torn from the earth, exposed and decaying. I hear the hushed roar of the waterfall and know that I am close. Close to what, I can't say, but I know that something will happen. It has to.

I can see it now, the waterfall, just beyond the edge of the trees. I can see that something is wrong with it. The water... it's red! I go to the water's edge in awe of the sight before me. The waterfall—the whole river—flows a deep crimson. I dip my hand in the water and, to my disgust, find that it is warm. When I draw my hand out, it is coated in the slick, red liquid. This is not algae, or pollution, or any other natural phenomenon. This is blood.

Then, I hear it... her song. It's all I can hear. The waterfall, even, is quiet, its gushing torrents silenced. I know, in that very instant, what I have come here for. I have come here to be with her. This is what I have wanted all these years, what has kept me from happiness. Her beauty, her love, however twisted, is greater than anything else this rotten world can offer me.

I see her now, in that same clearing through the trees where she stood all those years ago. She is looking right at me, smiling that same smile, and I am a child again, filled with dread and wonder and desire all at once. I am utterly in her thrall, totally powerless as my feet take one step after another towards her. With each step, I see her moonlight skin and fine, dark features more clearly. My Marie-Fleur. My one true love. She holds her arms out to me, welcoming me in. I embrace her, drinking in her sweet coldness, feeling for the first time in my life that I belong, that I am wanted. I am weeping now, my tears soaking into the cotton of her dress.

I hear her voice, but her lips don't move. She is speaking inside my head. Her voice, like her, is soft and sweet, but as cold as winter's breath.

"You will not be missed."

And with that, she begins to open. I watch in awe as a great fault line appears down the middle of her. Her arms tighten around me, crushing me, as the narrow crack widens to a chasm. Inside her is the hollow womb of death. I am fed into her void, surrounded by the long-dead shell of her, and as the fleshy walls close in around me, I feel the air sucked from my lungs, the light stolen from my eyes and the blood slowing in my veins. In the blackness, I hear the lilting sweetness of her song, a lullaby serenading me to sleep. Piece by piece, I am disintegrating. I am dissolving into her essence, just a tiny part of her whole, a lost soul in the ocean of lost souls that dwell inside her.

I am home now. I am finally home.

Tooth

BY

Thomas Staunton

Robert tiptoed around the Professor's study, snuffing out the candles as he went. The shadows danced as they flickered and died, until one lone candle remained alight, fluttering upon an imposing oak desk.

"Young Robert, come here a moment, please."

Robert approached the desk.

"Sir?" The Professor was studying a scroll.

"What a strange letter."

"Yes, sir, very strange."

"An old college friend of mine. It seems he's managed to worm his way into the Hellfire Club, up in the mountains."

"Rialto House, sir?"

"Indeed. 'Come join us for hunting, card games, and other sports of the most deplorable kind'." The Professor harrumphed.

Robert shifted on his feet, uncomfortable with the tone of the letter. He edged closer to the light.

"I've heard stories, sir, of strange rituals, sacrifices, devil-worship."

"Ha!" The Professor took his eyes away from the letter. "These people are nothing but drunks and scoundrels. They couldn't boil an egg, let alone raise the Devil. That isn't what puzzles me."

"No, sir?"

The Professor looked to the letter again.

"No, it seems they want my services."

"They wish for your counsel? On matters of the mind?"

"No, my other services. They want me to perform the incantations."

Robert's shoulders sank. He liked working for the Professor, and never took for granted the privilege that had been bestowed upon a lowly Catholic orphan. For the most part, his duties to the Professor were quite ordinary, but every so often, he was called to join the Professor on night-time excursions: card games, drinking, clandestine meetings. He had determined quite quickly under his employ that the Professor was a member of a secret society, but the details of its machinations were spared from him, thankfully. Robert was happy to wait by the carriage, pipe in hand, with a good book for company. All he knew was that the group was fascinated by the dark arts, particularly magick.

"They're dreadfully boring, these men, but I can't say that I'm not curious."

The Professor stood up from his desk, almost extinguishing the candle with his billowing gown.

"Be here early tomorrow. Pack some food and wine, and have Mr O'Reilly ready my carriage for 4 pm sharp."

"Shall I prepare your case, sir?"

The Professor picked up the candle and held it to his chest. The flames danced in his dark eyes.

"No, this requires a more detailed study. Unless you happen to know how to ward off evil spirits?"

o

Mr Levine and Mr Shaw were already quite drunk when the Professor's carriage arrived at the summit of Rialto Hill. They greeted the Professor with sham sobriety, cumbersome and heavy on the lean.

Mr Levine smiled awkwardly at the Professor.

"Professor Hopkins! My dear fellow! Come in at once."

The journey had been an unpleasant one. They had traversed ditch, bog and hill, ascending through the Dublin Mountains into the wilderness. The Professor spent the time leafing through enormous, black tomes, and hardly uttered a word, save for a few grumbles when the carriage hit a pothole and sent his texts flying. Robert sat opposite the Professor, his unease growing stronger the closer they drew to their destination.

Mr Reilly carried the Professor's luggage into Rialto House, leaving Robert alone in the late summer twilight. The house was an old, stone hunting lodge, but it had a certain ecclesiastical quality to it, a strange formality amidst these wild surroundings. Robert turned to observe the panorama. Down below, the city faintly glowed. He wished that he could be there now, amidst the comforting ebb and flow of the mundane. As Mr Reilly's carriage set off back down the hill, Robert took a deep breath to ready himself. It would be a long night.

o

Robert poured Mr Shaw another generous brandy and took his seat next to the hearth. The room was scant on furnishings, containing only a long, rustic table with simple, wooden chairs, a dusty Persian rug and a whiskey cask armchair on which Robert sat. Although it was not yet autumn, the room was bitterly cold.

The Professor and his two old companions sat around the table, reminiscing. Robert knew from his master's posture that he was thoroughly disinterested in the conversation. As the brandy flowed, Mr Levine grew garrulous and mad-eyed, while Mr Shaw sunk into a depressive stupor beside him. The Professor watched them both studiously.

"You say you're having trouble with spirits, Mr Levine?"

Mr Levine leaned in, his slate-grey eyes suddenly sharply focussed, and spoke with stark seriousness.

"We have gone to great lengths to ensure that our rituals are carried out with care and diligence. However, I fear—and Mr Shaw agrees with my theory—that the lodge was built over an ancient stone with some power, some significance beyond our understanding. We may have called up a more... exotic spirit than we intended."

The Professor delved further. "Exotic? How so?"

"Squealing!" said Mr Shaw, suddenly animated.

Mr Levine shot him a fierce look. "Be quiet, Mr Shaw."

"Squealing?" said the Professor.

"He did not say squealing," said Mr Levine.

The Professor turned to his assistant. "Robert, did he say squealing?"

"I heard the word squealing, sir."

Mr Levine was livid. "He did not mean to say that. He misspoke, didn't you, Mr Shaw?"

Mr Shaw fell silent, but his eyes revealed a deep disquiet that troubled Robert. Mr Levine rose from his chair and grabbed the brandy bottle.

"The pig farm down the lane. Perhaps this is what he was referring to?" said Robert.

The Professor gestured for Mr Levine to sit.

"I have not come here to interrogate you, Mr Levine, but you asked for my help. Now, as you know, I do not mince my words. A ceremony that you have performed has invoked an evil spirit, has it not?"

Mr Levine nodded and gulped a mouthful of brandy.

"I have warned you before, Mr Levine. You must perform these rituals with clear-headedness and thorough preparation. What cleansing has taken place?"

Mr Levine put his glass down. "Cleansing?"

The Professor's sigh was long and deep. He turned to Robert.

"Fetch me my case and wait outside until I call for you."

Relieved, Robert grabbed the case from beside his armchair, handed it to the Professor and then went to open the door. It took him a moment to notice the white face pressed against the glass. He leapt backwards in shock.

"Professor, the window!"

The Professor stood up and pointed his finger. "You there! Wait right where you are!"

Peering in from behind the glass was a gaunt, teenage boy.

"Robert, open the door and let him in."

○

The boy drank the soup straight from the bowl in noisy slurps, shivering under the Professor's heavy cloak. Robert tended to him, preparing a small meal from his master's basket.

The Professor puffed his pipe.

"Where have you come from?"

"Not far, sir. I look after Mr Delaney's flock. He asked me to find some strays that wandered up Rialto Hill, and I got lost in the dark. I feel stupid, really."

As Robert sat at the bench to prepare the cold meats and cheese, he noticed that Mr Levine and Shaw had sobered somewhat, and were staring at the boy with bewilderment.

"Do I know you, boy?" said Mr Shaw, cock-eyed and slurring.

Shrouded by the Professor's cloak, the boy turned his head to address Mr Shaw.

"I'm not sure. Are you from here?"

Mr Levine moved to the edge of his seat, his face a cold, sickly white.

"Professor, this boy cannot be here. We need to continue with our business."

"In time, Mr Levine. The boy must fill his belly and warm his bones before he departs."

"You look familiar, boy," said Mr Shaw. "Show me your face."

Panicked, Mr Levine shot up from this seat.

"He needs to leave now." His fist came down hard on the table, sending a wheel of cheese rolling onto the floor and under the bench.

The Professor met Mr Levine's terrified eyes.

"Fetch the cheese, Robert. We'll make this boy a package, clothe him and send him on his way."

Robert went to retrieve the cheese from under the bench and stopped abruptly. Below the boy's trouser cuffs were a pair of oily, black hooves.

"Professor, the boy..."

From beneath the boy's hood came an ungodly squeal. The men retreated to the far corners of the room.

The squeal grew in pitch and volume until it was almost unbearable.

"Show yourself, demon!" cried the Professor, his arms raised in defence.

For a brief moment, all was still and silent. Then, the boy floated up into the air, and came to land some feet behind. The men watched the scene unfold in terror.

The cloak began to stretch and tear until it was little more than a pile of rags on the floor, revealing the beast beneath. Standing before them was a seven-foot-tall humanoid figure with the head of a black pig. The hearth brimmed with raging hellfire.

Robert's terror was absolute. He stood frozen in paralytic fear as the demon commanded the room.

Mr Shaw cursed the demon and staggered towards the door. It was locked.

"Mr Shaw!" cried the Professor.

The demon grabbed Mr Shaw by his head, lifted him off the ground and slammed him down onto the table. Before the man had the chance to recover, the beast cleaved his legs and devoured his privates in a sudden, violent mess of blood and flesh.

Robert looked to the Professor for guidance and found him flipping feverishly through the pages of one of his spellbooks.

When the gorging had finished, the demon raised its head, and a rope of bloody intestine fell to the floor in soft, fleshly loops. Mr Shaw had forgotten to scream, so Mr Levine screamed for him. The demon roared.

The Professor caught Robert before his legs buckled.

"Not today, Robert!" said the Professor. "Stand behind me."

The Professor held his book aloft and uttered a strange incantation.

Out of the ether, a ghostly wall materialised, black as obsidian. It separated the demon from the men. Robert was mesmerised.

"Mr Levine, stand behind me." urged the Professor.

"Professor, where is the demon?" said Robert.

"We are safe, but only for a moment. We will trap it in this void."

The Professor resumed the incantation.

The black wall began to shrink, enveloping the demon inside it. It dwindled to an almost imperceptible dot floating in the air before collapsing in on itself. As it vanished, three pulses of bright red light radiated out and struck the three men in their foreheads. The world went dark.

When Robert woke, the Professor was standing over him.

"Mr Levine has absconded. We must leave this place immediately."

○

Robert awoke in a fit, lifted his head off the pillow, and immediately hunched over. There was an agonising cramp in his groin, and his head was burning hot. The nightmare lingered at the fringes of his consciousness. In the dream, the demon had found him hiding in a dark room. Robert was convinced that the beast had touched him somehow, for he felt a tactile pressure lingering still, day and night, in the spot where he had been struck. He drank the water at his bedside table and sat up in his bed to ruminate.

His encounter with the demon had changed him. His mood was mostly grey, and he was plagued by a dull, nagging ache that penetrated his entire body. However, it was the dreams that bothered him the most. Every night, the demon pursued him, coming ever closer to devouring him. In the last few days, the demon had begun to encroach on his waking life. As he tended to his duties, he would hear a faint grunting sound from somewhere behind him. When he went to investigate, he would find nothing there, but the feeling remained. He couldn't shake the sense that something awful was going to happen to him.

He got out of bed, lit a candle and walked to the living quarters. His shadow danced on the walls as he took his seat by the hearth. As the dying embers glowed softly beside him, he started to drift off, but just before sleep came, he felt a presence in the room.

Oink...

Standing by the scullery door was the farm boy, grey as slate and dressed in rags. Robert's body tightened. The boy stared at him silently for a while, then raised his hand and pointed to the front door. Robert heard nothing but the blood rushing through his ears. The boy smiled broadly, revealing a toothless mouth. Blood began to gush from the gums. Robert shot up from the chair and threw the candle at the vision, but it had already vanished. He began to cry, not out of fear, but pure exhaustion. He had no idea what any of these hallucinations meant. The only person who could help him had become a recluse.

○

"I'm not receiving visitors. Go away, thank you."

Robert stood outside the door of his master's study.

The Professor's new routine was to pass messages and instructions under the door, and he insisted that all food and drink be left outside for him to retrieve in his own time. Robert had pleaded to speak with him on several occasions, only to be greeted with stony silence, but now, drained of energy and inhibition, he closed his fist and thumped the study door until the wood began to warp.

"The demon, sir. Please! You have to help me. It's coming. It's COMING!"

Robert heard the shuffling of feet. The door opened abruptly, and he was pulled inside.

"You've seen it too?" said the Professor.

Robert had not dared to check his own appearance as of late, but he was quite sure that he did not look anywhere near as terrible as the Professor. The man was pale as death, his hair wild and his eyes bloodshot.

The study was dark, but for a small shaft of light streaming through a gap in the closed curtains. Books, sheets, manuscripts and ancient scrolls littered the floor. The Professor had been busy.

"I'm sorry for my present state, Robert, but I have been busy searching for answers. Unfortunately, all I have are more questions. I did not want you to be witness to this madness, and perhaps become infected with it too. I hope you understand."

"Sir, I think it has driven us both mad," said Robert. "We need to find Mr Levine. Perhaps there is something he can tell us."

"Don't you think I've tried that? He's vanished, and to add to my burdens, I now have Mr Shaw's family pursuing me incessantly." The Professor rubbed his face with his hand and sighed deeply.

"Pardon me, sir, but perhaps you may be the wrong person to look for Levine. I have some contacts, friendly faces, you know. Someone might know where he is hiding."

The Professor smiled, but it was a tired smile.

"Well then, young Robert. Lead the way."

○

The young nun escorted Robert and the Professor through a labyrinth of corridors and out into a barren, wintry courtyard. As they approached the door to the neighbouring convent building, she stopped suddenly and turned to face them.

"It is only because of Robert that I allow this, do you understand me, Professor? Mr Levine has asked for sanctuary, and we will provide it for as long as we can manage. Do not approach him or raise your voice."

The Professor cleared his throat and feigned a solemn tone.

"I understand. We will be brief."

Mr Levine was sitting on the floor in the tiny basement room when Robert and the Professor entered. His once-handsome face was sunken, ravaged by terror. When Mr Levine craned his head to look up at the Professor, Robert could see red patches of scalp where the man had pulled his hair out. The Professor sat down on a wooden chair, keeping his distance as the nun had requested.

Mr Levine squinted. "Are you the pig? I cannot tell anymore. I hear it squealing outside the room. Are you the pig?"

"I am not the pig, Mr Levine, but I warn you now, I will drag you back up to Rialto Hill, kicking and screaming, if you do not give me answers." said the Professor.

Robert winced, fearful that the Professor might lose his temper and ruin their chances of gleaning any information from the man.

Mr Levine rocked his head back and forth. His eyes widened, as if a fog had lifted, and he finally recognised the Professor.

"How did you find me?"

"That is not important. Now, listen to me carefully. Where did this demon come from?"

Mr Levine was silent for a moment, but then he started to whimper.

"You cannot stop it. You can't! It will not stop! We didn't mean for him to die, I swear to you!"

The Professor stood up from his chair and loomed over the trembling Mr Levine.

"What did you do, Mr Levine?"

Mr Levine wiped the tears from his puffy face.

"Mr Shaw, he... he took a liking to the farm boy. Invited him in and gave him whiskey. Oh, God help me!"

The Professor crouched down, grabbed Mr Levine by the jaw, and waited until the man was pacified.

"Tell me what happened."

"Mr Shaw was drunker than I've ever seen him. The boy was frightened of him! Petrified! He didn't care for his advances. He panicked. He... he tried to run. And Mr Shaw, he just lost his mind, he clobbered the poor boy over the head! Oh, God! He just lay there. He didn't move! I tried to wake him up, but he wouldn't wake up!"

Mr Levine curled into a ball and sobbed.

"Where is the body?"
"It's gone. We fed him to the pigs! Oh, God help me!"
The Professor turned away in disgust.
"We need to get to Rialto Hill, immediately."

°

The carriage ascended the last mile of the dirt track that led to the lodge. A dusting of snow had settled in patches on the peatlands. Robert turned away from the low, white, winter sun and tried to concentrate on the task at hand. The Professor had spent the entire journey preparing him for the ritual.

"The house must first be cleansed with oils and powders. You will hand them to me in the correct order when I ask for them. Be quick and careful. Then, I must read this text, and you must read the response. See here? Do not worry about the language; it is pronounced as it is written. Do not break away from your duties under any circumstances. No matter what happens, you must stay at your post."

Robert saw, in the distance, the grey stone outline of Rialto House. He looked to his tremorous hands and tried to suppress the urge to vomit. He turned to the Professor.

"Sir, why did they call for you? Mr Levine and Mr Shaw? Why not run away?"

"I suspect that they did run away, only to find themselves pursued by the spirit. It made sense for them to return to the house and try to clean up their mess. Unfortunately, they were too drunk, too foolish, and too guilty to accomplish an exorcism. So, they bestowed that task upon me."

"But we didn't do anything wrong!"

The Professor smiled, empathetically at Robert.

"Vengeance can be indiscriminate. The world is an unjust and cruel place, so why should the spirit world be any different? Now, ready yourself. We are here."

o

They had completed the cleansing without incident, and Robert watched in nervous anticipation as the Professor took a long, flowing, black gown from his satchel and donned it.

"The demon will appear imminently."

The Professor opened the book and motioned Robert to come closer as he read aloud the first line of the arcane text, and Robert followed with the response:

"Dalkankat Rokando"

Robert shuddered as a cold draught coiled around his neck. The air grew stale, followed immediately by a sickly, sweet smell. The room darkened with each passing line of text, until the men could barely make out the words on the page.

Oink...

With slow, fluid grace, the demon descended through the ceiling and alighted by the fire, hot steam billowing from its snout.

Robert tried, in desperation, to see the boy inside the monster before him, but the pig's eyes were dead and black and hungry for blood. The hearth threw up an enormous, smoking flame, and the demon roared in synchronicity.

Unmoved by the horrific display, the Professor continued with the text. He tugged at Robert's arm once again, and Robert responded.

"Dalkankat Rokando!"

Unflinching, the demon marched towards them and opened its great arms wide. Robert looked to the Professor, who, panicked, began to quicken his reading. Robert answered once again.

"Dalkankat Roka..."

The Professor was lifted off the ground before Robert could react. The demon dangled him in the air for a brief moment and then threw him across the room, effortlessly.

Robert ran to the Professor and turned his broken body over. Blood was pouring from his mouth and down his cheeks. Robert's heart sank, and he started to cry in anguish.

"Fool! Get up and leave! The spell holds the creature in this house forever."

The heavy thud of hooves signalled the approach of the demon behind Robert, but he no longer felt fear, only resignation. He was too exhausted to fight.

The Professor coughed a powdery mist of blood.

"Get up and leave. Get up and leave."

He smiled at Robert one last time and closed his eyes for good.

o

Delirious, Robert walked away from the house. Dawn was fast approaching, with the first touches of blue light glowing on the horizon. He trudged down the mucky hill, through thickets and heather, stopped at the gate and collapsed onto the ground. He was drained of tears, devoid of feelings and completely numb. Sweet death seemed so alluring now, and he thought about returning to the demon.

But, when he turned to look back through the bars of the gate, he saw the farm boy standing there. Just as before, his arm was raised and pointing. The boy smiled his toothless smile, all gums and blood. Robert got to his feet and looked to where the boy was pointing. Past the fork in the mountain trail sat a tidy, little farm. Robert had a realisation.

When he reached the farm, he snuck silently around the perimeter of the pigsty and jumped the fence. The hogs regarded him for a moment and then returned to their noisy sleep. He fell to his knees amidst their filth and plunged his hands straight in, pulling away piles and piles of dung, gagging as the smell hit his nostrils. As he reached the bottom, he felt something hard and pearly between his fingertips. He pulled his hand out, and saw that he had unearthed a single molar. He was right. The boy was here. He would dig all day and all night to find whatever else was left of him and bury it properly, in a place with some dignity. Maybe then the boy could rest, he thought.

The Curse Of Pinnilekk

BY

Sarah Daly

There is such a thing as natural order. So too is there a natural disorder, a propensity for anomalies to emerge, against all reason and seemingly in defiance of nature, but in truth, they are as natural as the air, the sky, the sun. Man has an instinctual revulsion towards chaos, towards deviation. It unsettles us to glimpse the breadth of all that is possible; the boundless horizons, too distant to grab hold of, the infinite potential for suffering. Yet, there they are, the anomalies, simmering just beneath the surface, waiting for that spark of chaos to ignite them into existence. This is the story of one such aberration.

o

One grey afternoon in October, Paul Rutherford took his dog for a walk on a quiet stretch of beach near his home in Stornoway. For those not familiar with the town, it is by far the largest on the Hebrides, a diverse archipelago off the west coast of Scotland, but is by no stretch of the imagination, a metropolis, with a mere eight thousand souls calling the far-flung settlement home. For Paul, it was heaven. Before moving north, he had lived for many years in London, a place that had almost killed him with its constant noise and demands, and the endemic loneliness that flourishes there despite its millions. London taught him that the worst kind of loneliness was the sort suffered while surrounded by people, by strangers to whom you were invisible. In Stornoway, he was isolated from the mainland, from current affairs, from the unrelenting onward march of progress, but he never for a moment felt alone.

Paul's three-year-old springer spaniel, Trixie, was one of the great joys of his new life. She never judged him, manipulated him, or made demands of him that he couldn't fulfil. She brought only boundless love, energy and affection. They would take each other for a good, long walk almost every afternoon, weather permitting. This particular afternoon was dull and flat, the dark drawing in already as autumn marched towards winter. It was neither warm nor cold. There was no wind to speak of. Even the sea seemed to have been hushed, its waves gently lapping at the sand rather than crashing towards it as they usually did on these brutal coasts. It was as if the day was holding its breath.

Trixie was skittish. She was not usually a nervous dog. In fact, she'd gotten herself into quite a few tricky situations thanks to her fearlessness. Today, though, she stayed close by her companion, yelping at things unseen. As they approached a crop of jagged, black rocks, a minor obstacle they faced almost daily on their walks, she refused to go any further.

"What's wrong, Trixie? Do you see something?"

She didn't make a sound, but stared into the distance, her gaze fixed on a particular spot by the rocks. There was something there. Paul could just about make it out, protruding from the sand. Could it be... a hand?

His heart pounding, Paul left Trixie behind, frantically barking her disapproval, and headed towards the buried thing, certain that the closer he got, the less it would look like what he feared it was. The opposite was true. Paul looked down, in horror at what was, undoubtedly, a human hand. The strange thing about it, aside from the obvious oddness of encountering a human body part on the beach, was that it was pink. Not blue, not black, not bloated or decaying in any way, but pink, the colour of living flesh. He knew that he had to touch it. However unlikely it was, he had to check if this person was, by some miracle, alive. So, he reached out and touched the fingers of the hand. They were warm! At this close range, he noticed something else odd. The man didn't seem to have any fingernails. Perhaps the poor chap was tortured before being buried here. As Paul thought on the horror of the imagined ordeal, the hand suddenly grabbed his, wrapping its strong fingers around it in a vice-like grip. This was not an act of violence, but of desperation.

Paul pulled his hand free and began to dig frantically. Guessing where the head must be, he ploughed through the coarse sand, tossing it behind him as fast as he could without fear of hurting the man trapped beneath.

Soon, he uncovered skin. And then more skin.

He must be lying face-down.

He kept digging, revealing the full head, perfectly smooth and hairless. The man was bald, fair enough, that wasn't unusual, but what was undeniably odd, was that the man didn't appear to have any ears—not that they had been removed or lost in an accident—but there simply weren't any. All that Paul could see was smooth, pink skin.

He heard the muffled sound of the buried man's cries, driving him to work faster still to get him out. He pulled away as much of the sand as he could, and, with all his strength, flipped the man over onto his back.

Paul had, of course, expected to see a face, but there was none. The man's 'front' was identical to his 'back'. This other side of the head was, again, covered in smooth, featureless skin, with no eyes or nose or mouth, or anything at all to distinguish one side of the head from the other. Paul let out a sharp gasp that had formed itself without him. There was something so unspeakably wrong about this 'man', this thing.

Paul stumbled backwards in the sand as the frontless, backless man got awkwardly to its feet. There was a hideous clumsiness to it, the way it couldn't seem to settle on which way to face. With every few wobbling steps it took, it would spin round, its hands and feet rotating to match each redirection, always with a little lag.

It held something in its left hand, something sharp. It was an ancient-looking dagger, with the dull patina of something that had spent a century underwater. Paul dragged himself backwards, the shock rendering him unable to stand as the thing approached him in awkward, jerky movements. Seeing Paul in trouble, Trixie overcame her fear and bounded towards the man-thing, snarling and barking and baring her teeth, but after just a few unsteady steps, the wretched creature ceased his lurching advance and raised the dagger to his 'face', roughly where a mouth should be. He clenched his other fist as he dragged the jagged blade across his skin, tearing a wide slit from one side of his head to the other. Once done, he dropped the blade, and let out a tortured, primal wail from his self-made mouth. He dropped to his knees, and his shoulders shook. It looked as if he was crying, but it was difficult to tell if a person was crying when they didn't have any eyes.

Paul could not contain the nausea that bloomed deep within his gut when he looked on the creature, but he was no longer afraid of the thing. It was pitiful above all else, and, like any living thing, deserved to be treated with kindness.

Carefully, Paul approached the man, putting a hand reassuringly on his 'back'.

"I'm going to get you some help, okay? It's going to be all right."

○

It was no more than a five-minute drive to the Western Isles Hospital, but with his perturbing passenger in tow, it felt like hours. Paul clenched the steering wheel with a white-knuckle grip and tried to focus on the fact that soon the man would be someone else's responsibility. He had so many questions, but didn't dare ask them for fear of what horrors might be revealed to him. In any case, the man, despite his makeshift mouth, could not speak. Try as he might, he could produce only garbled sounds that came from somewhere in his throat. He seemed to have a tongue, but no teeth, and no lips of course, only the flaps of skin that he had cut, which appeared already to be crusting over. So, the tongue lolled uselessly in the cavern of his mouth, unable to express whatever torment the man had endured. Paul was glad. A glimpse into the terror of the man's condition was more than enough.

"We're coming up to the hospital now. They'll look after you."

Paul led the man into the emergency room, his revulsion rising with each second spent in such close proximity to him. The man clung to Paul, like a newborn animal that had just been thrust into the world, blind and mewling, not yet understanding the mechanics of its own body, reaching desperately for its mother. The few souls in the waiting room barely reacted to the scene, preferring instead to fake interest in six-month-old copies of *Gardener's Weekly* or *Women's Health.* This was the British way. Keep your head down. Stay out of it. How Paul wished he could have been one of them, leafing through the pages of old magazines, finishing a half-completed crossword, waiting for a nurse to attend some minor injury. What bliss there was in their ignorance, in their God-given ability to 'stay out of it'!

He made it to the reception desk where a middle-aged woman typed furiously at a computer, her eyes dull from lack of sleep, or perhaps lack of interest.

"Excuse me." She carried on typing.

"Excuse me, can we get some help, please?"

She finished whatever sentence, paragraph, or perhaps, novella she had been working on, and finally looked up at them. For a moment, the apathy, the disinterest held, then came the confusion as she tried to make sense of the sight that confronted her. Finally, came abhorrence; that same primal disgust that Paul had felt the moment he first laid eyes on the man. The receptionist stared at him for a moment, transfixed, then returned to her usual officiousness. The emergency room was, as she saw it, a focal point for chaos and disorder. It was her job to create order within this disarray, to maintain a reassuring stoicism through the application of unflinchingly passionless bureaucracy.

"He'll have to fill this out."

"But he can't see! He can't... anything!"

"Then you'll have to fill it out for him."

"I don't know who he is. I found him like this and I brought him here. That's all."

"What's the problem here?" A doctor joined the conversation, a woman in her thirties with an immediate air of competency and kindness so profound that Paul could have wept.

"Please. I don't know what's wrong with him. I found him like this on the beach. He was buried in the sand."

The doctor assessed the man with concern, but, as yet, no obvious aversion.

"This laceration on the back of his head. How did he get it? Do you know?"

Paul understood then why she had not been repulsed. She didn't see it yet.

"That's not the back of his head. I mean... it's not the front either but..." He gently guided the man to turn around, so that the doctor could fully comprehend the man's condition. And there it was. Revulsion, fear, that dizzying punch-in-the-gut feeling of having everything you thought you understood about the world torn to shreds in a single, hideous moment.

"Thank you for taking him in."

He knew that she didn't mean it, of course. She wished, like him, that the abomination that stood before them could have passed her by, that she could instead have read about the strange incident in some obscure journal, an outside observer untouched by the brutal reality of the thing and all its gruesome details. This was not something she could leave behind at the end of her shift. This one would stay with her.

"I really have to go. I've left my dog in the car." Paul had never been so happy to have such an easy excuse to hand.

"We'll take care of him. Don't worry."

"I'll come back and check on him later," he said, not meaning a word of it. He turned to leave, but found his hand was gripped tightly. It was the frontless, backless man who held it. When the man let go, Paul found that he had pressed something into his palm... the dagger.

"I don't want this. Why are you...?"

The man was already being led away by the doctor. Paul was left to stare at the awful object in his hand, and guess at its wretched purpose. He saw a detail he hadn't noticed before, an inscription of some kind, etched into the handle:

PINNILEKK

o

Paul had hoped that, once he got home, the dreadful feeling would wear off, or at least thin a little, but it lingered, persistent as the island's rains. His cosy, little two-bedroom cottage by the sea had given him such solace, such security when he first made the move north. Now, his peaceful idyll had been tainted. He knew that he would not easily escape what he had seen that day. He would simply have to learn to forget it and move on.

To his surprise, sleep came easily. The adrenaline, he supposed, but it didn't last. He woke in the depth of night to a vicious, wet snarling and two eyes gleaming in the dark. Trixie stood at the end of his bed, teeth-bared, growling at him as if he was an intruder in his own home. He must smell differently, he thought. Perhaps the man had left some heinous odour on his skin that the dog could detect. He switched on the bedside lamp, sure that when Trixie saw him she would cease her misplaced aggression and jump into bed with him, as she often did.

She did not. Paul slowly got out of bed, careful not to make any sudden movements. He approached her just as carefully, but as soon as he got near the dog, she bolted, her bravado quickly melting away. She was afraid of him.

Paul convinced himself that she was still spooked from their earlier encounter. He certainly was. He'd slept a few hours, but his sleep had been plagued with fitful dreams, nothing coherent, just flashes; of the jagged slice across the middle of the man's faceless head, the smooth, waxy skin that completely enveloped him, the hideous, hopeless noises that caught in his throat. He was a walking nightmare.

Paul gave up on the idea of more sleep and went to the kitchen to make some tea. As the kettle boiled, he watched the sun appear over the horizon, its fiery edges spilling over the sea. The ocean always had such a calming effect on him. It made him feel comfortingly irrelevant, his problems puny in the face of such vastness. Today though, the sea took on a different hue. It was not the same landscape he had seen the morning before. There were dark, unseen currents snaking and coiling just under the surface of the water. It was not blue or green or silver, it was mercurial, and could no longer be relied upon.

An itch distracted him from his stream of thought, just the slightest tingle at his left eyelid. He scratched at it absent-mindedly, but found his efforts dissatisfying. Strange. He hadn't cut his nails for a while, yet when he scratched, he felt only skin on skin. He looked at his hands, at his fingertips, and frowned.

It was as if the nails on the right hand had become ingrown. The top of each nail was somehow buried in the flesh of the fingertip, the skin infringing on the nail edge. Skin where it shouldn't be. Skin encroaching past its borders. Skin! Skin! Skin! Panic set in fast. His mind raced to the most horrifying conclusions, as a sickening dread filled him from the bottom up and settled in his throat, choking him with the spine-searing terror of his predicament. He looked to the dagger that sat innocuously on the kitchen counter, and knew then why it had been given to him.

○

A million thoughts competed for space in his mind as he sped to the hospital, his foot a lead weight on the accelerator. Why hadn't he listened to Trixie's protestations and just turned back? Why didn't he call the police when he saw the hand rather than getting himself involved in something he had no business getting involved in? The question that screamed louder than all the others, however, was: *Can I be cured?* This was the question that had him barrelling down winding country roads in the half-light. He had to know what had happened to the man, if they had been able to help him.

He dashed past the few bleary-eyed souls in the waiting room, seeming, at a glance, unchanged from those of the previous day. The receptionist too was unchanged, to his dismay.

"What happened to the man I brought in yesterday?"

"Name?"

"I don't know his name. You don't remember me?"

"I see hundreds of patients every day."

Paul was quickly losing his patience, and his tenuous grip on sanity with it.

"How many do you see without a face?"

"If you're not family, I can't tell you anything anyway."

"Please, just let me speak to the doctor that saw him, the young woman. Is she here?"

The receptionist sighed and picked up the phone.

○

The doctor's office was cramped and made more claustrophobic still by the stacks of papers piled high on every available surface.

"Please don't judge me, Mr Rutherford. I inherited the mess, I didn't make it. The last chap wasn't exactly on top of his paperwork. Now lucky me has to go through it all." There was a nervousness to her small talk. She knew what was coming.

"Were you able to help him, Doctor? Is he going to be all right?"

"I'm afraid he passed shortly after you left. I'm sorry. There was nothing we could do."

"What happened? How did he die? Do you know what was wrong with him? Maybe... if it was detected sooner you could have—"

"Please, don't do that to yourself. The chances are, even if you'd found him earlier, the prognosis would have been the same. The... disease... it's like nothing we've ever seen before. At a guess, it's some genetic defect, some fault in his DNA that triggered his skin cells to multiply at an accelerated rate. In the end, that's all he was."

"What do you mean?"

"When they opened him up, for the autopsy, he was just skin. Layers upon layers of skin all the way down. No fat, no muscle, no organs. Just skin."

Paul was deathly pale and sweating.

"Are you all right, Mr Rutherford?"

"Can you please make sure... someone looks after my dog?"

And with that, he passed out.

○

Paul awoke to a profound, solitary darkness. It was not the gentle dark of night, but the smothering, black veil of blindness. He could not see. He drew his hands up to his face and, where his eyes should be, found only skin. He tried to scream, but found he had no mouth. Somehow, he could breathe still, against all reason. He was trapped in his own skin, a tortured, hideous parody of life! He found within him a terrible knowledge, perhaps transmitted along with the mutation, the knowledge that the affliction would not kill him, but instead let him fester inside the prison of his skin, perhaps forever, preserved by some nourishment beyond the bounds of science. How sweet death seemed then, a thing that he had always feared but now thought of with nothing but gratitude. Death was hope. Death was release.

He felt around him for the dagger, and finally felt the cold bone of it on the bedside locker beside him. With the cursed blade in his possession, he dragged his vile body out of the hospital bed, and fumbled his way to the door. He knew what he had to do.

○

Alison Steadford stopped to catch her breath. She had run almost the whole length of the beach, two miles. It was a long way off the thirteen miles ahead of her in the Isle of Harris half marathon, but better than the single mile she'd managed the week before. She was about to turn back, content with her progress, when she noticed something jutting out of the sand. She peered into the distance, and frowned as its form became apparent. Could it be... a hand?

The Reunion

BY

Thomas Staunton

I looked out the car window at the darkening sky. We were almost there. Martin kept his eyes on the road, pretending not to notice my nervous fidgeting, my obvious anxiety for what was ahead. As we climbed higher into the mountains, the view opened up. Huge, lavish houses whizzed by, all topiary and balusters. What would they make of me, the interloper?

Martin turned the last bend onto a long, winding driveway. Flanked by a row of oak trees, the road rose steadily uphill. As the car reached the crest, the country mansion was revealed in all its baronial glory.

"Please don't be nervous. These are the good friends, remember?" said Martin.

It wasn't his friends who made me nervous. They were very dear.

As we came to the stream that moated the garden, Martin slowed the car to a halt. Chalked across the bridge were two crossed lines with a small triangle at the convergence. It was a strange mark to see in such a proper place. "What is that?" I said. "I've seen it before, but I can't remember from where."

We drove across the little bridge and parked by the front door, where two strange figures awaited us. The most unusual of the pair was a tall, thin man in a shoddy Halloween mask, gowned in a black robe that fell just below his knees.

To his right stood a sour girl in a splashy party dress, unmoved. As I stepped out of the car, the masked man bounded forward with exaggerated pomp.

"Welcome, dear friends, to the reunion of the century!"

The sour girl rolled her eyes.

Martin rested his elbow on the roof of the car and sighed.

"Sarah, you remember Alan. And that's Etna."

Alan removed his mask, and a mop of greasy black hair fell down over his eyes. Stepping forward, he grabbed my hand and dragged me across the gravel. "Come on, Sarah, I bet you'll need a drink after a car journey with him."

o

I pondered how a lounge this enormous could be so crowded with uncomfortable furniture and untouchable antiques. On the abutting sofa, Alan swirled his brandy, took a careful sip, and failed to hide his revulsion. I smiled, thinking of a little boy wearing his father's suit jacket, trying to be grown up.

I had met Alan once before at a university ball and found him in a joyous mood. He had just quit his studies in medicine, a vocation which he had found stifling, a 'noose around his neck' he'd called it. Martin told me that Alan's parents had soon found a new noose to strangle him with; shame.

"Your mum and dad gone somewhere nice?" I said.

"Barbados," said Alan, a swig of brandy still in his mouth. "First time without me. He-ho."

"When do the rest arrive?" said Martin.

"Tomorrow afternoon," said Alan. "Etna, be a dear and call Richard. See what time the gang arrive."

Etna had been quietly nursing a drink in the corner. She shot up from her seat and stomped out to the hall with a parting swish from her dress.

Alan looked down into his brandy glass, his cheeks turning red.

"She's upset, but she'll be fine."

"What's the matter?" I said.

Alan leaned back in his seat.

"She just had a big fight with her parents over her... lifestyle choices."

"Jesus, have all of you been shunned by your parents?" I said.

"Wall-to-wall shunning in these parts. Even our greengrocer is a careers advisor," said Alan.

Martin got up from his seat and walked across the room.

"Let's have some music." He pulled a record out of its sleeve and placed it on the player.

The door swung open, and Etna poked her head around it.

"Turn that down!" she whispered.

"What's the matter?" said Alan.

"Look out the window!"

We got to our feet and gathered at the bay window. The sun was below the horizon, the sky flecked with tangerine and peach, and a dense fog was rolling up the front garden. It moved with eerie purposefulness. A strange feeling came over me, like the realisation that you are dreaming; the black void that materialises at its midpoint, ready to suck you down to the nightmare deep in your unconscious mind. Maybe I was still back home. Perhaps if I woke up, I'd find myself back in bed with Martin, our suitcases ready to go. I pinched my wrist but felt the sting.

"Is this normal?" I said. What a stupid question.

"I've been coming here every summer since I was born. I've never seen anything like it," said Alan.

The house was now enveloped in a cold, damp cloud, the lounge darkened to almost pitch black. It all felt so very wrong, the uninvited guest looming at the window, clawing to get in. Nobody said a word, we just stood there like gawking children caught in a moment beyond our comprehension.

"Look," said Etna, excitedly. "It's lifting!"

The fog climbed and thinned, then dissipated quietly into the night breeze. The vibrant orange sunset had given way to glorious moonlight.

"What in God's name is going on?" said Martin.

"Something's out there, look," said Alan.

At the far end of the front garden, on the bank of the little stream, an elegant, white shape came drifting towards the house. As it drew closer, I stood back from the window and nearly screeched. Soaring gracefully over a carpet of silky mist, was a ghostly woman in a flowing, white dress.

This has to be a dream. This has to be a dream. Wake up. Wake up now.

She came to a stop at the centre of the lawn and hovered silently. The grass beneath her feet began to rot and blacken. She turned and revealed to us a smooth, hairless head, pale skin and black eyes. Her mouth was a stretched grin of corrugated skin and transparent fangs, like a hideous, bottom-feeding fish.

I could not move, dared not move.

The white woman drew a deep breath and wailed a bone-shattering scream.

"Etna! No!" said Francis.

Before we could even begin to understand what was happening, Etna was already outside and sprinting down the driveway. The white woman lurched and glided across the lawn to cut her off.

"We have to do something!" I said, but it was an empty gesture. I was not moving. Nobody was moving.

The white woman intercepted Etna, hooked a ghostly arm around her body and pulled her into a tight embrace.

"What is happening?! What the hell is happening?" said Alan, pulling at his hair in manic frustration.

Etna was crying and hollering, kicking and screaming. She called our names, pleaded for our help, but we still did not move. The white woman sailed back to the centre of the lawn, clutching Etna under her arm, a mother lugging a fitful toddler.

I grabbed Martin's shoulder.

"We have to get out of here. Martin?"

Martin wasn't hearing me. He stared, transfixed.

"Martin!" I cried.

A scream of pure insanity filled the air. The white woman clasped Etna under her chin.

Wake up. Wake up. Wake up.

Alan backed away from the window and bolted from the room.

Etna's scream was clipped as her head came clean away from her body. The white woman held the bloody head aloft, and let out a hideous rattle, her teeth gleaming in the moonlight.

Alan skidded to his knees before the white woman. A fine layer of Etna's blood showered his face, stunning him momentarily. He spun around and started to crawl across the lawn, whimpering as he clambered. Martin and I stood watching, impotent onlookers in a shared nightmare. Alan's eyes stayed locked with ours as his head detached from his body.

With a strange, quiet calm, Martin turned to me, tears rolling down his face.

"I think we should close the door now."

o

We huddled together in the attic, completely still, not knowing what else to do. Down below, the white woman searched the house. Her wails rose and fell like passing sirens as she moved from room to room. Soon, she would be upstairs.

"I vote we run," I said. I was unexpectedly firm.

"Where?" said Martin.

"Anywhere. We just run."

"We won't make it. You saw how fast she is."

For the first time since we'd met, I felt alone.

"We die in this house, or we die running. I say we die running."

Martin meditated on my words. He scratched his head and let out a long, jittery sigh.

"How do we get out?"

"Have a look," I said, tapping the dormer window.

Directly below the sill lay a small, flat roof. Below that, the back garden opened out into the dark countryside.

The white woman's cries travelled up the stairs.

o

We crouched down on the flat roof, steadying our feet between the flimsy tiles.

"Are you ready?" I said.

Martin smiled. It was a nervous smile, an uncertain smile, but it was something.

"I'm ready."

With quiet care, we climbed down from the flat roof and onto the patio. Up above, the white woman loomed at the window and opened her mouth to scream. Martin grabbed my arm and thrust us out into the cold, open air. We fled across the back garden and into a meadow beyond. With our feet skidding in the long grass, the field took us downhill towards a ditch.

A flicker of relief passed over me. Maybe, just maybe, we could escape this. The air felt warmer and sweeter, as if we were pushing through the phantasm and back into the real world.

What a fool I was. I looked up to the sky and saw her soaring there above us, like a hawk in the night sky searching for two little mice.

"Martin!" I cried out.

"Keep going!"

The warm summer wind gave way again to cold. High above, the white woman passed by the pale face of the moon.

"Stop looking and keep going!" said Martin.

We came to the embankment. Martin climbed over the fence first, then reached out to grab my hand, smiling to reassure me. It happened so fast. His head slumped, and his eyes turned full and white. My hand slipped out of his, and he was lifted upwards in the talons of the flying demon. Silently, they disappeared into the darkness. A drop of blood fell onto my cheek.

I tumbled into the long grass and lay there, unable to think, or cry, or move. There was nothing in me anymore—no anger, no sorrow—just a kind of numb blackness. If this were still a nightmare, I would never sleep again.

I do not know how long I lay there, but when the wail came in the dark, I got to my feet and ran through the reeds. I ran and ran without looking back. After what felt like an eternity, I reached the brow of the hill and paused to catch my breath and get my bearings. To the west, where the summer dusk still clung to the sky, I saw a beacon.

o

The mansion was nestled in a grove of cherry blossoms, the skylights twinkling like welcoming eyes behind the branches. Music and singing drifted from the house. Filled with hope, I hurried down the hill.

The patio door opened soundlessly, and I slipped inside.

The lounge was a tasteless mix of marble and gold, shagpile carpet and vulgar Roman columns. At the rear, a little soiree was underway. A group of well-dressed partygoers huddled over a grand piano, singing a merry tune, arm in arm and drinks in hand. It took more than a minute for someone to notice me; the sweaty, blood-caked gatecrasher. The scream was all my own.

Elaine and Raymond, Martin's mother and father, were standing amongst the revellers. The piano went silent, and twenty heads turned at once. A row of blank, silvery eyes, smiling at me, unruffled.

"My dear Sarah, how are you?" said Elaine.

The revellers gawked.

"What's going on? What are you doing here?"

Elaine raised her flute. "We're celebrating!"

"I have to tell you something. Martin—"

"—is dead," said Elaine. "Yes, we know that. To Etna, Martin, and Alan. To their resurrection!"

"Hear, hear!" said the others.

Let the white woman take me, I thought. It was too much, too terrible.

Raymond nudged his way forward.

"How did you escape Magret?"

Elaine batted him away.

I knew that he was talking about the she-demon, and the more I thought about it, the more it all made sense. These people had summoned her.

"You murdered your own children?"

Elaine's smile couldn't hide the sneer. "Oh, they won't be dead for long. This is a rebirth."

A short man with a black moustache walked over to the lounge door, peeked behind it briefly, then turned back to the other guests and grinned. "We're ready."

Etna, Alan, and Martin shuffled into the room, clean, unblemished and beautifully dressed. Their soulless eyes stared through me.

Taking a step back, I put my hand behind me and wrapped my fingers around the handle of the patio door. The tears came this time, the sheer brutality of this endless trial taking its toll.

"Our failure was to have no boundaries, dear Sarah," said Elaine.

"They're captains of industry," said Raymond.

"Leaders!" said another, "Influencers!"

"With careful management," said Elaine, "these three will be completely revitalised. They will be driven. They will be successful. But, as always, there is a price. Nasty business, but Magret's way is the old way."

Somewhere outside, the white woman wailed.

With uncanny unity, the revellers stepped towards me.

"She's waiting for you, dear!" said Elaine, a sweet grin carved into her face.

Was my life really leading to this awful, pathetic moment? A shivering lamb in a house full of monsters?

The revellers formed a half-circle. Their pendants twinkled in the lamplight, the intersecting lines and triangle now clear for me to see.

"Run away now. Go!" urged Raymond, his eyes wide, filled with anticipation for the hunt.

I turned and opened the door. Somewhere out there in the darkness, a hungry mouth full of glittering teeth awaited me. I closed my eyes and stepped out into the night.

Black Santa

BY

Lawrie Brewster

Back in 2017, I spent Christmas Eve with my old high-school friend, Michael, who I hadn't seen for some years since we'd graduated. I'd left to go work in the city, and he'd stayed behind in our home town where he lived in the suburbs with his girlfriend, Nicole.

We enjoyed reminiscing, joking, and drinking, but after a while, Michael started to seem a little... off. He was agitated, nervous. He kept looking at his watch. Thinking that this was my cue to leave, I said my goodbyes, but, as I headed to the door, I noticed Michael in the kitchen, initiating a rather peculiar Christmas ritual.

Most of you will be familiar with the tradition of leaving a snack out for Santa Claus, perhaps a mince pie and a carrot for his reindeer, but this was something... different.

Instead of carrots or mince pies, Michael had placed a large chunk of meat, raw and bloody, on the kitchen table. When he saw me, he quickly kicked the door shut. As it closed, I could swear that his hand was dripping blood. Had he cut himself?

I caught Nicole's worried glance to the clock. It was 11:45 pm, just fifteen minutes before Christmas Day.

I had two choices; I could simply leave them to it, or I could interfere. Now, I am a naturally inquisitive person, and of course, I'd been drinking all night, so I chose the latter.

I gently nudged Nicole aside and made my way into the kitchen. She protested at first, then relented, with a peculiar hesitation. Perhaps she wanted me to investigate or challenge Michael's strange behaviour.

The door opened to reveal Michael hunched over the kitchen table, fist clenched as he eked out some extra drops of blood onto the meat. He looked at me with an expression that lay somewhere between embarrassment and fear, before wiping his hand with a kitchen towel. Nicole darted past me and opened a cupboard door to fetch a Band-Aid for the fresh cut on Michael's palm.

I was stunned, but, forever arrogant, I demanded an explanation. Michael smiled sadly at Nicole, a sign of resignation. She left us to it.

"I'm sorry, I know it looks weird, but it's a tradition. I've always done it, ever since I was a kid."

I couldn't take my eyes off the raw meat soaked in animal blood, and in my friend's blood too.

"But... why?" I asked.

"I wouldn't even know where to begin. Let's just say I do this because... I have to."

I laughed at him.

"Is this for Santa? Is he a hardcore carnivore?"

Michael didn't laugh. He looked around the room anxiously, as if he were listening out for a sign. He trembled, startled by something, and with an urgent expression, declared;

"I think you should go. Now."

In defiance, I folded my arms and explained that I wasn't going anywhere, not until he told me the truth. To this day, I wish I had heard him out properly, or just minded my own business.

But perhaps you would have laughed too, and trust me, you're about to laugh, just as I did, when I tell you exactly what came out of his mouth next.

"Since before I was born, my family has offered our blood to Black Santa."

In the hall behind me, Nicole shook her head, disappearing into the bedroom. Clearly, he was serious, and while I understand that now, at the time I could only ridicule him.

"Black Santa? What the hell's Black Santa? Is he like James Brown? Will he come down your chimney tonight?"

I rushed out of the kitchen and sang 'I Feel Good' into the fireplace, before turning to Michael with a condescending grin, a look that screamed its demand for a real answer.

But that was his only answer.

It was 12:05 am, making it Christmas Day. Frustrated by his obstinate refusal to answer, I decided that I would force a change in my friend's tradition. So, I went back to the kitchen, and before Michael could react, I grabbed the bloody steak and threw it into the fire.

In the process, I hadn't realised that the meat was skewered on a spike, and I had managed to cut myself, adding my own blood to his. Mesmerised at the sight of the meat sizzling on the fire, Michael stepped up beside me.

In a frightful tone, he whispered;

"What have you done?"

I turned to him.

"Fuck Black Santa."

He noticed the blood on my hand, and his lip quivered. I realise now the importance of the ritual, but at the time, I thought I had liberated my friend from an odd compulsion.

Michael tried half-heartedly to detain me with promises of an explanation about Black Santa, this strange boogeyman that he and his father and his father's father had appeased over the decades. I was having none of it. I say 'half-hearted' because there was a new-found relief in Michael, which I sensed from Nicole as well, as if I had lifted a great burden from them, for reasons I would soon discover.

I sped away in my car, disappointed to have left in such weird and unsettled circumstances, but also amused at the oddness of it all. I laughed as I drove, recalling the ridiculous name of Michael's boogeyman. The unexpected events of the evening had left me alert and very much awake, so I decided to head downtown, where I hoped there might still be bars open.

Black Santa indeed...

I can't remember the name of the bar, but it was surprisingly quiet, comprising mostly of middle-aged loners, the town's left-overs. Despite being from there, I had always retained a certain aloofness, which I guess made me stand out. A bristly-faced man with a plaid shirt leant over his stool at the bar to sneer, while a woman with pock-marked skin paused in her negotiation with the karaoke DJ to shoot me an inviting smile. You might wonder how I can recall all these little details, but trust me, the events of this night are forever imprinted upon my mind.

I went straight to the bar and ordered a drink, then chatted idly to the man in the plaid shirt, doing my best to ignore the caterwauling of the woman singing behind me.

The midi-electric music of the karaoke had a distinctly retro feel, as did the songs sung by the drunken siren. Then, quite gradually, I realised that the woman was no longer singing. Someone else had replaced her mid-song. It was a booming man's voice with a deep, gravelly resonance that imbued the lyrics of T'pau's 'China in Your Hand' with a strange fury.

I turned quickly to see who it was, almost knocking my drink in the process. As I did, the tune broke into the 'saxophone' solo, played out in staccato bleeps via the midi system. The performer danced slowly, sensually, swaying their hips in time to the music. This was not the drunk woman, but a large, bearded man in a Santa Claus outfit.

At the climax of the chorus, he reached out to me with the same dramatic flair one might expect from a performer before an audience of thousands. With unblinking eye contact, as a tear rolled down his bright red cheek, he blasted out the lines;

"Don't push too far, your dreams are china in your hand..."

I suddenly felt a nervous urge. My hand tightened around the glass I was holding. Why were his eyes so tiny, like shining pins?

"Don't wish too hard, because they may come true..."

Why is he now smiling so strangely at me—just me and nobody else? I was irritated by this, but no one else seemed to care or even acknowledge the outrageous scene.

"You don't know what you might have... set upon yourself."

I clenched my drink so hard that it shattered, showering me and the burly, plaid-shirt-wearing man with glass splinters. He pulled me off my stool, ready to punch me, then hesitated and let me go. With great relief, I patted myself dry and realised that the song had finally ended. I looked back at the stage and could see no sign of the peculiar performer, only the woman and the DJ from before.

I turned to the bartender, intending to order a Black Russian, but instead the words 'Black Santa' came out. He looked at me strangely and suggested that I should perhaps go home.

You don't know what you might have set upon yourself.

Why had the words the man sung sounded so threatening?

He had resembled an idealised version of Santa Claus, like you might expect from an old-fashioned Christmas card, or the Coca-Cola Christmas commercials. He would have looked perfect if it weren't for some subtle, sinister imperfections that produced an instinctual sense of repulsion. His cruel, cherubic grin and pinprick eyes somehow filled me with dread.

I fled to the restroom to steady my nerves. As I sat in the cubicle, taking deep breaths, I became aware that the cubicle next to me was not empty.

I can be a little self-conscious in public toilets, but the man beside me was decidedly not so. After producing a great volume of noise and smell, he made an outrageous, uproarious laugh.

It went like this; "Ho, Ho, Ho," then changed mid-way into an evil laugh, the type we might associate with a cartoon villain.

"Ho, Ho, Ho... muhahaha!"

The acoustics changed too, from a muffled echo to my left, to a sharp, clear sound right above me!

I jumped with fright and looked up to see, staring down at me over the cubicle wall, the bearded face from before. It was bright red with laughter, glaring at me with those beady, black eyes. Then I saw that he was holding something... a giant, rolled up ball of wet toilet paper, soaked in urine and excrement.

A second later it was thrown with tremendous force straight into my face. It hit me so hard that it knocked me off the toilet onto the floor. The horrifying object made me wretch with disgust. I was so shocked that I couldn't even scream or shout for help. I wiped the oozing mess off my face and dashed out of the cubicle, ready to punch this vile stranger.

His cubicle door was swinging wildly, but the man himself was nowhere to be seen. I rushed back into the bar, crashing straight into a patron, before feverishly shouting if anyone had seen him? The bartender, who was already convinced I'd drunk too many, signalled to the bouncers to kick me out, all of which played out to Foreigner's 'I Want to Know What Love Is'.

Stinking of crap, I stumbled past suspicious passers-by who quickly moved aside with looks of disgust. I must have resembled a vagrant, but nevertheless, I made my way back to the car.

Ah, my beautiful, silver, German-produced Audi A4. My pride and joy.

You can probably tell by those words that some strange fate befell it. Well, you still won't believe it.

In the window of a nearby department store was a bank of televisions, all set to the same channel. They were playing an episode of an unfamiliar game show, with a hysterical couple jumping up and down after having won the star prize. I stopped for a moment, because the man dashing to the prize podium was dressed in a Santa costume and resembled the man who attacked me. Well, he wasn't dressed quite like Santa exactly... the colour of his costume was too dark.

With a flourish, the man pulled off the sheet to reveal an Audi A4. The couple ran towards it, embracing the car like a lost child. I smiled, glad that this working-class couple could experience the luxury of a car only people like me could usually afford, but then, I noticed the license plate—the same number as mine!

The man dressed as Santa turned to the camera and began walking towards it until his face engulfed the screen. He was mouthing something through the glass, but I couldn't hear it. I leant in close until I could faintly hear words repeating over the buzz of the televisions. He was singing something.

"Don't push too far, your dreams are china in your hand..."

I ran as fast as I could, all the way back to my car, which, as you might expect, was not where I left it. There weren't even any marks in the snow to suggest it had ever been there.

Still smelling of crap and now without a car, I began the long trudge back to my motel. Despite my soiled state, I tried to hitch a ride, hoping some kind soul would take pity on me.

After about a hundred cars had sped past, at long last, a truck slowed to a crawl beside me. It was decorated in Christmas lights, yet, inside the cabin, it was pitch black.

The garish exterior and unsettling interior discouraged me, but with the snow now falling harder, I stepped up to enter the cabin. That was when the demonic man's face leered out suddenly from the darkness, the bristles of his beard scratching at my face.

"HOHOHO-Muhahahaha," he roared, as I tumbled backwards out of the cabin and fell into the snow. As I fell, my ankle struck a jagged rock, hard, shattering it inside. Searing pain engulfed me as I clambered up, hobbling away as fast as I could towards the motel.

The truck continued to crawl along the road beside me, its radio on full blast, playing 'China in Your Hand' on repeat.

Try as I might, I just couldn't go on. The pain had become too great and I collapsed with exhaustion. Looking to my foot, I could see that the injury was worse than I had first imagined. The bone was protruding from my skin, and my foot lay in a thick pool of blood.

The realisation hit me that this could be my final night. I could actually die like this. I was about to lose everything I had accomplished; the city career and the awesome car. I realised then that none of it had ever mattered, for here I was, a humble wretch crying in the snow, covered in blood and excrement.

The instinct to survive is a powerful thing, and I started to crawl once more, fighting to remain conscious.

Finally, my body gave out. I collapsed on my back and just lay there, looking up at the stars and the moon, at the waves of snowflakes spiralling gently towards me.

In the corner of my eye, I could see that the truck had stopped. The man, this demonic Santa Claus, was now effortlessly striding through the snow towards me, clenching a small fire axe.

He leant over me, sniffing loudly for the scent of blood, which soon led him to my crippled foot. Close up, I could see that this man's Santa costume was not red... but black.

He loomed over me, staring with those tiny, cruel eyes that shone like ancient stars, his body heaving with triumphant anticipation.

One month later, I awoke in the hospital, where I learned that I had been placed in an induced coma due to the extent of my injuries.

Within weeks, I could talk and move once more. Everything was as it should be... except for my left foot. They told me that it had been hacked off, and that something had eaten it, leaving only the bones beside my body.

It's now Christmas Eve, 2019, and I can get around well enough with my new prosthetic foot. I make my way to the kitchen, where I will prepare two snacks. One is a mince pie for Santa Claus, and the other, a steak tartare with a dash of my own blood, for Black Santa.

The Mould

BY

Thomas Staunton

The smell came first—a musty, pungent odour. Shielding my nose, I peeled a strip of wallpaper off of the ceiling, and there, in all its revolting glory, was a moist, brown patch of mould as big as a dinner plate. The ceiling sagged abruptly, as if relieved of a tight-fitting corset, sending me crashing down off the ladder and onto the floor. I stared at the mould with grave suspicion. Beads of water began to roll across its fur, then converge at the crown and drop to the floor in heavy splashes. I moved out of the way just in time to miss a giant, brown droplet. The stink began to fill the room: rotten vegetation at first, then dirty socks, and finally, a meaty smell, like raw chicken on the turn.

I sat on a bundle of uprooted linoleum in the hallway, feeling deflated. Would I ever finish this damned apartment? Each new endeavour revealed more of its withering structure— little booby traps of stress and expense, waiting to be set off at every turn. Now I felt violated, infected almost. I would have to rid the place of this grotesque and disturbing mould before I could do anything else.

An investigation of the attic proved fruitless. After finding my bearings, I marked the spot above the mould and pulled a section of fibreglass insulation away, but found nothing. There were no leaks, no water damage, no trace of where this mould was coming from. It made no sense.

I returned to the spare room, intending to observe the fungus with some semblance of detachment. Maybe reason would return to me now that the initial shock and revulsion had worn off. Perhaps I'd kick myself for being so dramatic. As I contemplated this, the thing began to pulse softly. And had it grown larger? How was that possible? It was unlike any other mould I'd ever encountered or even heard of. It was a nightmare.

Outside, the street lights came on, and I realised that I had been standing there in the spare room all evening, just staring at the thing. As I went to leave the room, I heard it give a little sigh. I shivered in disgust.

I would kill the beast tomorrow. I would drown it with chemicals until it was no more.

o

MOULD KILLER PLUS ONE - GETS THE JOB DONE.

I sat on the floor of the spare room with a dozen cans of anti-mould spray and considered the present size of the fungus—a little bigger than my coffee table now. With a can in each hand, I climbed the ladder and opened fire on the beast, unloading the contents of both cans, and leaving a thick, oily iridescence on its furry membrane. Just seconds later, the fungus had absorbed the poison completely and grown another inch, just to spite me. With two fresh cans, I climbed higher and edged closer, and then, aiming at the fattest part of the monster, I attacked it again. A cloud of rasping toxins swirled around me. Feeling it invade my lungs, I retreated back down the ladder and sat on the floor, breathless. The mould was impregnable, and I was not feeling at all well. The operation had been a total failure. As I sat there, despairing, the thing groaned passively, like an animal stirring from its slumber. I jumped to my feet, fled the room and shut the door.

°

THE SPECIALIST

"Holy Jesus," said the Specialist. He scratched his backside, took a deep breath, and climbed the ladder.

"What kind of mould is it?" I said, from the doorway. I didn't dare get any closer.

"I've been doing this for fifteen years, and I've never seen anything like it." He took out a little pen and prodded the thing.

My muscles tensed. Would this aggravate the beast? I didn't want to be there to find out.

"Coffee?" I said, rather urgently.

"Milk and four sugars, please," said the Specialist. "I'll need to make a phone call."

I stood watching the kettle boil, my mind swimming with visions of horror and decay.

The whole ceiling will have to go—the apartment condemned. I'll have to be quarantined, then I'll die.

I imagined my dreams going up in smoke, my little apartment, my life savings—the works. I wouldn't get to see the kids, not without a home. She'd think I wasn't fit to see them now. She'd keep them all for herself. Could I blame her?

I dropped four sugars into the coffee and headed back upstairs.

"Hope this isn't too much milk..."

The mug swung around my index finger and crashed to the ground. Dangling over my head, was the Specialist, his head plunged deep inside the mould, his legs gently swinging. I stood with my mouth agape, trying to comprehend what I was seeing. The fungus drooped and folded over the man's Adam's apple.

SUCK. SUCK. SUCK.

I wrapped my arms around his thighs and pulled. The mould clasped tighter. With all my strength, I pulled again. The creature relented, letting out a watery gurgle, and the Specialist's head slipped from its sphincteral maw.

He flopped over, sending us both crashing to the ground with a bang. The fungus contracted, and I got to my feet and pulled his limp body into the hallway.

The Specialist was covered in a thick, pungent slime, but to my relief, he was breathing. I gave his cheek a light slap. He shook his head and opened his eyes.

"Are you okay?" I said.

"Yeah, I'm fine. Must have had a fall."

I thought for a moment, about how I could possibly begin to explain to him what had just happened. None of it made sense. I had tumbled headfirst into an unthinkable nightmare.

"I should probably call you an ambulance," I said, "just to be on the safe side."

"Don't do that," he said. "I'm fine."

"I really think we should phone an ambulance."

He got to his feet, dusted himself off, and put his hand on the wall for balance.

"I'll be back tomorrow. With a team."

He stumbled out the door, and all was quiet again.

I couldn't bear to be there anymore, not with that thing. I would pack a bag and check into a hotel until it was gone.

As I headed to the bathroom to clean myself up, I looked out the hall window to the street below. The Specialist was sitting in his van, staring directly ahead with a worryingly vacant expression. It was a full hour before he drove away.

○

THE NIGHT CALLER

I stood in the hallway, my bag at my feet, listening. The spare room had been quiet for hours, but as the last light of day disappeared, a cacophony of odd and unnatural sounds erupted—spine-chilling, alien sounds of no discernible animal or human origin.

I took out my phone to call a cab.

Knock Knock

Oh, Christ. What have I forgotten? Is it my turn this weekend? Wait... she doesn't even know I'm here. Does she?

I opened the door, and standing there, in the same state as I had left him, was the Specialist. He stepped into the light of the hall, his eyes fixed on me.

"I thought I'd come by and take another look at the problem. I forgot to take pictures. The boss won't send a team until I show him what we're dealing with."

"It's pretty late," I said. "Perhaps you could come back early tomorrow? I'm heading out."

"Don't do that," he said, stepping over the threshold. A snaking streak of black passed over the white of his left eye. "It'll just take a second."

I looked at his clenched fists and saw a man ready to attack.

"C-Come in."

"Where is the light switch?" he said, walking down the hall to the spare room.

What is this? A trap? I could run now. I could run out that front door, right now. Why am I not running?

"It's just behind the door, to the left," I said.

"If you wouldn't mind switching it on for me," he said. "I left my glasses in the car."

For the life of me, I cannot explain why I did as he asked, but there was an authority in his voice that somehow demanded compliance.

As I opened the door and reached for the light switch, I felt a strange, warm sensation on the left side of my chest. I only noticed the knife when the man pulled it out, slick with blood... my blood. The warmth turned into stinging, and then the stinging turned to searing pain. My knees went, and the rest of me followed. The Specialist stepped over my body, walked into the room, and shut the door.

○

THE ROOM

The spare room was alive with awful vibrations. First, I heard a colossal thud, then a squelching noise, followed by stretching; like rubber being pulled to its limit. Next came the breathing, hollow and deep. The wall was brutally hot. Beads of condensation rolled down the bare plaster. I checked my wound. I had been saved, just barely, by a rib.

If I got out of here, who would believe what I had seen? And even if someone did come, would the mould still be here? How would I explain myself then? I'd never see my kids, I'd be locked up in a psychiatric hospital, and that would be that. I needed to know what was happening in that room. I looked to the ceiling and thought of a plan.

The attic was unbearably humid, like I'd just stepped into a tropical hothouse. Down below, the strange noises and groans continued. I tiptoed across the beams and over to the loose floorboard.

I hooked my fingers under the board and pulled it upwards. A thin skin of plaster lay beneath. What was I doing? I punched a hole into the plaster, and a waft of wretched air rose up and met my nostrils. The stench was pure, rotten decay. Struggling not to vomit, I peered into the hole. Down below was a room completely filled with brown, sweating fur. It pulsated and throbbed in one heaving mass, kissing the walls and ceilings, filling every nook and cranny. Scattered here and there were the dismembered remains of the Specialist. The mould was so enormous that I felt the floor begin to lift slightly.

I stumbled away from the hole, vaulted over the beams and crashed down the ladder. The door to the spare room was coming apart. A small crack in the wood quickly grew to a giant split. Soon, it would break through.

Frantic thoughts consumed me. How big could it get? Would it just keep expanding until it had devoured everyone? Could this heinous organism ever be destroyed? Apocalyptic visions played out in my mind of a leviathan fungus pulling entire skyscrapers into its cruel, undulating mass. I had to do something.

o

THE END

The mould had broken through the door and was inching its way over the threshold. I emptied the last of the petrol on the hallway floor and snapped the lighter open with a click. I cursed the mould. Along with its foul mass, the flames would take everything I had, all hopes I had for the future, but I knew that this was what I must do.

The mould slithered down the hallway towards me, consuming everything it touched. I flicked the switch, and the flame danced into life. I tossed the lighter onto the floor and ran. A deafening, unnatural roar thundered behind me as the fire took hold of the creature. I felt the heat of the blaze behind me as I walked out into the night. I didn't look back.

Dig For Fire

BY

Thomas Staunton

The demon had no name, only a word that it uttered incessantly: *Dig*.

I was eleven, and my parents had bought a big old house in rural Connecticut. The place was a dump, or a 'fixer-upper,' as they called it. The long-neglected roof sagged troublingly and the window frames were rotten, the panes riddled with cracks and fissures. Decrepit though it was, still there was a sense that it was alive, that it breathed somehow; deep, moaning breaths that strained the rotten timbers. I felt uneasy from the moment we drove through the gates. Being so young, I couldn't put my finger on what exactly was wrong with the place, I only knew that it felt ancient... and evil.

My bedroom was on the top floor, two flights up, and far from the warmth and safety of the living room. Big houses are always terrifying to children, especially at night, when they take on a heavy, brooding quality that transforms the very fabric of the building into something dangerous and otherworldly. What is charming in the light of day can so suddenly turn sinister at nightfall. I slept uneasily, hiding my face from the gaze of the preposterously large wardrobe that loomed in the corner of the room. I counted myself lucky if I didn't hear the strange and disturbing sounds that emanated from the house at these late hours: creaks, groans and gurgling noises, mysterious whooshing sounds, like old men sighing... They conspired to keep me from ever sleeping soundly.

My father, sensing my growing discomfort, tried to soothe me.

"Julia, sweetheart, it'll take time. I promise you, you won't know yourself in a couple of weeks. You'll be running this place."

Kind words, but they provided little comfort. I knew that soon, too soon, he would be gone, and I would be alone in the darkness once again.

Then came the night of the demon. I was lying in the dark, listening to the building's chilling orchestra of sounds, when I felt a strange pull, as if the room was sinking, tumbling away from reality and into a dark and dangerous dimension out of time. The rushing stopped, and an eerie silence followed. The scant moonlight in the room had turned a sickening rust-brown. From the far corner of the room came a scuttling sound. Something scuttled through the walls and around the back of my headboard.

"Rats. It has to be rats," I thought. I lay on my back and looked up. The wall behind my bed was stretching outwards like plasticine, and impressed upon the surface of the protrusion was the face of a demon, sharp-toothed and crowned with horns. It sniffed the room from side to side, hissing like the static of an old television. Was it purring? Then, it spoke.

"DIG."

Like an axe sunk deep into a block of wood, the word was now buried in my skull.

DIG.

The demon retreated back into the wall, leaving behind a single, smoking scorch mark. I don't remember the rest of that night.

o

Over the next two months, I saw more psychiatrists than I could count. They tried to get me to talk. Unfortunately for them, I was a determined mute.

My parents were devastated. The country house had been their dream: the peace and quiet, the beautiful scenery, and all that space! They saw me as their future poet, and the house as a gift for my inspiration, but that dream was dead, and I was a shell.

One of the odd things about being mute is not ever hearing your own voice. Under normal circumstances, your inner voice takes over, but the demon had a different plan for me. That strange, static hiss, awful and inscrutable, was now playing endlessly inside my head. It overwhelmed my senses with a blinding fog of noise that never lifted. Over and over again, that word penetrated my mind: *DIG*.

Disturbing thoughts became compulsions. I acquired a newfound fascination for knives and other sharp objects. I drew them out of drawers and stared at them, sometimes for hours, if nobody was watching. As the blades glimmered in my hand, the only thoughts that came to mind were: *sharper, thinner, sharper, thinner*. I looked at my arms and legs and imagined chopping them off. It felt like the exact right thing to do.

My parents weren't fools. They saw what was happening to me. Their little girl was, for want of a better word, possessed.

And then, one day, a removal truck arrived. My parents were solemn, defeated, as they packed in silence, while I, conversely, felt a twinge of relief growing inside me. I ran to my room with a mix of panic and excitement, an anxious feeling that drove me to pack my things as quickly as I could, in case my parents changed their minds, or worse, the demon emerged from the walls and took me.

Years later, I asked my mother why we left the house. I feared the answer, as I was pretty certain that it was because of me. She said nothing for a while, just stared into her cup of coffee. Then, she turned to me, and I saw something in her eyes, a familiar fear.

"There's something wrong with that house," she said.

○

The world outside the comforter was grey and uninviting. It was early afternoon, and I was still in bed, a not uncommon occurrence throughout my adult life. I felt heavy again, with that old, familiar dread, the kind that urged me to move my bed away from the walls, just in case. My phone was already clutched in my hand when it started to vibrate. It was my dad. I perked up a little, more out of surprise than joy. They never called me. Especially when they were on vacation. They didn't want me ruining the mood.

"We need a favour. The Gardners haven't picked up their phone in two weeks. Their rent is overdue, and we need it for the rest of our stay. Can you go to the old house and find out what the hell is going on?"

I felt myself sinking as my dad uttered the words 'old house'. With the kind of desperate instinct that only a traumatised mind would possess, I searched feverishly for excuses: I'm sick, I'm away this weekend, I'm working double shift... anything! I even considered giving them a loan to tide them over, but then I remembered that I was completely broke. Dammit! I'm twenty years old and scared of a house. A house that my parents couldn't fully let go of.

After we moved, they rented the place out, even though it remained mostly unoccupied. Tenants came and quickly went, usually sending apologetic emails to Mom and Dad from some motel far, far away, begging them not to sue. Then, in the summer of last year, their old friends Robert and Edna Gardner called out of the blue and asked to see the place. They had just lost their business down in New Orleans and needed a fresh start. I gave them four months before they bailed, but, much to my surprise, they stuck it out longer than anyone else, including us.

I should have known that someday I would have to go back. I had always felt a sense of unfinished business, but I dreaded the prospect of seeing the old house again, and of it seeing me. Ever since that awful night, I had been desperately searching for some reasonable explanation: it was an overactive imagination, I was hallucinating, I was poisoned... but then, every once in a while, my ears would sting, and I would hear, faintly, that unique and terrifying hiss.

Why was I going to say yes to this? I couldn't figure it out. It had taken years to get to the stage where I could talk confidently to anyone but my parents, and now I was allowing myself to be thrown back into hell.

I muttered something affirmative, hung up the phone, and realised that my hands were shaking.

○

I parked behind the Gardner's minivan and turned the engine off. I stared straight ahead, not wanting to meet the gaze of the house. Some foolish part of me felt like, if I didn't look at it, then I wasn't really here, and I could just turn around and go back the way I came. I went to restart the car, but stopped at the turn of the key. I grabbed the steering wheel, clasped it tightly, and watched my knuckles whiten.

With my keys firmly in hand, I stepped out of the car, and with all the mental strength I could manage, I raised my head to finally look at the house. I'm not sure why I was surprised, but it hadn't changed at all, except that now it was strangled by a mass of red ivy, which wrapped around the entire house like a tangle of twisted arteries. The pale autumn sun warmed the walls, but the windows remained defiantly dark, devouring the soft light like black holes.

I thought, hopefully, that if the Gardners were in, then maybe I wouldn't have to set foot in the place at all. Eagerly, I called out.

"Hello? Robert? Edna? Tom? Anybody home?"

My voice carried across the vale, but the echo that returned was different; it was deeper and somehow less human. I shuddered.

The back door was unlocked. I stepped into the laundry room, calling out the Gardners' names, sternly. Surely they wouldn't have gone out without locking the door?

Dirty dishes were piled high inside the sink, and as I approached the kitchen door, I could smell the sweet odour of moulding bread. I knocked on the door as I opened it, annoyed at my meek politeness.

The room was a bloodbath. Knives of every kind lay neatly across the breakfast table, all slick with blood. A blowtorch sat next to them. The smell of death hung in the air. I clasped my mouth and nose tightly, turned around, and made for the door, propelled by shock and horror.

BANG!

The door slammed shut and locked by itself. I tried to open it, but it wouldn't budge. A peculiar feeling of emptiness washed over me. Something cruel and dark and relentless was returning to infect my psyche once again. I heard it then, its robotic awfulness piercing my eardrums.

"DIG!"

I looked to the kitchen wall and saw the beginnings of a protuberance. It coiled and contorted itself into the shape of an evil, mocking grin. I stood aghast. *I have to run!*

I darted out of the kitchen, through the hall, and slammed into the front door. Locked. I called for the Gardners one last time, my feeble attempt at denial. "Robert? Edna? Tom? Where are you?"

Next to me, nestled under the telephone table, was a thick wooden chair. I grabbed it by the armrests and raised it aloft, ready to take aim at the door, but just as I was about to strike, an unseen force slammed the chair back down, shattering it into splinters. The demon's voice grew louder.

"DIIIIIIIIIIG!"

The word lingered, reverberating in the walls. A strange sensation came over me, a terrible itch that ran from my head down into my left arm. The itch needled continuously until I couldn't bear it any longer. I felt a deep and morbid craving, my thoughts turning to knives and razors, guillotines and piano wire. *Stop it!* But I couldn't stop it, and nothing but blades would do. *Thinner, thinner, sharper, sharper. Flesh, flesh, flesh!*

There was a strange clarity in this madness. I didn't have to make my own choices any longer. The demon was my commander, and my arm had to go.

○

As evening set in, I sat at the breakfast table and stared blankly at the cauterised nub that was once my arm. I wondered why I had not felt any pain during the ordeal, just incremental, almost pleasurable relief. It all felt like a dream, like someone else had been at the helm, and I could only watch as the knife went clean through the flesh and then struggled with the bone. I was drenched with sweat, I realised. The blowtorch had been used heavily. If I had known madness in my childhood, then it was only a kind of half madness. I was now beyond the pale. The demon lurked above me, somewhere in the ceiling, swimming through the plaster. I didn't have to see its terrible grin to know that it was pleased; I could sense it. What would come next?

I was just about to slip away when the itch returned. Again, it started in my head, but this time it travelled down into my left leg. Please, no. Not this. What are you doing to me?! I can't die here, all alone in this awful place. And my poor parents! They would return from their holiday to find my mutilated body. How could they ever cope?

I love them so much.

Wait.

The itching began to peter out, replaced by a growing pain in my nub. The demon's psychic link was waning.

I love them so much.

I stood up from the chair, faltering in my weakened state. Overhead, the demon roared in raging disbelief. It tried to unite with me again, with greater force and urgency, flooding my brain with images of knives—hundreds and thousands of shining blades, sharp and thin. With all my might, I pushed the twisted thoughts away. I pictured my parents. They were smiling at me.

Now or never. I ran for the kitchen door and unlocked it, then bolted through the laundry room and out into the garden.

The last of the light was draining from the sky as I ran through the long, dense grass. I was off-balance, keeling sideways. I saw something up ahead, but my legs didn't stop in time, and I fell down a deep well into a waiting light.

o

The fire pit burned at the centre of the cave, its mighty orange glow sending shadows dancing across the walls. I wiped the dirt from my face, patted myself down with my one remaining arm, and found that I was unhurt. I had landed on a mattress that was placed beneath the hole above. With blurry eyes, I saw a figure crawling towards me. As the shape drew closer, Tom Gardner came into focus, his face completely covered in brown dirt, accentuating his fierce blue eyes. He smiled at me.

"Have you come to help us? We're almost finished!"

He had a pickaxe in his right hand.

"Mom told me to come see what the noise was. We've been so busy!"

Tom had always been chubby, but now he was painfully thin. His left arm and both his legs were severed just below the joints. The poor boy. The demon had made short work of him.

He smiled again.

"Tom..."

"Come with me."

With some deftness, he rolled himself over and crawled towards the back of the cave. I looked up to the perfect circle of night sky above. There was no way up and no way out. Where else could I go? I followed him, resigned and defeated once again.

Robert and Edna Garner sat together in the shadows at the back of the cave. They didn't seem to notice me at all. Save for their right arms, they too had removed their limbs. They were digging, quietly but attentively, at a long, smooth slab of black rock. It looked like a pharaoh's sarcophagus.

"Robert? Edna? It's me, it's Julia." I stepped closer, but they didn't hear me.

Robert slammed his pickaxe into the black rock and pulled a large chunk away in one swift pull. A jet of hot steam burst out of the cavity. It cooled and dissipated, and with the light of the fire pit behind me, I saw a recognisable face within. It was the demon in the flesh. Its skin was a deep blue, with intricate white lines branching across its face and ram-like horns spiralling upwards. The eyes were shut, but it was grinning all the same. The room started to spin.

The Gardners had heard the call to dig and answered it dutifully. Now, they sat before a smoking, black rock, mindlessly possessed—crippled diggers for a sleeping demon. Tom crawled excitedly towards the black slab and joined his parents in the excavation. Huge shards of stone fell away as they struck the rock with relentless enthusiasm. Soon, the demon would be released. I had to do something.

I looked around, searching for something, anything. In the shadows by my feet, a pickaxe glimmered. It was blunt.

I picked it up and charged for the demon's head. Somehow, Tom had anticipated this, and he grabbed my ankle.

"NOOOOOO!!!" he yelled. "He must be freed!"

His frail hand could not hold me, and I escaped his grasp. The whole pitiful family looked to me, their pleading eyes begging for their master's life.

"He must be freed, he MUST be freed!"

I stood over the demon and took aim.

"He shall be freed."

I plunged the pickaxe into its skull and out came a stream of blue light.

An earthquake shook the cave, and I was thrown backwards, slamming onto the ground with a dull thud. All went black.

I don't know how long I was out for, but when I opened my eyes, I could see a trickle of daylight coming from the hole above. I looked up and saw the Gardners sitting there, staring at me, like lost ghosts.

Tom crawled closer, sat himself up, and asked a simple question.

"What do we do now?"

The Bog

by

Thomas Staunton

The freezing cold air bit John around the nape of his neck. He pulled his hood up tightly and gazed across the vast bog, an endless sea of black land dotted with pools of water that shimmered weakly in the last light of dusk. His hands burned from the cold, but he managed to steady his map just enough to trace a route with his finger. He was sure this was the only way. He put the map in his pocket, checked his watch with a resigned sigh, and turned to his two travelling companions. How had he become the expert in all of this?

"Frank, I know you're in a lot of pain right now, but we don't have much time."

Frank sat up uncomfortably and winced. "What are we doing?"

"We can't go back the way we came. Not now, it's too dark. Too many ledges and cliffs. We have to go through the bog."

Callum crossed his arms. "You—"

"It's not ideal, but we can't stay here. It's too exposed. If we cross the bog, we could be onto a road within a few hours. Two, maybe three. We just take our time."

The sun had all but disappeared by the time the men reached the bog. A thin strip of orange and magenta lay across the horizon line. The descent had been a long ordeal. John and Callum carried Frank down in carefully orchestrated steps, avoiding any movement that could make his ankle worse. They rested at the bottom. John knew that hikers would stick to the dry, higher sections of the bog, but they had the benefit of the bright light of day. Beyond them in the vast blackness lay marshes, pits, and sinkholes. He panicked a little, as he knew that Callum was looking for any hint of uncertainty, any excuse to swoop in and take over. In the distance, he could faintly see a ridgeway, a high path above the wet turf. He smiled to himself.

"Over there, this way."

The last of the light was swallowed by the horizon, so John took out his flashlight. The bog was dead silent, except for the faint trickling of water. Occasionally, they heard a rustling sound from somewhere, and when John scanned with his torch, a pair of eyes would glow and then scatter. Not far into their painfully slow march, the ridge was starting to narrow, and the dirt beneath their feet loosened and tumbled down the slopes. Frank held onto Callum for balance, taking slow, deliberate steps.

John swore under his breath. This had been his idea—a day of bonding with the colleagues. Callum and Frank were mystified by the idea of hiking. Back in the dusty office of the flour mill, they had listened with disinterested expressions as John described the fresh air and breathtaking scenery of the mountain. They had never even heard of the mountain, even though it was visible on a clear day from the top of the factory. They finally relented when John promised them drinks at a local pub after. John cursed under his breath again, feeling the pressure building.

○

The darkness now was absolute, the moon and stars hidden behind a column of thick cloud. The flashlight gave John some comfort, but it only showed him what lay straight ahead. He dared not think about what was in his periphery.

The trickling water became a steady flow, and when John scanned with his flashlight, he saw little streams pouring into the embankments around the ridge. He noticed then that the peak was now sloping downwards into the peatland. He stopped and thought for a moment.

"What's the problem?" said Callum.

"There's no more ridge." said John.

Callum helped Frank to sit down, dusted himself off, and marched over to John.

"So, what now? We walk through this treacherous sludge for hours? Is that it?"

John knew that Callum was itching for an argument. Everyone was tired and frustrated, but John had to keep them moving.

"The bog road is straight across this stretch. We'll help Frank down and take turns supporting him."

John was already moving to take Frank before Callum could reply. "You ready?"

Frank shifted uncomfortably. "Yeah."

Poor Frank, John thought. It wasn't fair on any of them, but Frank had really gotten the raw deal. John lifted him up and put his arm around his neck. "How is it?"

"Getting worse; it's really swelling up."

"Do you want to go back?"

"No. Let's go."

The bog slowed their walk to a crawl. Many diversions were made as they encountered ponds, streams, and ditches, with each new route sending them further away from dry, rocky terrain. Callum swung the flashlight around with panicked frenzy at every sound emanating from the bog, be it a wet belch from a pond or a croak from a frog. John was far behind, sweating under the weight of Frank's heavyset frame. Still, they plodded along, going deeper and deeper into the centre of the bog.

Then the fog came, a thick blanket of white moving so fast that it barely seemed real. It bloomed and then rolled forward like an exploding bomb, the air cooling sharply, the atmosphere heavy with damp. John stopped and propped Frank up into a standing position. They were now completely surrounded by the fog. John felt an uneasy presence, like eyes watching from a window in an abandoned town.

"Callum, stop." John couldn't see five feet in front of him. There was a silence, and then the sound of soft footsteps as Callum appeared before them. "There's a fire up ahead."

Frank adjusted his posture. "A what?"

As quick as it had come, the fog lifted, and sure enough, as they walked into the clear night air, a small orange glow glinted in the distance. John was nervous. He could see it in Frank and Callum too. The light approached them.

Frank turned to John. "What do we do?"

"I don't know." John looked at Callum. "Farmer, maybe?"

"On a bog? At this hour?" Callum smirked at his little jibe, but John made every effort not to react.

The light was upon them. The bearer emerged from the black, an emaciated man dressed in a battered tunic, his skin like tanned leather, stretched over his skeleton. He stood before them with sad and frightened eyes. The light he held was a burning sod of turf impaled on a metal rod, and as he lowered it to the ground, John had no idea what to do, apart from stare. This man wasn't old, he was ancient, like a reanimated bog body. With a weak and breathless drone, he spoke.

"Alms for the poor?"

The man looked to Callum, then to Frank, and back to John, his white Mohawk glimmering in the firelight. John felt his body sink into the marsh. He could run now. All it would take is a quick push to Frank, and he would be away from all of this.

Callum stepped forward timidly.

"Sorry, we can't help, we..." Callum trailed off, his voice stuttering and useless. Frank squeezed John's back and then tapped him repeatedly.

"We have to go," said John.

Frank moved first, detaching himself from John's side. He marched over the wet ground like a man possessed. Callum quickly followed. John stood alone with the emaciated man. He wanted to say something else, but the inherent oddness of the situation had muted him. As he walked past the strange man, he thought he saw a faint smirk etched on his sunken face. John quickly joined the others, and their slow march across the bog became an urgent trot of huge, squelching steps.

o

The orange glow had long disappeared behind them. The clouds had parted, and moonlight washed over the bog, its milky blue lines marking the undulating land ahead of them. Callum led the pack, although he seemed to be wandering aimlessly, swinging the flashlight around like a frightened child. Frank was still managing to walk unaided, but the adrenaline surge had waned, and his face was now deeply pained. Eventually, he stopped and keeled over with a heavy, wet thud.

"I need to take this off. Help me take it off!" John stooped down and carefully slipped Frank's boot off.

"Callum, shine the light over here."

Frank's ankle was a balloon of red and purple. Callum circled them both nervously.

"We can't stay here. That man could come back."

Frank looked ready to heave. "I shouldn't have done that, I should have waited for you to help me."

John grasped Frank's arm. "Stop it, Frank. Callum, we're lost."

Callum was hyperventilating. "And whose fault is that? You stupid moron! God, this is a nightmare."

"The bog is not that big. We just continue heading this way, and we'll reach a road."

"Says you. You don't have a clue what you're doing." And with that, Callum walked away, taking the flashlight with him.

John turned to Frank, "Wait here," and took off running after Callum.

An immense collapsing sound thundered from the bog. Frank was already sinking by the time John turned around. A pit was forming in front of John's feet, masses of wet soil and vegetation cascading inwards in one fell swoop. Losing his footing, he tipped over the crater's edge, only to be hauled back from the brink by Callum. They fell onto their backs as Frank's desperate scream pierced the air. John grabbed the flashlight and crawled to the rim of the crater to find Frank sliding further into the pit. At the bottom, a monster was lurking.

The emaciated man was protruding out of the earth, a hideous worm gawking hungrily at the prey falling into his trap. In one horrifying jerk, his jaws opened wide, the cheeks stretching until they were almost transparent. Frank clawed feebly at the wet peat, but he was lost. The emaciated man moaned in pleasure as Frank slid down his throat. John and Callum watched on silently, impotent in the face of such horror. The monster slipped softly back under the ground, and Frank let out a final sigh as his face sank under the black sludge.

○

John saw the house first, a solitary cottage with its whitewashed walls glowing in the moonlight. There were no lights on, but that hardly mattered now. Callum followed behind him, broken and silent.

They climbed over the stone wall that surrounded the cottage, and circled the little building. John knocked on a back window.

"Hello?"

The silence seemed to agitate Callum, and so he screamed, "HELLOOOOOOOOO!"

A curtain was flung open to reveal a dark figure standing inside. The barrel of his rifle kissed the window.

"I can promise you now," said the man, "I will shoot you if you set foot in this house."

John raised his hands slowly. "We're not robbers, we're hikers, we need—"

"You don't need anything except to get off my property!"

Callum was crumbling under his panic attack. He lunged forward and slapped his hands against the window. "Please! He's coming for us!"

The figure went for his rifle bolt. John grabbed Callum and slammed him onto the ground, and with an assertiveness he never imagined he possessed, he straddled Callum's chest and slapped him clean across the face. "Stop... this... NOW!"

Callum sobered instantly. John rolled off him and turned to face the window. The dark figure had lowered his rifle, and the window was now half-open.

"I can't let you in. Not with *him* out there. It's his time of the year. He has the bog now, and I'm safe if I stay off it. Take the little road around the front and keep walking until you see the old rail track. Follow it and it'll bring you towards the town. You'll be safe as long as you stick to the track. Don't go near the bog."

John stood up slowly. "What about our friend? He took our friend."

"Your friend is gone. Don't walk onto the bog, you understand? Go!"

°

John and Callum were being mocked by the emaciated man. His hyena laugh came out of the darkness, from the left, from the right, from everywhere.

"Alms for the poor... aaaahhh-hahahahaha!"

He stalked them unceasingly, a lion in the dark, vanishing in and out of existence. Sometimes, John would catch a flash of his gaunt frame, walking on all fours like a hairless wolf.

"Brother Frank was fat and juicy... aaaahhh-hahahahaha!"

John was drained. He kept his attention on the gravel road laid out before him, desperate to block out the cruel taunts. It was all he could do to stop Frank's face appearing in front of him.

"I belched his bones out... aaaahhh-hahahahaha!"

Callum's sanity was evaporating. He whimpered and hollered and came in and out of delirium. Sometimes, he would let out a little sigh and say "Frank, oh God." John could only keep him from accidentally wandering off the road.

The railway embankment came into view a few hundred yards up ahead, intersecting the little road and continuing east into the faint light of dawn. As they got closer, John's stomach sank into his bowels. The gravel disappeared to nothing, and between them and the embankment was a stretch of soggy marshland. Somewhere in the dark, the emaciated man howled and squealed with laughter.

John grasped Callum by his arms and shook him to attention.

"Look at me, Callum," he whispered, firmly. "We need to run. A few more yards and we're free. Okay?"

Callum took a burst of short, shrill breaths. "Okay. Okay. Okay. Okay."

All sound was drowned out by the pounding of John's heart. It flushed through his ears and his face. He pocketed the flashlight, put his arm around Callum, and with one great push they bolted across the marsh. Each stride went deeper into the earth, and they lost their momentum. Soon, they were hauling their legs out of the mud.

When they were halfway across, Callum went down in one great squelching slap. John grabbed his hands and pulled, and Callum let out an agonising wail. He was already being eaten. The emaciated man wrapped his enormous mouth cleanly around Callum's legs, slowly enveloping more and more of him until all that was left was his head, a pale pupa protruding out of a cocoon. The emaciated man descended underground, gurgling like a baby. The bog was silent, once again.

John couldn't remember how he'd gotten to the embankment. He seemed to be walking, but he wasn't really there. From above, he watched himself move along the rail line, and then he was on the main road into town. Car headlights appeared over the hill and the car sped down towards him. He rolled into the ditch, and with the last of his strength, he waved the car down. He hoped, hoped beyond all wishes that it would stop.

The Owlman

BY

Lawrie Brewster

In my career as a horror filmmaker, I've made many friends among fellow directors, actors, and aspiring creatives. I often keep in touch with them through Facebook, where we'll chat about the challenges we face in trying to make independent films.

For me, working in horror is a way of exploring supernatural beliefs and possibilities, and while I could never claim to be an absolute believer, one indie filmmaking friend of mine, Christopher, most certainly was.

How that belief became an obsession is something which I feel deeply responsible for.

The most popular of my films featured a character called 'The Owlman', a godlike monster that could grant wishes to those willing to murder the ones they love. It resembled a tall man dressed in a dark Victorian tailcoat, with long, razor-sharp claws, and a giant owl's head with round, bulbous eyes. Inspired by the god Moloch, the Owlman was a master manipulator that spoke with an erudite intelligence both ancient and terrible.

Late into the night, Christopher and I would talk about the limitless possibilities of the universe, of what entities or deities might exist out there... somewhere. He was adamant that he didn't believe in God, but that he might believe in *the gods.*

Apart from our shared interests, I really knew nothing at all of Christopher's personal life, except that, like me, he was from the United Kingdom. His Facebook profile showed no photographs of himself, no pictures of friends or family, and displayed no location. I assumed that he was a loner, eccentric perhaps, but otherwise harmless. The only thing I really knew about him was that he was a huge fan of the Owlman, especially the prank videos.

The Owlman prank videos were produced to promote our movies, and we would spend weeks planning and executing these pranks on the unwary public. Our favourite location for filming was a centuries-old fever hospital for children. It had been abandoned for decades, and was located in a wasteland some miles out of town.

As the months went by, the topic of conversation shifted from the limitless possibilities of the universe, to the Owlman. All Christopher wanted to chat about was what had inspired us to create him, when the next video would be produced, even if he could 'meet him'. Eventually, his correspondence became relentless and, sadly, I was forced to ignore his messages. This agitated him, but after a while, the messages stopped, and for a couple of months there was no contact at all, until...

One night, he sent a single image that chilled my blood. Taken at night, the image was difficult to discern, but I could tell that the background was the children's hospital. In the centre of the image was a person standing some distance away, facing straight towards the camera.

The figure was wearing a hood which covered their face. There appeared to be something scrawled on it, three letters, but I couldn't make out what they were.

I don't think I wanted to make it out, as the image was deeply unsettling. Why had Christopher sent me this, and how had he discovered the location of our pranks, so close to where I lived? I lived with my partner in a small house by the forest, just out of town, beautiful, but remote. Getting up from the computer, I moved cautiously from room to room to check that the windows were latched shut, and finally, my front door, which, thank God, was locked.

As I returned to the computer, I grabbed a kitchen knife and kept it by my desk. Loading up the image in Photoshop, I decided to investigate the strange letters I had seen on the figure's hood. First, I adjusted the brightness, revealing little. Then, I increased the contrast, which helped, but the letters were still unclear. Finally, I added a sharpening effect, and the letters emerged from the darkness: the first was 'M', followed by 'L', then 'K'.

That sequence of letters, 'M.L.K.' had a terrible significance for me, as I knew from my research into the Owlman character that those letters were an ancient reference to Moloch. Often scrawled across the walls of archaic temples and forbidden ruins, the cursed religion of Moloch identified itself by the letters MLK.

Did Christopher believe that the Owlman was real?

My fingers hovered over the keyboard. Part of me wanted to reply to his message, to draw some comfort that perhaps this was all a practical joke made in poor taste.

A horrific realisation dawned on me as I noticed that Christopher and I suddenly shared a new mutual friend... my partner, Sarah.

Had he messaged her as well? It was 10:35 pm. She was out with friends and would probably not be back until late. I sent her a message to warn her of the strange image that I'd received and urged her to return home.

As the seconds passed with no response, my mouth became dry. Then, to my relief, I could see the *dot dot dot* icons in our chat window, signalling her imminent reply.

Another picture? My stomach turned. It was a photograph of a red Toyota, parked by the side of a road long-since surrendered to the undergrowth. Sarah's car. Behind it was a towering structure, the main building of the abandoned children's hospital.

I sent her many more desperate messages, but no reply came. Never have I felt such despair and helplessness as I did at that moment. Christopher must have tricked her into meeting him, and now she was trapped there, in the dark, with this psychopath.

I replied to Christopher's first message.

"Please don't hurt Sarah. Just tell me what you want."

As I waited, my mind raced with mad, anxious plans. Should I call my friends and go with them to try and rescue her? Or surely I should call the police? But what if he murdered her before help arrived? What if I couldn't save her? What if she was already dead? I rushed to the kitchen and retched over the sink, vomiting in pathetic terror at the situation I found myself in.

When I staggered back to my computer, I saw that Christopher had replied.

"I want you to believe."

More *dot dot dots* appeared.

"Come alone. I shall show you the proof of God."

I was afraid, but also determined to save her. While I waited for the taxi, I put on a long, black coat and concealed a kitchen knife in one of the pockets. Christopher might be watching from a hiding spot at the hospital, which consisted of a whole complex of crumbling brick buildings, and Sarah could be in any one of them.

Headlights swept through the blinds of my bedroom as the taxi rumbled to a stop outside. It was time to go. Facing whatever horrors lay ahead, I stepped out into the wintry night. The icy wind was so cold that my breath swirled like smoke. I said nothing to the driver, despite his best efforts to initiate conversation, and soon we arrived at the desolate outskirts of town. I would walk the rest of the way on foot, down a pitch-black track of abandoned road, towards whatever fate had in store for me.

The freezing wind blasted my face, blowing away my tears of rage and frustration. I passed Sarah's car by the side of the road. It lay empty, its doors unlocked. There was no sign of a struggle, at least as far as I could tell.

About a hundred feet ahead of me, looming over a horizon of overgrown forest, was the crooked assembly of hospital ruins, each building more foreboding than the last. Before them stood an imposing iron gate, the view beyond it obscured by a twisted jungle of weeds. The moon provided little help, silhouetting instead of illuminating the buildings ahead, which, over the tree-tops, resembled a sort of infernal Mount Rushmore of monstrous heads.

My phone showed no new messages, and as I made my way into the centre of the complex, I could see no sign of life. It was deathly quiet. The only sound was the wind whistling through broken windows.

I switched on my phone torch, guiding it to the surrounding buildings. Most of them were single-storey, brick-built sheds, their roofs sagging inwards, ready to collapse at any second. I aimed the beam of light at the windows and doorways, desperately seeking some sign that Sarah was here, and that she was alright.

My phone flashed—a message. It was from Christopher.

"Turn off your torch."

I did as instructed, and looked all around me, exposed and fully vulnerable. If he were intent on killing me, he could come from any direction, then all would be lost. A lump formed in my throat as I slid my hand into my coat, gripping the kitchen knife in preparation for whatever might come next.

Of all the buildings, there was one that stood out from the rest. It wasn't the largest, but it was the most remarkable. It resembled a church, with a stone tower and adjoining hall. I couldn't help but sense that Christopher might be hiding in there, in the most grandiose of the ruins, and the most suitable venue for his supposed proof of God.

Stone steps led to a collapsed door, and beyond it, a great hall, once a hospital ward to countless sick children, in decades, and even centuries past. Shafts of moonlight streamed through the broken windows, illuminating slivers of debris, collapsing floorboards, and a white feather.

A white feather?

In my original film featuring the Owlman, the protagonist would discover feathers, serving as clues or deadly reminders that 'it' was coming. Everything in the place was covered in soot and dust from the fire that had doomed the building to decay... everything except for the feather, that is. I picked it up and called out to Christopher.

"Christopher, I've followed your clues! I've done what you asked!"

Moments later, a message flashed on my phone.

"Look up."

I looked up immediately, but could see nothing but the moonlight piercing through the holes in the broken roof. I switched on my phone torch once again and shone it around the hall, but nothing stood out to me.

I was about to reply to Christopher when the torchlight landed on a small doorway I had missed before. I approached it and observed a set of stairs leading upwards, probably towards the attic. The narrow stairwell had plastered walls, black with rot and decay. The ascent was claustrophobic, the rotten wood under my feet making each step perilous. At the top of the stairs I could see a closed door, green with a brass handle... and another single feather.

My phone pinged—a message from Christopher.

"Open the door and meet your God."

I had reached the summit of horror. I looked back and winced at the sight of the staircase I'd climbed vanishing into darkness.

This was it. I took out the kitchen knife and grasped it tightly, ready to strike if I had to. Thoughts of Sarah flashed before me.

Please, God, I thought, *just let her be safe. Take me if you have to.*

It was like watching someone else as my hand twisted the brass handle of the green door, as it creaked and cracked, opening slowly.

Beyond the door was total and utter blackness. I was effectively blind. I fumbled again for my phone and shone my torch into the darkness.

And then... I saw God.

The Owlman.

THE OWLMAN!

Shrieking in horror, I stepped back, tripping on the warped wooden floor. I found myself tumbling backwards, down the steps of the narrow staircase. As I landed at the bottom of the stairs, a chunk of jagged debris pierced my arm, slashing through the skin. Having dropped my phone, I could see little in the darkness. My mind raced with panic and fury.

I could barely take my eyes away from the black void at the top of the stairs, waiting, wondering with horror whether the Owlman might now come for me.

I shouted in rage and terror.

"Christopher!"

I heard footsteps. Not from the top of the stairs, but from the main hall below. Without thinking, I dragged myself up. My left arm was soaked in blood and felt like it was broken. Nevertheless, I charged into the main hall, and there I saw Christopher, running out into the night.

I still had the kitchen knife. I charged after him into the courtyard, shouting and swinging the blade, but by the time I got there, he was gone. I could see no sign of him, nothing except an abandoned cloak that he must have thrown to the ground as he ran, the hood emblazoned with MLK.

In the minutes that passed, the injury I suffered began to affect me, slowing me down, blurring my vision. Thoughts of Sarah raced through my mind, and I called out to her while fighting to remain conscious.

Returning to the main building, I staggered back into the main hall. To my shock, I saw the Owlman shuffling in the dark, but this 'Owlman' looked different, not like the startling vision I had seen at the top of the stairs.

By some instinct, I approached it. This was a costume much like the type I used in our prank videos. I removed the head gently, and there, inside, was Sarah, her mouth taped shut.

Once I untied her, she helped me back to the car, explaining how she too had been lured there, and then forced by a masked stranger to adorn a costume he had constructed.

As she drove me to the hospital, I asked her how she had managed to get down the collapsed set of stairs. She looked at me strangely, a look that I will never forget, and said;

"I was on the ground floor the whole time..."

By the time I had returned home, Christopher had deleted what little remained of his internet presence. I never saw or heard from him again. Neither me, nor Sarah will ever forget the horror of what we experienced that night, and I still live in fear for the day that I might encounter a white feather, or a question of sanity of the likes that was presented to me that night... by the Owlman.

BALDURROCK

BY

SARAH DALY

In the end, it was such a small thing that tipped the balance. After everything: the oil shortages, the rising cost of food, the punishing public spending cuts, no one could have guessed that taxing the internet would bring civilised society as we knew it tumbling down.

Across the country, disparate groups mobilised into a spontaneous uprising that escalated into full-blown anarchy in a matter of weeks. Peaceful protests turned to violence when met with violence from heavy-handed police. The military were drafted in to counter looting and rioting in all major cities and, before long, a police state was declared as civil disorder took hold. It was a similar story all over Europe. Although the triggers in each country were different, the result was the same. Revolution spread like a virus. We passed the point of no return with no warning and now we must each fight for our own survival in a new and dangerous world.

Before it all kicked off, my boyfriend Callum and I had been planning our wedding. After five years of subtle and not-so-subtle hints, I'd eventually agreed that perhaps marriage wasn't such a stupid institution after all. After a few short weeks of engagement, the rioting began, and all our plans, hopes and dreams went out the window. We'd actually taken part in the protests in the beginning. We weren't political creatures by any stretch of the imagination, but things had gotten so bad that we felt compelled to do something about it. As the demonstrations became increasingly violent, however, we retreated to the comparative safety of our flat and holed up there, hoping things would settle down before too long. For the first few weeks we managed alright by staying indoors, only venturing out early in the morning when the night's looting had subsided. Then, the violence came to us. A gang broke into the flat downstairs, directly below us. They ransacked the place and brutally attacked the old woman who lived there. It was a stern warning, both heartbreaking and terrifying. We knew then that we couldn't carry on living in the city. There was nothing left for us there but the constant threat of violence. It was Shay, Callum's best friend, who suggested that we go to Baldurrock.

When my father first inherited Baldurrock House, fifteen years ago, our family was elated, and shocked. We'd never even heard of the place, or of its deceased owner James Findlay. As it turned out, he was my father's cousin, and my father his only living relative. Being accustomed to scraping by on the modest income from my parents' small business, we couldn't quite believe our good fortune.

Our excitement soon faded when we went to see the place. After a torturous drive to the remote highland estate, we were dejected to find the house and grounds in a terrible condition. It had obviously once been a grand home, but now it was crumbling. Its ominous façade was smothered by decades of creeping ivy, its windows were half rotten, and its roof riddled with holes. This was no goldmine; it was a money pit. Of course, I didn't understand that then; I was just ten years old. All I knew was that the place filled me with a sense of dread so thick that I could barely breathe. I prayed to the god I no longer believe in that I would never have to return.

We put the house up for sale, but as the months and then the years went by, it became clear that nobody wanted it. We dropped the price again and again, but still there was no interest. Baldurrock was our burden to bear, and when my father died last year, that burden was passed on to me.

Before long, I was to return there willingly, desperately hoping that my place of nightmares could become my refuge, blissfully oblivious of the horrors to come.

o

We set off just before dawn, hoping to avoid trouble. There were five of us: myself, Callum, his mother Mai, Shay and his girlfriend Samantha. It was never in question whether we would take Mai with us. She was an unshakable little Vietnamese woman in her seventies who had been a constant source of solace and stability to us, but to me especially, since I had no parents left myself. Her husband George, a Scotsman, died days before Callum was born, and she had raised him all by herself in what was then a strange country. I admired her greatly and thanked her frequently for teaching Callum to cook the incredible food he conjured up almost nightly.

The decision to bring Shay and Samantha, however, had been a more difficult one. Shay was Callum's oldest friend, but he and I had never really seen eye to eye. It had always been a bit of a tug of war between the two of us, with Callum in the middle. As for Samantha, I didn't know her very well and suspected that no one really did. It was possible that she had hidden depths but, if so, then she was incredibly talented at concealing them. She was undoubtedly a very sweet-natured girl, but irritatingly delicate and reserved. Knowing what I know now, I am not ashamed to say that I was against taking them with us, but, at the time, the choice made sense. Aside from the fact that Shay had suggested the endeavour, he had also stowed away a few gallons of fuel when he saw what was coming. This was a godsend, as it meant we wouldn't have to risk the notorious queues at what petrol stations were left. Armed guards now manned the stations, and deaths were common among the waiting drivers, who were often stuck in queues for days on end, only to be told that the well had run dry. So, on practical grounds, I agreed that all five of us would go together. Looking back on that decision, I desperately wish that I had gone with my gut.

Once we set off, our main problem was the abandoned vehicles clogging the roads. We wound around them as best we could, but occasionally we were forced to get out and push them out of the way. This was a nerve-wracking experience, as it left us open to attack, and our precious fuel vulnerable to the siphons of the new gangs. Although progress was painfully slow, we were lucky and managed to avoid any major trouble. After ten solid hours of driving, running on our final fumes of petrol, we made it to Baldurrock.

It was dark when we pulled up into the winding, tree-lined drive, not dark like it got in the city, but a pure, dense, unflinching blackness that filled me with a primal panic the second I switched the headlights off. The house loomed out of the darkness, an ancient and commanding presence.

The panic subsided once we entered the house, only to be replaced by that old, familiar fear and a cloying dread in the pit of my stomach. It was just as I remembered it. The large entrance hall was adorned with the dusty antlers of long-dead stags and austere portraits of long-dead ancestors, their dull eyes looking down on us with scorn. The air was stale and loaded with clouds of acrid dust, disturbed into life by our entrance. It felt more like a crypt than a home, a place of death rather than a safe haven.

It was far from the welcoming retreat I knew the others had expected, despite my warnings. No one would admit it, but we were all depressed by the place, all dreading the thought of making it our home, all except Shay that is. Shay was fascinated by every period feature, every macabre oddity. He explored the house with a giddy, childish excitement; a boundless enthusiasm that he exuded to the point of being unnerving. The rest of us left him to it and went to choose our rooms.

The house was a maze spread over three floors. It was so vast that the five of us could easily live together and hardly ever see each other, yet we chose three bedrooms in close proximity. I suppose you could call it the herd mentality at work, but in reality, we were afraid, and keeping close made us less so.

o

Despite our fears, we all slept well that first night and faced the new day with a little more positivity. We quickly set about making the place habitable. Living up to gender stereotypes, Callum and Shay went off to cut wood and attempt to catch some fish in the nearby lake, while Samantha, Mai, and I got stuck into the monumental task of cleaning the place. We knew it would take weeks to get the house in order, but we weren't daunted by the work. In fact, we were all glad of having something to do. It was what came after that frightened us. How would we fill our days? What purpose would drive us? Would we be safe here, or would other desperate or dangerous people find our sanctuary and want it for themselves? Nothing was certain. We just had to keep our heads down and get on with what needed to be done; take it day by day.

After about a week, we had 'settled in', or at least grown accustomed to the idea that this was our home now. We had our daily routine of chores to keep us sane and give us structure. Everyone pulled their weight, even Mai, who must have struggled to keep up but never once showed it. She bore all the changes better than anyone, perhaps because she'd lived through a war. Born and raised in Vietnam, Mai was just a child in the sixties when it all kicked off, and so her formative years were filled with death, violence, and upheaval. She'd seen far worse times than these, and we all looked to her for strength.

Samantha found it most difficult; the hard work as well as the emotional adjustment. She had always reminded me of a porcelain doll, beautiful, but dangerously fragile (and, as I said before, a little lacking in terms of personality). She was the epitome of 'nice', all smiles and polite small talk, but despite the ordeal we were facing together, I still hadn't managed to forge any real friendship with her. Regarding her difficulty adapting, I supposed that because she'd led quite a privileged life, she hadn't developed the necessary coping mechanisms for dealing with such hardship. On this front, Shay was no help to her whatsoever. In fact, he made things worse with his unerring positivity. Ever since we'd arrived he'd maintained that same strange enthusiasm for our new situation. He seemed almost to glow with an eagerness, a lust for life I'd never seen in him before. Perhaps it should have been encouraging to see someone approach adversity in such a way, but, in reality, there was something deeply unsettling about Shay's new *joie de vivre*. I couldn't make out whether his attitude was an act, a manifestation of subconscious denial, or if it really was genuine, but whatever it was, it had the effect of making him horribly unsympathetic to Samantha's problems. He either couldn't or didn't want to understand why she was struggling. It was disturbing to watch this dynamic play out, but the events that came next were infinitely more troubling.

It started with just a few odd incidents; small things, but they bothered me nonetheless. One particular night, I was having trouble sleeping, so I went downstairs to make a cup of tea, as I often did. Although I was frightened at the thought of walking the shadowy corridors alone, I wouldn't allow myself to be ruled by fear. If I wanted a cup of tea, I would have one. With each nighttime excursion, my confidence had grown, but this trip was different. On my way to the kitchen, I heard a muffled voice, a lone sound in the otherwise profound silence. I stopped dead and listened. It was coming from the sitting room. I tiptoed to the closed door and placed my ear against the wood, careful not to make a noise. There was a voice alright; Shay's voice. It sounded as if he was speaking *to* someone, yet I could hear only one voice. Was he talking to himself? There was a worrying thought. Or was he on the phone perhaps? None of the rest of us had gotten any phone signal since arriving, so that was unlikely. I kept my ear to the door, intensely curious as to what he was doing still up, and perturbed by the strange, one-sided conversation. The heavy, old door was solid enough that I couldn't make out what he was saying, but the longer I listened, the more I was convinced that I could hear another voice along with his. It was another man's voice; a low, rumbling drone that sounded nothing like Callum, who I knew was still in bed upstairs in any case. I should have just opened the door and solved the mystery there and then, but some instinctive voice within me told me I should get away instead. I trusted my gut and went straight back to bed, no longer feeling like being alone in the kitchen. All I wanted was to feel Callum's warm, familiar body next to mine, and forget everything else.

The next incident happened when Callum and Shay were out hunting. Yes, hunting—we had devolved that far. We had begun to grow vegetables, but of course it would be months before they were ripe for eating, and the lake had proven itself void of any edible aquatic life. In the meantime, rabbit and venison were our main food sources. This was another cause of upset for Samantha who had, up until then, been a committed vegetarian, but needs must. She never seemed to have much of an appetite in any case.

Callum and Shay had stepped up and quickly proven themselves to be capable hunters. One day, however, Callum returned from the hunt with a worrying story to tell. He and Shay had been in the woods, waiting it out in a good spot where they'd been lucky before, when Shay took an odd turn all of a sudden. According to Callum, Shay had been on edge and acting strange all day, culminating in a weird episode where he ran around pretending to be some kind of commando. Callum went along with the joke at first, thought it was funny; any kind of release was welcome back then, even if it seems reckless in hindsight. After a short while, Callum started to feel uncomfortable with how Shay was acting. He was getting a little too 'into' the performance apparently. After reciting an intense and deeply disquieting monologue, Shay aimed his rifle at Callum. Understandably, Callum panicked. If this was a joke, Shay had taken it too far. He held Callum in his sights for something like thirty seconds, then broke into uproarious laughter, claiming it was all a prank, and ridiculing Callum for buying it. Maybe it was just a laddish wind-up, but the look on Callum's face when he told me about the incident was enough to convince me that something was very wrong. Callum was not one for drama or exaggeration, so if he was concerned about something, then we needed to take heed. We had to keep a closer eye on Shay.

So, that night when I heard Shay leave his room, I decided to follow him. I'd heard him wandering about a number of times in the small hours, almost every night, in fact, and it was time to get to the bottom of it. On my way down the stairs, I heard the front door open and shut. Why was he going outside? It was freezing out there, and pitch black. I went to the window that overlooked the front lawn, expecting to see Shay out there, but he was nowhere to be seen. There was someone out there, however. Or something.

I peered into the dark, my eyes adjusting to it, and the figure came into focus. The thing stood stock-still under a gnarled, old oak; so still that it could almost be a statue. He or *it* wore an old-fashioned morning suit, its unnaturally long arms protruding out of the ragged sleeves and ending in what looked like enormous, sharp talons. The most horrifying thing about the creature, however, was its head, which looked for all the world like the head of a giant owl. The head turned, slowly, slowly, until the owl man's shiny, black eyes seemed to be staring right at me, right *into* me.

Too afraid to scream, or even move an inch, I stood frozen in terror, locked in a staring contest with the monstrous thing on the lawn. After what felt like minutes, but could only have been seconds, it turned its head and directed its cruel gaze elsewhere. When I finally regained the use of my limbs and stepped back from the window, I heard the front door open. I turned to run back up the stairs, terrified that the creature was coming for me, but when I glanced down, I saw that it was Shay coming through the door. My mind went into overdrive trying to make sense of it all, and the conclusion I came to filled me with rage. It had been a trick, some kind of sick prank. Of course it had! He'd really crossed the line now!

I stormed down the stairs to confront Shay, screaming blue murder at the fright he'd given me, but he flat out denied that it was him. He told me I'd lost it, that I was seeing things. He claimed that he'd just gone out to get some air, that he'd been having trouble sleeping and the night air helped to clear his head. He suggested that maybe I should do the same. I refused to believe him. I knew what I'd seen, and the only logical explanation was that he was playing tricks again. What else could it possibly have been but a cruel trickster in a costume? We were about to find out, and the revelation would change all of our lives forever.

○

Tempers started to fray over the next few days, and our concerns about Shay were pushed aside as we struggled with what seemed like more pressing problems. We hadn't had any fruit or vegetables for weeks and were all starting to get run down. We had no medical supplies, which was a growing concern, and we were running out of all the little things that we'd taken for granted in our old lives: toothpaste, soap, tea, sugar. We were living like cavemen in a grand mansion. As usual, Mai weathered the storm best, but we could see that she wasn't well, even if she wouldn't admit it. Samantha though, was doing very badly. She had lost a lot of weight and looked gaunt, weak. She barely said a word, except to complain of the various pains that now plagued her and, with no medical supplies, there was nothing we could do except to suggest that she rest in bed. She spent most of her days there now, and each time she emerged, she looked worse. Shay still seemed to neglect her, hardly visiting her during the day, and acting almost as if she didn't exist. Terrible though it was, I was really starting to wish we hadn't brought them with us. We'd felt compelled since the move was Shay's idea, but I didn't know how much longer we could all live together like this. Our tentative dream for a better life was fast becoming a nightmare.

Yet, there were times still when we would laugh about the strangeness of it all, enjoy ourselves even. It was those moments that made the trials bearable. One evening, Callum, Mai, and I lit a bonfire outside and told stories about the old days, reminding each other that this life wasn't all we were about. We had to be careful not to lose ourselves in the hopeless drudgery of it all. Otherwise, what was the point in even trying to survive? For a couple of golden hours, we were ourselves again, but when night came, and a storm with it, reality crept back in as it always did, and the party was over. That was the night it happened.

○

The house creaked and groaned as the wind gained strength. These nights were the worst, when every little sound became a nightmarish threat in my tired mind. I knew that I would get no sleep, so I didn't even try. I occupied myself with a tattered, old book I'd found on the history of Baldurrock. It made for fascinating reading, but was hardly the most comforting tome to delve into on a stormy night. In its five-hundred-year history, the house had seen more than its fair share of tragedy. As I read further, I discovered that I wasn't the only Findlay to seek refuge here, and find nothing of the sort. I was filled with the oppressive sense of a pattern repeating, a dark and unstoppable force shaping my fate. The north wind howled through the crumbling chimneys of this cursed place.

It was about 3 am when I heard the familiar sound of Shay setting off on one of his nighttime jaunts. I hadn't dared follow him since that first night, terrified of what I might see. I had convinced myself at this point that I had simply imagined the figure, but nonetheless, I certainly didn't want another vision like it, so I stayed put. Then I heard another noise amidst the wailing winds; it was the sound of something being dragged. *What was he up to?* I listened closely and heard what sounded like a moan, barely audible, but enough for me to wake Callum and tell him about it. Callum groggily pulled a t-shirt over his head and agreed to go investigate. I insisted on going with him, mostly because my fear of what was out there was less than my fear of being left alone in the room.

We crept out into the hall and toward the grand staircase, encountering nothing untoward. We peered into Shay and Samantha's room and saw Samantha sleeping there alone, her breath worryingly ragged. I don't know why, but I wanted to check on Mai too, so I quietly pushed open the door of her room and looked in. She wasn't there. We hurried down the stairs to find the front door wide open and an icy wind blasting through the house. We looked at one another and ran for the door.

The storm raged outside, the winds so violent that the roots of the ancient trees rose out of the ground like skeletal hands reaching upward from shallow graves. The ferocious gale whipped our faces, and sleet blurred our already weak vision. We could barely see a thing in the pitch-black night, but the faint light of a torch in the distance drew our attention. We followed the beam, both filled with an intense dread at what it was we might be running towards.

The beam stopped dead. Whoever was holding it had put it down by the edge of the lake. We were almost there. From about fifty yards away, I could begin to see what was happening. Shay was dragging something, someone, into the lake. Whoever it was, they were unconscious or dead. Something glinted in the pale moonlight... a blade? An axe. Shay was carrying an axe. My stomach flipped and my heart seemed to stop beating. I prayed to that old God that somehow it would all be okay, but I knew there was no way anything could ever be okay again. The body was in the water now, and Shay was holding it under. He was drowning her. He was drowning Mai.

As Callum drew nearer, Shay raised the axe and warned us not to come any closer. I was crying now, as I could see Mai just under the surface of the black water, and few bubbles coming from her nose. If, by some miracle, she was still alive, she wouldn't be for long. I begged Shay to let her go, but there was no reason left in him. He looked and sounded nothing like the Shay I knew. This was a desperate man, a man driven to the edge of madness... but by what? He was screaming something about how he "had to do it," that he "had no choice," that it was "the only way to save her."

"But you're killing her!" I screamed.

"Not Mai," he said, "Samantha."

It made no sense, but this was no time for making sense. Callum charged at Shay, driven by a wild instinct to protect his mother. I screamed at him to stay back, but there was no stopping him. Shay let go of Mai for just a second in order to better hold the axe. Seeing my chance, I ran to her, and as the men fought, I managed to pull her limp body to the shore. I turned her on her side, hoping that this would help the water to drain out, and then, perhaps wrongly, went to Callum's aid. I was terrified that Shay would kill him, then what would I be left with?

Shay swung the axe wildly, fighting Callum off with a vicious abandon. He managed to slash Callum's shoulder with the axe. My stomach lurched as Callum fell, blood already oozing from the vicious wound. Shay raised his weapon and prepared to strike, to murder his own best friend and the man I loved. I couldn't let this happen. I crept up behind Shay, my heart thumping in my chest and a jagged rock clutched in my hand. Driven by wild instinct, I slammed the rock hard against the back of Shay's head. He slumped to the ground, and Callum rolled out of the way just in time to avoid the falling blade.

Callum rushed to take care of his mother. He knew just what to do, and in a few seconds had her coughing up the water she'd ingested. It seemed that Mai was even tougher than I gave her credit for. Shay's eyes opened just as she came round. He looked over at her sadly, all the fight gone from him. He sobbed, muttering something about how he had failed. Furious, Callum picked up the axe, and was about to bury it in Shay's chest when Shay said something odd, odd enough for Callum to stop and hear him out.

"Please don't let him take me."

"Who?" I asked, "Who's *he*?"

"The Owl Man," he moaned. Suddenly I couldn't breathe.

"You've lost it, mate." Callum shook his head.

"He told me, he told me months ago that if I brought you here, if I gave him what he wanted, he'd save Samantha."

"Save her from what?" Callum spat.

"Cancer... she's dying." Callum and I looked at each other. "I had to give him Mai in her place. That was the deal. I know it's awful... I know that, but she's old. She'll die soon anyway." Shay looked right into Callum's eyes, imploring. "You would have done the same for her."

He gestured to me. Callum looked at me with an expression I'd never seen on his face before, lifted the axe high above his head, and planted it firmly in Shay's chest with a sickening crunch. I felt the vomit rising in my throat. How had it come to this? How had we found ourselves in this living nightmare? In any other time, I would have walked away from Callum then and never looked back, but these were new times, different times, with different rules. We were cave men now and cave men kill to protect their own.

o

Callum and I carried his mother back to the house in silence. I wondered how we would ever speak to each other again after what we'd seen and done that night. We made it back to the house and warmed some water over the fire to bathe Mai in. We wrapped her in all the blankets we could find and hoped that it would be enough to keep her with us. Still without saying a word, I tended to Callum's wound, which, luckily, wasn't as deep as I had feared. When I had finished cleaning and bandaging, I went to fill a hot-water bottle for Mai. On my way past the large window in the hall, I caught a glimpse of something moving through the night, something with a sharp beak and round, black eyes. It moved gracefully across the lawn towards Shay's body. Mesmerised, I watched as it pulled the axe out of Shay's chest with its taloned hands, raised the axe high, and in one sharp movement, brought it down hard on Shay's white neck, chopping the head clean off. Then, the creature picked up the head, turned to look directly at me, and held the vile thing up for me to see.

I must have fainted, because the next thing I remember is Callum calling for me to come quickly. I shook myself out of it and went to help him with Mai, who was shaking violently. I wouldn't trouble him with my vision now; I had to hold it together, even though inside I was falling apart.

We made Mai comfortable, and then, somehow, we slept. We curled up on the floor by her bed and held each other until we both passed out. When we woke the next morning, it was to the sound of fat frying and the smell of venison. After checking on Mai, who seemed to be recovering nicely, we went downstairs to find a very rosy-cheeked Samantha cooking up a storm. She was glowing, smiling, a different person to the sickly waif I'd seen just the day before. She was brimming with excitement about her transformation, and her newfound happiness was infectious. It almost felt for a moment that things were looking up, until she asked:

"Where's Shay? Have you seen him?"

o

So, it seemed that, in dying, he had saved the one he loved. Perhaps we would have called it a heroic act had he done it willingly. Instead, we snuck out while Samantha cooked our breakfast and buried what was left of the body. Callum wouldn't believe my story about how Shay lost his head, but couldn't offer up a better explanation. He agreed that we would keep the house locked and never venture out at night in case the man came back, but I knew that it was no mere man. It was the Owl Man.

He never did bother us again. I suppose he'd gotten what he wanted. And as for Shay, we let Samantha believe that he'd left one night to find medicines for her and never came back. We wanted her to know how much he loved her, but not just how far he had gone. In time, she found the strength to move on. To her, every day on this Earth was a gift, no matter how bleak it might have seemed to the rest of us. Her attitude helped us all to cope in the days and weeks and months to come. There were many dark days, but none as dark as the day the Owl Man came for his offering.

Mom & Pop

BY

Lawrie Brewster

All my life, I've struggled with depression, a result of my failure to deal with an event from my childhood so disturbing that it's left me unsure of my own mind, even after forty years.

I have no siblings, and my real mother and father have long since departed, lost to the treachery of an icy road. Mother... Father... when I think of them, my heart should light up with the flickering warmth of joyous memories. How I loved them, yet, when I visit their grave each year and look upon the cold, grey stone that bears their names, memories of two others corrupt my cherished recollections... two strangers who called themselves 'Mom' and 'Pop'.

I've fought my whole life to erase their pale faces from my mind, but now I know that I must risk everything to return to my old childhood home, to rid myself of them, once and for all.

First, you must understand that these... watchers... were not my parents. Even saying their names conjures the worst images imaginable. Looking out the windscreen of my car, I can see the fateful red sky before me, impatient to devour me. Tonight, I must drive fast, to reach the old house before nightfall.

As the road races under the wheels of my car, a can of petrol jostles loudly in the trunk. Tonight, our journey will end with fire, but first I must tell you how it began.

When I was seven years old, we lived in the suburbs of a small factory town. Our home was the full package: white picket fence, two storeys and four bedrooms—a perfect home with a perfect middle-class family inside, or should I say, trapped inside.

My father was an administrator at the factory, a job he hated but couldn't afford to quit. This unhappiness caused many arguments between my parents, during which I'd hide in my bedroom upstairs.

I consoled myself with toys, recreating scenes from movies with police cars whizzing in hot pursuit of some villain, or fighting great wars among the ranks of my plastic soldiers. Despite my attempts at escapism, I remained a sorrowful child, with a constant feeling of loneliness, both at home and school.

One Sunday afternoon, it was raining hard, and my parents were fighting again. I suddenly couldn't take it any longer. I dropped my toys, fell to the floor, and cried my eyes out. A feminine sigh, gentle and sympathetic, surprised me. I had thought that I was alone. I turned around and was startled by the sight before me.

Blurred through my tears, I could see two figures, standing, watching me.

This is the moment when you'll think I'm mad, when you might stop reading, but I'm sure of what I saw: a beautiful woman, dressed in 1950s attire, with a smile so infectious that I couldn't resist smiling back, frightened though I was. Next to her stood a man in a blue blazer and slacks, his collar adorned with a bow-tie, smiling with the same wide-eyed delight. They resembled the couples you'd see in adverts for new kitchens in old magazines, and perhaps like the pages of those magazines, they possessed a slightly uncanny two-dimensional quality.

I can't remember the precise words they said, as they spoke in a quick murmur that seemed to translate itself inside my head. I only recall that they wanted me to call them 'Mom' and 'Pop'. Strange as it may seem, with them I experienced a level of contentment and security I'd never known before. Whatever utterances they made echoed inside me, filling me with a sense of love that would send me to sleep excited at the prospect of seeing them again the next day.

In the days and weeks that followed, I soon trusted my new parents to be there for me, more than my actual mother and father. After dinner, I would race upstairs to be with them, so that I could hear Pop's adventure tales, or better yet, so Mom could tuck me into bed and read me bedtime stories, all while my real parents shouted at one another downstairs.

Nothing, not the bullies that plagued me or my parents' constant arguing, could discourage my new-found joy. Every evening when I returned from school, Mom and Pop would be waiting, waving cheerfully from my bedroom window, with smiles that never faded.

Until the night they did.

One bedtime, as Mom tucked me in as usual, she seemed distracted, like someone with a secret they're desperate to share. That night, I had a terrible dream, a nightmare that saw me lost and alone in a great void.

I could see only a black horizon without end, and such was the terror I felt at this that I awoke. It was still night-time, and it took a moment for my eyes to adjust to the darkness. At the foot of my bed, I could see shapes, first one and then another. I slowly made out their features, and with some fear, I recognised that it was Mom and Pop, standing at the end of the bed, watching me.

Did they watch me like this every night? Mom and Pop saw that I was awake and glided towards me. Leaning in close, they explained that they had spent all night coming to an important decision about the future of our 'family'.

"Do you want to be with us forever?" they asked.

The street light outside glowed orange, painting their faces with warmth. Their kind eyes shimmered with emotion. How could I refuse? I was an outcast at school, a lonely boy without a friend in the world, and here I was, with the two most wonderful people I knew, and they were asking *me* to be with *them.*

I can't remember the exact words they said, but I can remember mine, and I can still hear my seven-year-old self fatefully whispering...

"Yes."

Then, I blacked out, and what happened next is a blur. From what I was told, it seems my parents were roused from their sleep by the sound of me rummaging in the kitchen. When they came to investigate, they were shocked to discover me lying on the floor, attempting to force the prongs of a fork into an electrical wall socket. I have no memory of this, but I remember how upset my parents were and how scared I was when they explained how close I had been to killing myself. They didn't want to leave me alone that night, so they took me to bed with them.

As my mother and father hugged and embraced me, I could think only of my bedroom just down the hall, where I considered with dread who would be waiting at the foot of my bed.

I need not have worried, because in the days that followed, I did not see Mom and Pop again, neither at the foot of my bed or at my bedroom window as I left for school. This was a golden age for me, and at school I even began making friends, while my parents reconciled the issues that had put their marriage in jeopardy.

But one night in October, in the midst of a gale, I awoke to find Mom standing by my bed, concealed in shadow but for the moment a flash of lightning illuminated her. She didn't speak, but just watched me with eyes that burrowed into mine. She was smiling as always, but I realised that it was never really a smile. It twisted strangely at the corners. It was a crude mask that hid a grin filled with malicious intent. Enraged by my rejection, I could see that Mom was now relishing the prospect of whatever she had in store for me. Trembling in horror, I thrust myself under the bedsheets, terrified of what might come next.

A second bolt of lightning revealed Pop, who stood by the window, which was now wide open. The wind blasted in, lifting the curtains over the rails and spraying a torrent of rain across the room. The fury of the storm was overwhelming, but not for Mom and Pop, who stood there, unaffected by the wind, not a hair blown out of place.

I peered out from under the bed covers at the open window across the room. Pop was there, beckoning me towards it, his thin fingers bending unnaturally towards the fate they had in store for me. It was clear what he wanted me to do: to leap out the second floor window to my death.

Then I would be with them forever.

I tried to scream, but the air had been crushed out of my lungs, lost to the terror that gripped me. I looked to Mom, perhaps hoping for mercy, but her eyes, once so radiant with love, now twinkled like those of a demented lunatic. I could take it no longer and shook my head, whispering with what little defiance I could muster:

"No... no, Mom... Pop... I can't."

I will never forget what happened next. Mom switched like a slide in a projector into a horror beyond imagination. She glided towards me, her eyes draining of colour, her jaw unhinging to reveal a cavernous, black hole which emitted a shriek so terrifying that I covered my ears and dived back under the sheets.

Through the thin fabric, I could see them, illuminated by flashes of lightning as they circled me, before standing together at the foot of my bed.

The commotion had alerted my father, who burst into the room, rushed straight to the window and slammed it shut. Close behind was Mother, who scooped me out of bed and rushed me downstairs. They had not seen Mom and Pop, who vanished the second my parents entered.

I thought that these events had taken minutes, but it seems I had been exposed to the elements for hours. I was freezing cold, probably in shock. My father ran a hot bath, while my mother prepared me a mug of hot chocolate.

I was so out of it that I was almost catatonic. I remember Mother blowing on my hot chocolate to help cool it down, and then giving me small sips, so as not to burn me. She stroked my hair, and was so attentive and loving, but I couldn't trust it; I thought she could change suddenly like Mom had. Perhaps this was a trick and they were just pretending to be my real parents. To feel so paranoid about the only ones you have left is the loneliest feeling in the world.

Once the bath was ready, Father carried me upstairs, gently lowering me into the warm water. The heat of it came as a shock to my ice-cold bones. As steam filled the room, a sense of relief set in, or perhaps it was exhaustion. In the soothing water, I felt I could sleep for a hundred years. They left the bathroom door half-open, and I drew great comfort from the sound of their voices, even though they were discussing whether to call out the doctor. My behaviour must have frightened them deeply. They must have wondered what had gone wrong with their boy. I wondered too, what it was that I had done to deserve this, and why Mom and Pop had chosen me.

After a while, the humidity of the bathroom produced enough haze to obscure the door, which, I noticed, was now closed. I could still hear my parents outside, but then the sound of their voices became faint, replaced eventually by silence.

Our bathroom was small and narrow with tiled walls. The tiles were decorated with nautical pictures: ships and fish, now obscured by the enveloping haze. The pictures, obscured as they were, appeared to change, and to the left and right of me were pictures of people, one on the left wall and the other on my right. Ships? No, and not sailors either. I recognised the face of Mom, staring at me from the wall. Pop was on my right, both of them attached to the walls like wallpaper.

The white pupils of their grey eyes were fixed squarely on mine, their expressionless faces bereft of humanity. Their skin and clothes were grey too, drained of almost all their colour. Before I could scream, Mom began to peel down the wall, her body curling until her head was upside down, her eyes never leaving me. Their necks stretched out, unnaturally long, as their faces leant closer and closer towards my own, their white eyes glowing like lost stars.

I screamed, thrashing my arms and legs with all my might. My parents heard the noise and rushed to get into the bathroom, but found the door locked, latched shut from the inside. As they fought to smash their way in, another force was pinning my head under the bathwater. I can remember shrieking as the water flooded my lungs, and my eyes burning as I fought to keep them open. Distorted by the rippling water, I could see their pale faces watching me die.

They were smiling.

The door collapsed off its hinges, and my father dragged me out of the bath. I kicked and screamed, and no matter which room my parents took me to, all I could see when I opened my eyes were Mom and Pop staring at me... just inches away.

As I waited for the doctor, I refused to open my eyes. Even then, I could still feel their presence close by, the prickling sensation of their breath on the nape of my neck. When the doctor arrived, I was whisked away to a local clinic, where I received a psychological evaluation. I tried my best to explain what had happened, but how does a seven-year-old articulate a phenomenon such as this? My story was inevitably misinterpreted, and I was soon placed into protective social care, during which time I stayed with a number of foster parents.

I saw many therapists who placed me on drugs that no child should endure, until, finally, after a year, I was returned to my parents. By this time, they had moved out of town, since many in the local community suspected them of abusing me, whether spoken publicly or revealed by a judgemental look.

Fortunately, I enjoyed a thoroughly ordinary adolescence, with the usual fixations on video arcades and girls. During this time, I had come to believe that Mom and Pop were not real, but the manifestation of a breakdown brought about by the stress of my parents' marital problems, and our move to a new town. It seemed reasonable to assume this, not only because my memories of childhood were so clouded, but because so much of it was unfathomably surreal. The white faces that haunted me became as vague as a startling scene one might recall from a horror movie they'd watched years ago.

I was so convinced of my theory that I was quite unconcerned when, during a road trip with friends, we passed through my old home town. I hadn't seen it since I was a child, and while I might have felt some trepidation, I was mostly curious about which diners were still open, and spared little thought for the monsters I'd consigned to childhood delusion.

We passed through the main street around dusk, and made it to the suburbs close to my former home shortly after. The years had not been kind to the town, which had experienced hard times since the closure of the factory. Those aspirational, middle-class homes, once adorned with white picket fences, were now half-empty, with many sporting protective bars on their windows.

I saw my old home loom towards us on the road.

A strange instinct wanted me to stop, to make my friend turn the car around, but I fought it. After all, what did I have to fear now?

Instead, I asked my friend to slow down, and the car crawled along the kerb past my former home. The place looked decrepit, its rooms now empty, with most of the windows broken and boarded up. It appeared so tragic, in fact, that it looked almost disappointingly harmless, as if I had misspent my time mythologising whatever had occurred there in my childhood.

I gave a sudden laugh, which surprised even myself. My friend grinned at me as he switched on the car radio and speeded up. As the music played, I smiled at the wing mirror, at the sight of my old home shrinking fast behind us. I felt on top of the world, and decided to turn around to give the place one last look before it vanished for good.

No... it couldn't be...

Two shapes, silhouetted by the sun, stood at my old bedroom window. I couldn't make them out, but they looked like people. I could feel my stomach plummet with dread as I recalled Mom and Pop. Back then, I had even forgotten what I used to call them. As our car turned at the end of the street, I struggled to fight the nausea rising within me. My friend offered to stop the car, concerned that I might be sick, but I shouted at him, begged him, in fact, to keep driving at all costs.

He must have thought I was crazy, and I probably was.

As the years rolled by, I became obsessed with what I'd seen that day. Was it two figures by the window, or perhaps a trick of the light? In a perverse irony, it was not Mom and Pop, whether real or not, that ended up ruining my life; I managed that all by myself.

After college, I pursued a normal life, anything that would keep me from being alone with my thoughts and fears, anything to prevent my loneliness. I settled down with the first woman who would marry me, rushed her to have kids, the works. I worked a normal job; a low-level, white-collar position at a local manufacturer. I ended up hating my job, hating my wife, hating everything, but I couldn't leave them for fear of being alone with myself.

Eventually, I was fired when the economy went south, after which I fell into a spell of heavy drinking. My wife did her best to help, but in the end, nobody could save me. She left, taking the kids with her to live on the West Coast, hundreds of miles from me. I'm glad she did, for their sake and her own. Not long after my marriage fell apart, my parents passed away in a tragic road accident.

I was truly alone, just as lonely as I'd been as a nervous kid hiding upstairs in my room while my parents argued downstairs.

One night, after a bout of heavy drinking, I made a pitiful and devastating realisation. I was a lost cause, perhaps I'd always been, yet nobody took away the pain of loneliness like Mom and Pop had. In my unexceptional life that had amounted to nothing but tedious mediocrity, only they were truly exceptional, and, remarkable though they were, they'd chosen me. I'm ignored by the world, and yet, they found something special and worthwhile in me.

Mom and Pop...

Now, the red sky is black, and as my car rolls up to the front of my childhood home, I know what I must do, what I wasn't brave enough to do as a child.

I step out of the car and look upon the derelict building before me. My old home is condemned for demolition, much like the rest of the town. I take the can of petrol from the boot of my car and look up to my bedroom window.

I can't see them yet, but I know they'll be waiting.

The Below

BY

Thomas Staunton

For the first time in twenty years, I'm trembling with terror, rooted to my chair and unable to move. A newspaper sits on my lap, a coffee stain now spreading slowly across it. The front-page photograph shows a group standing in front of an imposing, medieval building... Dunville Castle.

I was 17 years old when I first set foot inside the castle. It had always been a place of myth and legend, out of bounds for most of its history, and for good reason; it was reputedly the most haunted estate in all of Ireland. Nestled deep in an ancient forest that bordered our little town, the turrets loomed over the canopy of oak trees like a sentinel. Perhaps as some sort of childhood hazing ritual, my friends and I would trudge through miles of farmland to find a weak spot in the ruined perimeter wall and then dare each other to climb over it into the woodland beyond. Those brave enough to venture over would do so only for the briefest of moments, for the forest itself had a dreadful and uncanny chill that sent you clambering back to safety.

It was on one of these childhood outings that I first saw the creature. I was sitting on top of the boundary wall while my friends played below. As I gazed into the distance, a shadowy figure emerged from the dark of the woods. It hovered just off the ground, taller than anything I had ever seen, maybe nine feet high, and gowned in a long, black cloak. It moved into a clearing a few yards from where I sat, and stopped to regard me, cocking its head up in a strange, jerking motion. Its face was featureless and waxy white. The forest dimmed to twilight, and I fell into a paralysing trance. The creature grew taller, each spurt producing a cracking sound like bone breaking. It swam downwards and then hoisted itself upward to meet my eyes. My friends hollered at me to come down, but I was too mesmerised to look away, until, finally, I broke free from its spell and plummeted to the ground.

My friends demanded answers. What had I seen? I didn't speak for the rest of the day.

My father was not surprised by the story when I finally confided in him. On the contrary, he had persistently warned me to stay away from Dunville, but, being a curious child, I had found the place too intriguing to resist.

He told me that, long ago, against the warnings of the locals who believed the site to hold great importance to the ancient Druids, the wealthy Dunville family had cleared a large patch of woodland and built their castle home in the style of their medieval ancestors. From then on, each generation of the Dunville family had been plagued by misfortune: illness, accidents, disappearances, suicides. Even the most cynical locals believed the family to be cursed. The most recent and notorious event happened in 1970. John Dunville, the patriarch at that time, fell from the top of the grand central staircase to his death. It was ruled an accident, another tragedy cruelly bestowed upon the family. John, a keen astronomer, had left a note in the castle observatory, minutes before the fall. It contained a drawing of a hooded figure and a chilling warning:

Beware of Dolgad!

By the time I started working at the castle, now a hotel, the Dunville family had long since gone, and the rumours and legends had been quietly quashed by the hotelier, Mr Mitchell. My father told me I was mad to set foot in there again, no matter how good the money was. He was probably right.

But something about the place called out to me as if to say: *I have what you're looking for*. Somewhere in my heart, I knew that the creature I saw was connected to that word: DOLGAD.

○

"You'll do well here, Richard. You keep your mouth shut," said Brian, the burly master bartender on my second month working in Dunville.

He was a kindly man, but his positivity was usually spiked with a warning about the castle.

"Just remember to let someone know when you're going down to the cellar. Remember that if nothing else."

Indeed, the cellar had a terrifying reputation. It housed the boarded-up entrance to an old escape tunnel which howled furiously, day and night. Over the years, many staff had accidentally locked themselves in the room, only to be found minutes later, screaming in terror. Quite recently, a young barman was trapped inside for an entire night. Brian, who found him the next morning, confessed that the near-catatonic barman had been muttering under his breath, repeating the words 'black cloak' while chipping pieces of his fingernails off.

"He wasn't the same after," said Brian, shaking his head in resignation, "Such a shame."

Mr Mitchell, taking no further chances, removed the cellar door from its hinges.

It was on one of my visits to the cellar that I stumbled on something that made me uneasy. I dragged a box of wine out from against a wall and discovered a word crudely engraved in the stonework: D O L GAD. I backed away and ran out of the cellar.

○

A notice was placed on the staff board in early October, my third month working at Dunville. The morning crew had gathered in a circle to read it.

> *The Dunville Castle Hotel will be closed to the public from Sunday, 28th October until Monday, 5th November. The Cathbad Astronomical Society will hold a private week-long event at the hotel during this time.*

All staff on duty during this event must observe the following rules. Failure to adhere to the strict code of conduct during this event will be met with IMMEDIATE DISMISSAL.

1. *All staff will work and break in pairs at all times. Working alone is STRICTLY FORBIDDEN.*
2. *Staff must leave the castle grounds before 7pm SHARP each night. A bus service will depart at 6.30 pm. DO NOT BE LATE.*
3. *Do not approach or speak to any member of the Cathbad Society under any circumstances. Any questions or issues MUST be directed to the manager.*
4. *The Conference Room and Observatory are OUT OF BOUNDS TO ALL STAFF during this event.*

Further instructions will be given in due time.

Most of the staff shrugged at the notice.

"Typical looney Mitchell," one muttered.

Others, like myself, were baffled. I pestered the senior staff for answers, but most brushed me off or pretended not to hear. Everyone was far too busy making preparations, including emptying the hotel of the remaining guests.

As we approached the week of the conference, Mr Mitchell singled out the staff he wanted to work the event. Despite being very green, I was on the list, news which filled me with excitement and unease in equal measure. What sort of event would require such exclusivity?

○

"Look at them, they look ill," whispered Joe, a colleague, under his breath.

All the staff had lined up outside to greet our guests, the Cathbad Astronomical Society, who arrived in a fleet of black cars and marched into the reception area without speaking a word, all of them looking, as Joe had pointed out, quite ill. Some used Zimmer frames, others limped, some wore large hats and glasses to hide blemishes and lesions. A tall, slender man in a well-fitted suit trailed a little behind the procession and gave us all a courteous nod.

The first two days went smoothly. The guests slept till late afternoon, and in the evening, they dined, before retiring to the conference room. As ordered, the staff worked in pairs, silently and without fuss, and left the castle at the designated time.

After day two, the strangeness began. We arrived on the third morning to find the smouldering remains of a massive bonfire in the garden, with half-burnt clothes scattered around it. Chalk markings appeared on the walls, odd inscriptions in a language we couldn't identify. We heard screaming and shouting from the bedrooms at various intervals.

On the fourth day, Mr Carruthers, the elderly founder of the Cathbad Society, walked up to me as I smoked a cigarette with Joe on the steps outside the front door. He looked gravely ill.

"It has taken me all of my life to get here," he said, "and now I fear I will never see the fruits of my labour. Do you know the work of Dolgad?"

Mr Carruthers was lifted off his feet by the tall, slender man, who appeared out of nowhere to take him away. His feet dragged across the stone steps as he was carried back inside the castle.

How did he know about Dolgad? For years I had searched for that name and found nothing, and now, out of the blue, a stranger mentions his name in passing, only to be taken away before I can get some answers. What was going on?

"That was Mr West, the Club Secretary," Joe whispered, "the guy who took Mr Carruthers away."

When dinner commenced that evening, things were tense. The society ate in silence, and Mr Carruthers was noticeably absent. With the drinks served, we left them to their business and headed back to the kitchen. It was then that we came across the open door of the conference room.

Inside, Mr West was leaning over a massive book. Behind him, a projector displayed a collage of images: a yellow star with black lines intersecting it, row upon row of dense, indecipherable hieroglyphs, and a slew of mathematical problems. In the last quadrant, an archaic drawing caught my eye; a jet-black cloak shrouding a featureless, white face with one terrifying word written sharply underneath: DOLGAD. Before my knees gave way, Joe caught me and pulled me away down the corridor.

o

"You're mad," said Joe, incredulously.

I didn't blame him. I had stuttered uncontrollably while trying to explain what I had seen in the conference room. I told him about the creature called Dolgad, and its connection to the Dunville estate. Joe, being Joe, dismissed it, and returned to puffing his cigarette.

Something sinister was going on at Dunville. The Cathbad Society were not simply astronomers, as they had claimed, not with Dolgad involved. I had to know what they were here for. I had to get into that conference room.

Joe wasn't moved. "I'm not going back up there. Look, if it'll get you to stop talking crazy, I'll give you five minutes. I need to grab some stock for the kitchen. We meet there, okay? Don't get me in trouble. We're not supposed to be on our own."

We broke the rules and went our separate ways. I climbed the servants' stairwell and came out onto the deserted corridor. I pressed my ear up to the now-locked conference room door. Faint mutterings came from within, but the door was too thick to make anything out. I turned to leave.

Then, a word came through; a chant, in unison, repeated over and over again. The chant grew thunderous, and all at once, the murmurings formed a single word.

"Do... ga... Dol... ga... Dol... gad... Dolgad... Dolgad... Dolgad... Dolgad."

A hand clamped down on my wrist, and I was pulled away from the door and slammed onto the ground. Mr West stood over me, his wiry shadow looming.

"Where is your partner?" he said.

"Sorry?" I said, shakily.

Mr West's eyes locked onto mine. "Leave this floor immediately and return to your appointed partner. Consider yourself reported."

I bolted for the stairwell and hurried down to the kitchen. Joe wasn't there. I looked at my watch and saw that it was 6:16 pm. The bus would be leaving soon, and I was missing my partner. Knowing that I was in deep trouble, I snuck to the front door to take a peek. The staff were waiting in the yard, but Joe was nowhere to be seen. My heart sank. I had to check the cellar.

I descended the stairs into the bowels of the castle. A cold, biting wind was coming from the cellar. I peered inside.

"Joe?"

I shook away my stupor and started down the ancient, stone steps.

"Joe!"

I turned the last corner and stumbled over the broken fragments of the wooden board that had sealed the old escape tunnel. How could this be? Had someone broken in or broken out? There was no time for questions.

I shouted into the darkness, "Joe!"

My voice was lost in the thunderous howl that roared from the mouth of the tunnel. I edged closer to it, the dark void groaning. A white face came floating out of the black. I stumbled backwards and felt a sudden, searing pain. The creature glided out of the tunnel and into the cellar, its cloak billowing with the violent power of the wind behind it. I tried to crawl backwards, but the ground was slick with debris. For the first time, I could see the detail of its face, a gaunt and sexless mask, with sad blue eyes set deep in its sockets. And then I heard that familiar noise, that awful cracking of bones as the creature grew and grew like a feeding black hole. The cellar walls melted away to become the blackness of outer space, with dim stars dotted sparsely across it.

The abyss erupted in a choir of tormented groans. The creature opened its great black cloak, revealing a hideous mass of anguished faces squirming and wailing beneath. One of them was Joe. His tortured grimace protruded out of the frightful melee of screaming heads and then receded back to join the multitude. Then there were arms, flailing and reaching outward to grab me, and I was slipping away.

I felt a slap across my face, followed by an angry, but familiar, voice.

"Wake up! What the hell are you doing down here?!"

I opened my eyes, and I was back in the cellar. The world was quiet. Mr Mitchell was standing over me, his face twisted in indignation.

"What are you doing on the floor? Where's Joe?"

I sat up, drew a deep breath, and started to cough uncontrollably. It felt as if my lungs were full of dust. What had happened to me?

"I... I... the creature..." I trailed off.

Mr Mitchell grabbed my shirt and pulled me up to his level. "Where is Joe?"

I pointed to the tunnel.

"The bus is waiting for you," he said. "Get up and leave, right now, and don't speak a single word to anyone."

I was too weak to protest.

Nobody spoke to me on the journey home. The minibus chugged along the tree-lined road, and I looked on blankly, my body sinking further into despair and paranoia. Did they know about Joe? They had to suspect that something was wrong. He wasn't on the bus, and that meant that we had broken the rules. Was Joe gone forever, trapped in the unspeakable hell of the creature's cloak like all the other tortured souls? The only thing I was sure of was that the dark figure and Dolgad were one and the same.

Late that night, I woke to find myself clutching my neck. The house was quiet, except for my father's snores, but I could have sworn that I'd heard Joe calling to me. Had it been a dream? There was blackness at first, and then, high up above, a star materialised. It turned on its axis to reveal Dolgad's terrible, inhuman face, and the night sky became its cloak. Joe whispered my name, endlessly, until I woke.

As my father slept peacefully down the corridor, I cupped my head in my hands and wept.

The bedside phone rang.

"Hello?" I said, clearing my throat. I sat up, now fully awake.

"Your contract has been terminated. Do not report to work tomorrow," said the voice.

"What about Joe?"

"Stay away from Dunville and don't ever try to contact us again. This is your only warning."

Joe was reported missing on the last night of the conference. In the months that followed, the Cathbad Society became the heroes of my town. They headed up the search party, paid for the posters, and made televised appeals on behalf of Joe's parents. They became so well-known, and so universally lauded, that confessing what I had seen to anyone would have been utterly futile. I remained silent, despite all the questions and interrogations.

For two years, all I saw were posters of Joe, a constant reminder of my guilt and shame.

○

Years have gone by, and my life lies in tatters. I have lived alone all this time, an outcast in my own town, and now I learn from the local newspaper that the Cathbad Society has returned. Has Dolgad returned too?

After 15 years, the Cathbad Astronomical Society makes a welcome return to Dunville Castle to honour the memory of club founder William Carruthers. Club Secretary Mr West spoke to us about the reason for their return.

"The Dunvilles were generous patrons of the sciences, particularly in the field of astronomy, and this castle holds great significance for us in many ways. So, rather fittingly, Billie Carruthers chose it to host one of our yearly club excursions. It has everything we need: clean air, privacy, minimal light pollution, and of course, a fantastic telescope!"

The return to Dunville, however, is a bittersweet one. Joe Doyle, a young employee of Dunville Castle, was reported missing during the last Cathbad event and has never been found. In 2018, he was declared legally dead.

The Cathbad Society was praised for its assistance and cooperation throughout the search, and Mr West hopes that the town has found some peace after all these years.

"It was such an extraordinarily tragic event, and one that we have never forgotten. We were truly amazed by how the community came together to help with the search. We hope that this trip, in some way, commemorates Joe, and that his family has found peace."

Before our conversation ended, we asked Mr West about some of the rumours that have circulated about the society in recent years, chiefly the bizarre allegation that they are secretly a pagan cult and worship an obscure entity called Dolgad.

"What a load of nonsense!" Mr West lets out a hearty guffaw. "The name of our society references the druids, who were the astronomers of their time. I think the misconceptions stem from that. As for Dolgad, well, apparently he held the secret to eternal life, which isn't exactly in the spirit of science, now, is it?"

I'm about to shred the newspaper into a million pieces, but then I see it, the photograph. Posing in front of the castle, I see the familiar faces of Cathbad. They look trim, healthy, younger.

As I inspect the photograph more closely, I see, at the window over the main castle door, a familiar, white face, watching, waiting to feed.

A whisper returns to my ear.

Dolgad... Dolgad... Dolgad...

INFERNAL
PRINCESS

The Immortal Princess

BY

Lawrie Brewster

I

Scottish-born inventor Alexander Mackintosh achieved such extraordinary feats in his early career that by the age of thirty he was hailed as one of the most prodigious figures of the Enlightenment era. Before long, however, he would be exposed as its most heinous fraud.

His rise and fall would follow in the mechanical footsteps of his incredible and controversial creation, the 'Immortal Princess', or as she later became known, the 'Infernal Princess'.

What truth is there behind the myth of this contentious inventor and his nemesis, the aristocratic Prussian military general, Ernst von Heinrich? The struggle between these two men—artist versus aristocrat—would manifest through the creation of a legend of such notoriety that it is remembered still, centuries later.

Alexander was born on the 12th of May, 1743, in the Scottish town of Inverness, a foreboding place surrounded by the misty glens of the Highlands. He was born into a bourgeois family of some esteem, having made their name and their fortune in the design and manufacture of clockwork devices.

His mother and father, Sarah and Robert Mackintosh, endeavoured to provide their son with an education that might befit a man of prospect in rank and society. They invested in the hope that Alexander might one day follow in the footsteps of his father by expanding the family business throughout Britain. In 1757, at just fourteen years of age, Alexander began to reveal the tantalising aptitude for technical ingenuity which would later make him famous. The first recorded Mackintosh invention is the 'Sleeping Dormouse', so named for its realistic emulation of the beating heart of a mouse. Customers marvelled at the modest creation, displayed in the workshop of Alexander's proud father.

Such was the calibre of his creation that by the age of sixteen Alexander had won prestigious commissions to produce two small songbird automata, one for Robert Ker, 2nd Duke of Roxburghe, and the second for Charles Hedworth, Lord Provost of Edinburgh. The marvellous birds were reportedly capable of flapping their wings and emitting a whistling tune with uncanny realism.

Alexander would consequently secure the personal support of Charles Hedworth, earning the young man entry into the University of Edinburgh, and a weekly allowance of fourteen shillings. He began his formal studies at the historic institution on the 12th of March, 1760, at the age of just seventeen.

During this time, the outside world persisted in the scientific progress of the steam-engine, a technology pioneered by fellow Scotsman, James Watt. Watt's accomplishments appear to have deterred Alexander from further study in the field of mechanical engineering, diverting him instead towards the aesthetic aspects of the discipline. We can discern the sentiments that prompted his change of mind in this passage from a private letter sent to his father in 1761:

> *What value dwells within the minds of those who shape the machines of tomorrow when pitted against the eternal divine that empowers the spirit of the artist? For only he armed with sacred purpose can guide his fellow man through the corporeal abyss of mundanity unto God, while the other might learn how to grind flour a little faster.*

The University of Edinburgh archives show that during his later years at the institution, Alexander focussed on the study of ancient history, theology and classical languages.

In 1762, the Inverness Parish Records reveal that Alexander's father, Robert Mackintosh succumbed quite suddenly to 'red fever'. Shortly afterwards, Alexander abandoned his studies and married the widow Janet Osborne, from whom he attained a small dowry, which he used to purchase a workshop in the Canongate area of Edinburgh.

Disapproving of her son's marriage, Sarah Mackintosh ended the family's small allowance of two shillings a week, as evidenced by a letter of complaint that Alexander sent her. Free of the burden of study, Alexander could now devote himself to his workshop, where he produced and sold mechanical novelties.

Little is known regarding the events which took place between the years 1762 and 1766, except that, by the age of twenty-three, the business that Alexander had built met an abrupt end. There is no official record as to why this occurred, but we can speculate that it came as a result of the personal tragedies that beset Alexander in that final year.

In the winter of 1766, Sarah Mackintosh finally succumbed, after a long period of illness, to 'consumption', a disease now known as tuberculosis. Within months of Alexander's bereavement, the parish records of the Canongate Church of Edinburgh show a submission for divorce signed by the Legal Lord Advocate John Pym, along with an affidavit consisting of many personal accusations, signed by Janet. The charges included: 'ungodly behaviours and rampant hooliganism', as well as 'acts of ill-repute and financial impropriety'.

While these extracts do not articulate the specific deviations in question, we may reasonably assume that they included alcoholism, sexual promiscuity, and gambling. Alexander was either unable or unmoved to challenge the divorce submission, which was granted by the Canongate Church of Edinburgh in the summer of 1777.

At the age of twenty-four, Alexander now carried a substantial burden of debt with little hope of repayment. The young man was at risk of falling prey to the notorious debtors' prison and spent many months lodging in different residences around the city. The Sheriff Court of the Canongate still retains the official application for the right of arrest lodged by the debt collection firm, Dundas & Baille Collectors. Had they captured him, he may have found himself transported to the Caribbean, where he would be forced to repay his debts in the sweltering heat of a sugar plantation. This dreadful servitude could easily have been his fate, if not for the remarkable decision he made next.

In the spring of 1768, Alexander fled his native Scotland to begin a new life in France. He brought with him his most prized clockwork creations and began touring them across the northern countryside. In this new country, Alexander would encounter a deeper appreciation for his artistry, and it did not take long for him to garner some modest patrons.

A surviving pamphlet from 1769, written in the German language, announces that Alexander and his 'Carnival of the Mystique' will visit Westphalia and the Kingdom of Hesse. Alexander spent much of that year travelling through the German states, at that time comprised of a political confederation known as the Holy Roman Empire.

The story of Alexander Mackintosh may well have ended there, like that of so many travelling artists, spending their lives on the road, entertaining crowds at the village squares and smaller courts of Europe. However, an event was to occur that would forever set Alexander apart, and on an altogether different path to his contemporaries. In 1770, Alexander received a personal invitation to attend the court of King Frederick II of Prussia, perhaps more famously known as Frederick the Great. Frederick II was a distinguished monarch who had already achieved great renown on account of his nation's victory in the Seven Years' War.

The world had changed for Alexander, who now stood at the cusp of royal patronage, an assured route to immense riches and acclaim. An apocryphal story states that during their first meeting, Frederick proposed that Alexander could enjoy a permanent place at court if he could produce a clockwork marvel to surpass the intricacy of the famous mechanical theatre of Hellbrunn Palace. A technological wonder built in 1750, the theatre was commissioned by Archbishop Andreas Jakob von Dietrichstein, and featured over two hundred miniature automatons depicting characters from all levels of society working in harmony.

As the story goes, Alexander boasted as follows: "Let the good Archbishop of Hellbrunn indulge in his box of two hundred toys while we maintain the fellowship of men."

This statement piqued the interest of Frederick, who insisted that Alexander should elaborate, and he dutifully obliged. Instead of producing a theatre with two hundred tiny figures, Alexander would design and build a full-size clockwork man.

Frederick was a monarch with a deep interest in the arts and sciences, often with a view to their military application; the Prussian army and society were well known for their strict discipline and militaristic tendencies. French writer François-Marie Arouet, better known as Voltaire, described Prussia in the following terms: "Where some states possess an army, the Prussian Army possesses a state."

To a famed military commander and strict disciplinarian, the prospect of building a clockwork man was, of course, supremely exciting. In 1770, Alexander was invited to join the Royal Court, where he was accommodated in the palace and received an ample allowance from the king's purse.

In 1771, Alexander unveiled his 'Clockwork Man', presenting it to the court at Sanssouci Palace in Potsdam. Records from the court reveal that the creation was only two feet tall, but was reportedly capable of marching forwards and could even salute on command.

Unfortunately, Mackintosh's Clockwork Man has been lost to history, and the palace records include no illustration of how it might have looked. One key document has survived, however, in the form of a report written to the Royal Chaplain Sigmund Homburg from the king's private secretary, Captain Friedrich von Beust:

> *It appears that you good church folk have little need for godly concern in the matter of this charlatan who claims the power to create man, but instead produces an odious offspring, a stunted beast that stands no taller than my breeches, resplendent with a face so hideous that a monkey might swoon upon gazing at it.*
>
> *Be assured that his majesty was decidedly unimpressed by the so-called 'wonder', and joked that a regiment of such creations might be better suited for the armies of France.*

This letter provides evidence that Alexander attracted some antipathy from those at court during his brief time at the palace. It is perhaps worth clarifying that Frederick's comparison of the Clockwork Man to the armies of France, at that time the enemy of Prussia, is not favourable.

Within a month of the unveiling of the Clockwork Man, Alexander suffered a reduction in his allowance and was conveyed into modest lodgings outside the palace. Alexander was undeterred, and continued to visit the palace often to request an audience with the king. He was eager to present his design for an enhanced version of the Clockwork Man. The palace records show that the king's private secretary, Captain Friedrich von Beust, went to exceptional lengths to ensure that no such meetings would or could occur.

The situation finally came to a head on August 12th, 1771, when Alexander was abruptly removed from his lodgings and escorted under armed guard from the palace grounds, his patronage coming to a dramatic end.

Alexander was an ambitious man of infectious enthusiasm, but also an intemperate man who often quarrelled among his peers at the Royal Court, ultimately leading to the conspiracy between Captain Friedrich von Beust and the Royal Chaplain Sigmund Homburg to remove this 'interloper' once and for all. In a surviving extract from a sermon written by the Royal Chaplain, he complains about a type of man we might infer to represent Alexander:

> *Let no man call himself a genius who cannot walk through the corridors of power without fouling the air with decadent promises and debauched flagrancies, for such a man is not a man, but a mere interloper to the common good.*

Another letter written by a junior officer to Captain Friedrich von Beust provides an insight into the discrete observations made of Alexander: "This morning, the so-called genius who behaves as a lout has once again offended ministers and overstayed his welcome."

One can imagine that the accusations laid against Alexander were similar to those made by his former wife Janet several years before. Had the stress of the king's demands and his inability to deliver led him down a path of confrontation, alcoholism, and debauchery? Unfortunately, we may never know the precise answer, for even enemies rarely tell such truths of a man.

It was in the winter of 1771 that Alexander was unceremoniously expelled from Prussia, stolen under guard and dumped across the border into the icy wilderness of Westphalia.

Alexander made a threadbare living producing toys incognito, travelling from village to village to sell his creations. He was assiduous in avoiding any authorship of the toys he produced during this period, eager to distance himself from the notoriety now associated with his name.

Alexander despaired as a new wave of clockwork masters such as Jacques de Vaucanson gained accolades, fame, and riches. The Frenchman's most famous creation, the 'digesting duck', was declared a feat of scientific wonder, while Alexander's creations were played with by village children.

Alexander remained a frustrated toy trader touring the minor German kingdoms under various names and in relative poverty until 1778, when a short period of illness led him to fall into substantial debt. At thirty-five years old, his creations had expended much of their novelty, and despite attempts to ingratiate himself at various Royal Courts, his requests for an audience were repeatedly refused.

Baron Gottfried von Kaspar of Blamberg, a minor aristocrat of the Holy Roman Empire, writes to his mother about the 'peculiar, tall man':

> *There is an intemperate Scotsman at my front gate each morning with an assortment of childish creations that he claims are the product of genius, but which, to my inexpert eye, resemble the naive toys of my darling daughter Marie. This peculiar fellow even claims to be a member of the Prussian court, despite looking like a tavern keep, and smelling like one to boot.*

After showing such exceptional promise, this might have been the end of Alexander, a footnote in history fading into obscurity, but fate would intervene once more, with startling results.

In 1779, Alexander was urgently summoned to the court of King Frederick II, where the king's physicians immediately attended to his malnutrition and 'nervous temper'. He received the full reinstatement of his patronage and was even provided luxurious lodgings at the palace, near the royal suite occupied by the king.

What had brought about this tremendous change of fortune?

The secret was revealed when Frederick introduced Alexander to his most trusted military commander, General Ernst von Heinrich. Frederick and 'The General', as he was known, shared a passion for the utilitarian philosophy of the Spartan military code, along with a keen interest in military technology.

Frederick wanted Alexander to design and manufacture an incredible gift to celebrate the approaching birthday of The General's daughter, Talia. Frederick wished to bestow this honour on The General's daughter as a means of praising the commander for his countless years of venerable service to the kingdom. Alexander was tasked with creating a life-size automaton in a perfect likeness of the young woman, which would be presented at court before the nobility of the nation later that year.

Alexander was allowed to examine Talia so that he could achieve a perfect representation that encompassed the 'radiant innocence' of this 'beautiful creature'. Specific to the demands of the king, Alexander was to make the automaton capable of performing five 'incredible feats' to be presented before the nobility of Europe, so that Prussia's scientific achievements might become the envy of the world.

During his time with Talia, The General and his agents would act as chaperone, and Alexander would have at his disposal a workshop close to the palace, garrisoned by a small legion of artists and craftsmen paid for by the Royal Purse.

Never before had an automaton of such ambition or complexity been attempted. Alexander accepted the commission without question, and such was the bounty he received, that after only a month, he had repaid both his European and Scottish debtors, as evidenced by receipts written by Dundas & Baille Collectors in 1778.

We can imagine the surprise of Sigmund Homburg and Friedrich von Beust on seeing their old rival striding once more through the ornate halls of the Sanssouci Palace, adorned in fine silks and extravagant powder wigs.

Friedrich writes in a personal letter to Sigmund, dated December 12th, 1778:

> *What a marvellous Christmas gift it would be for this returning hero to stumble down a well, or better yet, fall under a horse, but alas, this rake dressed as a lady-in-waiting with the manners of a peasant must be tolerated with the patience of Saint Augustine.*

During the winter, it would seem that Alexander had quickly returned to health and regained his bravado. Over the course of the season, he and Talia became quite inseparable. Rumours were rife that the artist and his muse were in the midst of an affair, yet despite the growing tensions and distractions, the automaton known as the Immortal Princess began to take shape.

The Immortal Princess attracted artists, scholars, and philosophers from around Europe, including the famed French philosopher Voltaire, who attended the studio to admire the masterpiece that many claimed only God's wonder could rival. The workers toiled day and night, at such great expense that some efforts were made by palace ministers to obscure the mounting costs. Experts have calculated that, taking into account inflation, the Immortal Princess would today cost over twenty million US dollars.

It soon became clear that the automaton would not be completed in time for Talia's birthday, and by that time the project had blossomed into one of national importance.

As work continued into the spring of 1779, a curious report from the archive of the palace guard, written by adjutant to The General, Captain Erich von Wurzel, provides evidence of some mounting suspicion against Alexander: "With special instruction from Lord Ernst von Heinrich, the palace guard is advised that on no account is his daughter to be left unattended in the company of the Scottish inventor."

The persistence of the rumours at the Royal Palace indicates that whatever vigils the guards maintained proved futile at frustrating the blossoming affair between Alexander and Talia.

The grand unveiling of the Immortal Princess was set for August 1st, 1780, with invitations dispatched to all the great houses of Europe. Amidst a sense of terrific anticipation, the whole nation awaited the unveiling of the mechanical demigoddess, capable of five impossible feats of wonder that would make Prussia the envy of Europe.

However, just weeks before the unveiling was set to take place, there occurred a series of tragic and unexpected events which would inspire the automaton's legendary moniker, the 'Infernal Princess'.

The first of these tragic events occurred on July 15th, 1780, and is described in an alarming report from the Palace Guard by Captain Erich von Wurzel: "The Palace Guard is instructed to recall every available man, so that no thread nor hair is spared in the search for the missing daughter of his Lordship."

The General's daughter Talia had inexplicably vanished, and would never be seen nor heard from again.

Much suspicion fell upon Alexander, as many at court with an axe to grind spread rumours about his culpability. Within days, he was confined to the workshop by armed guards until the automaton was completed.

Had Talia vanished to be with her lover? Did she leave of her own volition, or was she the victim of some dark plan?

The legend of the Infernal Princess posits such a strange and disturbing account that we cannot arrive at a coherent conclusion without first examining the life of Alexander Mackintosh's adversary, Ernst von Heinrich, and the strange fate that would bind these men forever.

II

One cannot fully understand the legend of the Immortal Princess without studying both the Scottish inventor, Alexander Mackintosh, and the man who would become his nemesis, Prussian aristocrat and military officer, Lord Ernst von Heinrich.

In 1702, forty-three years before the birth of Alexander, Ernst was born in the capital city of Königsberg, Prussia. Like Alexander, he too was an only child. His father was the highly-esteemed Leopold III, Duke of Livonia, and his mother Marie-Louise was princess of the Duchy of Baden.

Ernst was raised from an early age in the school of Prussian military doctrine, and soon secured the rank of Junior Adjutant, serving as the personal assistant to many great Prussian generals. During this time, the young man sought combat experience outside the commander's tent, often risking his life with courageous actions on the battlefield, against the express orders of his superiors.

He saw active service in the Great Northern War of 1721, in which Prussia fought Sweden. Ernst won commendations for valour, and earned notoriety for his brutality, in particular for his handling of enemy captives. One apocryphal legend describes Ernst, at that time only a lieutenant and observer to the allied forces of Saxony, ordering the execution of several soldiers who too readily surrendered.

By the end of the Great Northern War, Ernst had attained the rank of captain, which was considered an excellent achievement for a man of just 19.

In the spring of 1722, Ernst inherited the territories of his father Leopold III, acquiring the title and riches of the Dukedom of Livonia.

Ernst proved himself a capable and ruthless administrator. He threw himself into the domestic affairs of his estate, dramatically expanding its wealth and power within the Kingdom of Prussia. His contemporaries mused that he achieved such efficiency among the peasantry by demanding of them the same ruthless discipline as was expected of the Prussian army.

Charles Alexander, Duke of Württemberg, remarked years later in his diary about the response he received from an unnamed acquaintance after he enquired into how The General maintained such efficiency on his estate: "No serf moves faster in his toil than he who has caught the gaze of The General, for his eyes cut so sharp they might snap a sabre!"

In 1728, parish records from the city of Riga, the capital of the Duchy of Livonia, reveal that a legal complaint was submitted to the Bishop of Riga by the burgher merchant classes. They accused Ernst of implementing extra-judicial punishments against their workers without proper legal process. Held in Prussia, the case was led by King Frederick-William I, whose ruling censured Ernst, with an immediate demand that he submit to the authority of the local courts of Livonia. Parish records would indicate that Ernst complied with the order and ended his extra-judicial punishments, choosing henceforth to ignore the business of his estate and instead preoccupy himself with the search for a wife.

Ernst would not have to search for long. In 1729, he married Josephine, heiress to the Duchy of Saxe-Weimar-Eisenach, a small but affluent territory in the nearby Germanic Kingdom of Saxony. Their marriage was not to be a happy one, despite the large dowry paid to Ernst. We can only speculate as to the causes of their marital strife, as there are no recorded details of their trials and tribulations. What we do know is that the management of the Duchy of Livonia, once Ernst's primary concern, was no longer a preoccupation, leading to a period of stagnation which would last almost a decade. Throughout this period, Ernst remained in seclusion at Riga Castle on the banks of the River Daugava, where he produced little in the way of written correspondence.

We may speculate that the failure to produce an heir, coupled with the censure placed upon him by King Frederick-William had instigated a deep depression. In the autumn of 1740, after almost twelve years of marriage, the parish record of Riga notes with some innuendo, that the Duchess Josephine von Heinrich left Livonia to return home to her family in Saxony:

> *In the year 1740, on the fourteenth day of August, the Duchess of Livonia has departed our lands without bearing an heir for our benevolent ruler Duke Ernst von Heinrich. She left swiftly, and while no answer is forthcoming from the attendants of our master, we pray nonetheless for an end to the solitude and strife that has denied him both descendants and peace.*

Upon her return to the Duchy of Saxe-Weimar-Eisenach, court records show that she remained secluded in her bedchamber for months while attended to by expert physicians sent for from France.

While there are, unfortunately, no reports providing further details of the precise nature of her condition, the presence of famed French physician and philosopher Julien Offray de La Mettrie does perhaps give us some insight. Julien was a doctor whose specialisms included the treatment of mental disorders, which begs the question: could Ernst have caused this?

Josephine and Ernst never saw one another again. After several years of seclusion and apparent mental illness, clues to her demise were recently uncovered in an entry in the Leipzig Parish record of November 1744. The entry cites 'Josephine of Saxony', without her full name and title, as being interred in unconsecrated ground, which might indicate that the cause of death was suicide.

In the years that followed, Duke Biden II of the Duchy Saxe-Weimar-Eisenach issued a series of formal complaints to the Prussian court, demanding further censures against Ernst for the failed marriage and calling for monetary damages.

These complaints related to the considerable dowry paid for the unsuccessful marriage, which now left both territories without heirs. Ernst repaid the dowry piece by piece, aided by loans provided to him by his friend, the recently-crowned King Frederick II.

During that time, enemies of his rule in the Duchy of Livonia, with support from Duke Biden II, made claims that Ernst had acted 'against ordinary moral conduct', and that he was, as one pamphlet put it, 'a man consumed by devils with an appetite for innocence'. One such propagandist pamphlet still exists today in the museum of Kaliningrad (the modern-day name for the city of Königsberg). It depicts The General standing tall atop the backs of two crouched devils, with a horsewhip raised above his head, preparing to strike a terrified young woman cowering on the ground. Despite enjoying a cordial relationship with Frederick II, such was the damage caused by this political campaign, that he could not lobby the king to remove the censure that his father, King Frederick-William, had placed upon him.

With the censure in place, without an heir, and successfully demonised by his enemies, Ernst remained ostracised from the Prussian Royal Court, and was forced to return to his self-imposed exile in Castle Riga.

Duke Ernst von Heinrich may well have grown old and perished in that castle, slipping into obscurity like so many of his fellow nobles, were it not for a series of momentous events that would soon rock the very foundations of Europe.

In 1740, the War of Austrian Succession had begun, promptly pitching two large factions against one another in a conflict that would encompass all of the great European powers. The death of Charles VI ignited the spark of war, as two heirs now vied to succeed him for the rule of the Holy Roman Empire. On one side was the Archduchess Maria Theresa of Austria, who claimed the right to replace her father. On the other side was Prince Charles Albert of Bavaria, who fought to deny Austria any chance of increasing its hegemony over the rest of the German states that comprised the Holy Roman Empire.

Maria Theresa led Austria with support from Great Britain, Holland, and Russia, while Charles-Albert led Bavaria with the backing of Prussia, France, Spain, and Sweden.

The escalation of the war provided Ernst with a new lease of life, and at thirty-eight years old, he attained the rank of colonel in gratitude for the enormous levy of men he raised from his estates. Ernst presented two regiments, claiming to have gathered from his estates 'every living soul with the loins to do battle'.

Ernst also made a considerable contribution to the Prussian war fund. So significant was his pledge that he almost bankrupted his estate. Such generosity would not go unrewarded by the king, and at the start of spring 1745, Ernst relished in the removal of the censure laid against him by King Frederick-William eighteen years before.

Even more good news was to come, as King Frederick II permitted Ernst to accompany him onto the battlefield. He was commanded to lead his troops in a string of violent struggles against the forces of Austria in the mountainous lands of Silesia.

In 1745, during the notable Battle of Hohenfriedberg, in which over 120,000 soldiers fought, Colonel von Heinrich led his regiment in an unexpected charge that caught the enemy entirely off guard. The rout of the Austrians turned the tide of the battle, completing the Prussian victory.

The defeat of the Austrian army propelled Ernst into the pages of military lore, and earned him his legendary moniker 'The General', an affectionate name afforded to him by King Frederick II.

In 1748, after eight years of death and destruction, the war finally came to an end with the Treaty of Aix-la-Chapelle. As with most wars, the original objectives had grown arms and legs, with the question of which heir should inherit the offices of the Holy Roman Empire obscured by the territorial disputes of the many warring parties. The war parties enjoyed meagre spoils, as Maria Theresa prevailed in retaining the rule of Austria, while her husband Francis I assumed the office of Holy Roman Emperor. By a stroke of luck, her rival claimant, Charles-Albert of Bavaria, had perished from gout in 1745. The cost of victory had been high, however, and there would be many years of recovery.

While the nations quarrelled over their slender gains, Prussia proved itself a singular exception, doubling its lands and population as it absorbed many of the smaller Germanic kingdoms that had allied with Austria.

Austria was no longer the undisputed master of the German states, and for his triumphs in the war, King Frederick II of Prussia was hailed as a truly mighty leader, cementing his power and position. Yet, none of this would have occurred were it not for the extraordinary efforts of his loyal servant, Ernst von Heinrich.

Ernst was no longer tarnished by the poor reputation that had so affected him. Now he was a war hero and a favourite of the king, which made him an enticing prospect for the unmarried daughters of the aristocracy.

In the spring of 1749, at the age of forty-seven, Ernst married his second wife, seventeen-year-old Theodora Saxe-Bergen of the Baronial House of Saxe-Bergen. Their wedding inspired considerable speculation that there might, at last, be a successor to the significant estates and fortune of the Duchy of Livonia.

Ernst had no intention of abandoning the position of king's favourite by returning to his estates in Livonia, and instead took permanent residence at the Sanssouci Palace at Königsberg.

Contemporary accounts define their marriage as tempestuous, with records from the office of the Royal Chaplain describing several interventions that sought to bring about the reconciliation of Ernst and Theodora. These earnest attempts on the part of Chaplain Sigmund Homburg would come to nothing. After just two years of marriage, Ernst ordered Theodora back to the Duchy of Livonia under the pretence of having her administer those lands.

The House of Saxe-Bergen took great offence at this slight, which all but declared to the aristocracy of the country that the marriage was a failure, and that there would be little chance of Theodora producing an heir to Ernst's fortune. King Frederick II received two petitions from the House of Saxe-Bergen, demanding that Theodora be recalled to the palace to join her husband. These pleas were ignored until the Crisis of 1753, when taxes were withheld from the Royal Purse until a settlement was agreed. Negotiations led by the king's Secretary, Captain Friedrich von Beust, resulted in a compromise in which Ernst would visit his wife twice a year in Livonia, intending to produce an heir. This provides further evidence of the strength of the bond between the two men, that Frederick II was willing to battle Royal Houses inside the kingdom to protect his friend, The General.

Ernst's twice-yearly visits to Livonia proved fruitless, and during the 1750s, it was widely assumed that Ernst would die without producing an heir. A press pamphlet cartoon from July 1756 depicts Ernst as a venerated war-hero, adorned with medals, fleeing across a battlefield... pursued by his wife. Pamphlets produced by his political enemies went much further, suggesting that Ernst was either infertile, or worse, consumed by a love affair with King Frederick II. It is worth noting that for most of his reign, King Frederick II was dogged by rumours of homosexuality, resulting from the notorious Katte affair of 1730. The previous king, Frederick-William I discovered his son, Frederick II, and a young army officer, Hans Hermann von Katte, in an adolescent tryst. The pair attempted to escape to Britain but were captured, and Frederick II, at the age of just eighteen, was forced to witness the execution by decapitation of his friend and possible lover—an incident which would haunt the future king for the rest of his life.

When von Katte was dragged out into the prison yard for execution, Frederick II shouted in French, "*Veuillez pardonner mon cher Katte, au nom de Dieu, pardonne-moi!*" This translates as: 'Please forgive my dear Katte, in God's name, forgive me'. Katte shouted back in the same language, "There is nothing to forgive, I die for you with joy in my heart!" after which Frederick II fainted.

An extract survives from a letter Hans Hermann von Katte wrote to his father Hans Heinrich Graf von Katte, which reads as follows:

> *At once, everything is falling apart; and how sadly is the scenery of my life coming to an end; and how is my current state distinguished from that with which my thoughts have gone. I must, instead of promenading the way of honour and reputation—walk the path of disgrace and shameful death. Get strong again, my father, and believe me, God is with me in this game, without whose will nothing happens, not even a sparrow on the earth may fall! Meanwhile, I thank you with filial respect for all the fatherly loyalty shown to me, from my childhood to the present hour. Now nothing is left for me but to close with this consolation. Even though, my father, you haven't experienced anything high and distinguished from me in this world, oh! So please be assured that you will find even higher in heaven. Your faithful until death son.*

In later life, King Frederick II became quite inscrutable, and there is little evidence to indicate why, in the autumn of 1760, he ordered Ernst to make a permanent return to Livonia. However, the return would be short-lived, as Theodora became pregnant in the course of that year, and Ernst was allowed to return to the palace. Propaganda against Ernst and the king would relent in 1761 with the announcement of the birth of a daughter—Talia.

Theodora tragically perished during childbirth, leading the House of Saxe-Bergen to renew its petitions to the crown, this time with the demand that Talia should be allowed to inherit the Duchy of Livonia outwith the laws of primogeniture. Ernst made no defence against the petition, which led to an extraordinary settlement, reflected in changes made to the deeds of the Duchy of Livonia in the spring of 1762. By this agreement, Ernst would spend the rest of his life as the king's official companion, with a permanent position at the Royal Court at Königsberg, while the House of Saxe-Bergen would take on the administration of the Duchy of Livonia.

This peace would be short-lived. In the summer of 1763, while Talia was at the palace, Ernst made a spectacular decision that would stun the Royal Court and bring the Kingdom of Prussia to the brink of civil war. At the stroke of a signature, Ernst changed his will, and with immediate effect, bequeathed his titles and the Duchy of Livonia to the Prussian Crown.

The magnitude of this betrayal led to a violent renewal of the feud between Ernst and the House of Saxe-Bergen. Unprotected in the Duchy of Livonia, The General's former allies were quickly rounded up and arrested by the forces of the House of Saxe-Bergen. Many of them were killed.

The other Royal Houses of the Kingdom of Prussia were quick to align themselves against the Crown, and demanded the reinstatement of the agreement. They suspected that the king had orchestrated the change in an attempt to seize wealth and lands, though there is no evidence to suggest that King Frederick II had any idea of what Ernst had planned.

The enormous gift from Ernst to his sovereign made the king's own Royal House, the House of Hohenzollern, the wealthiest in central Europe. In an instant, Ernst ensured that Frederick's lands and riches made any future challenge to his rule unlikely to succeed.

None of this would come to much had a settlement between the king and the House of Saxe-Bergen not been possible. Open conflict was avoided, but a spate of assassinations struck right to the heart of the Royal Court, including an attempt on the life of Captain Friedrich von Beust.

Though he was not killed, Friedrich von Beust became so incapacitated that most of his duties were assumed by allies of Ernst, such as his former adjutant, Captain Erich von Wurzel, while Ernst himself became an official advisor to the king.

During this tumult, Ernst had demonstrated his incredible generosity to the king by bequeathing him the Duchy of Livonia. However, one might also posit that his actions were an exercise in realpolitik. Through the sacrifice of his lands, Ernst had become an inseparable ally to the king, making him the second most powerful man in the nation, eventually earning him the modern-day moniker, 'the Prussian Richelieu'. Like Richelieu, Ernst was quick to place a network of trusted allies and spies at the highest levels of government.

Talia would become a permanent resident, or perhaps, hostage, of the Royal Court at Königsberg. Her vulnerability would lead to the eventual truce between the Royal Crown and the House of Saxe-Bergen.

An agreement was negotiated over the course of two years, in which Frederick II and his advisors promised that Talia would be taken care of until she came of age, upon which time she would be promised to the Royal Heir, whomever that might be. As a dowry, the House of Saxe-Bergen would receive, in perpetuity, half the collected tax revenues from the Duchy of Livonia as well as various royal appointments in government relating to commerce and trade.

Many who have studied The General would say that the internal crisis of 1761–1765 was his most significant victory.

During this period, there occurred another seismic political event which cemented the position and power that Ernst enjoyed at the Prussian Court. War erupted once more among the great powers of Europe. Between 1756 and 1763, the defeated nations of the Austrian War of Succession sought their revenge in a new, global conflict that would become known as the Seven Years' War.

Maria Theresa, Empress of Austria, sought to achieve hegemony over the Germanic Kingdoms, but to do so, she had to defeat her great rival, Prussia. Among her allies, she could count France, Spain, Russia, Sweden, and the Kingdom of Saxony. Standing against her was Frederick II of Prussia and his allies, Great Britain and Portugal.

This war, just like the Austrian War of Succession before it, would grow to encompass multiple theatres of operation, from the old world to the new, across land and sea.

Ernst was eager to serve his king once more, and he quickly secured command of the Royal 4th Army, which he led in a series of bloody battles. However, at the age of fifty-five and beset by illness and fatigue, the old general began to make mistakes, which resulted in his defeat in the Battle of Kay versus Count Pyotr Semyonovich Saltykov of Russia.

Prussian forces of some 26,000 men were en route to secure strategic high grounds around the town of Kay when they were ambushed by a much larger Russian army of 41,000, which had entrenched itself along treelines and ridges.

Determined to achieve the strategic objective of the high ground, Ernst ordered repeated assaults against the entrenched Russian positions, only to be bloodily repulsed over the course of the day. By the end of the battle, the Prussians had lost over 8,300 men, along with several experienced commanders, including Major General Moritz Franz Kasimir von Wobersnow, who was a personal friend to the king, and cavalry commander Lieutenant General Heinrich von Manteuffel.

Frederick II blamed his men for the Prussian defeat, calling them 'cowards and scoundrels', but not their commander, his friend Ernst.

The General's military woes were set to worsen after Frederick II, frustrated by the defeat of his army at the Battle of Kay, came to supervise command at the much larger battle of Kunersdorf. This climactic battle, fought only fifty miles south of Berlin, aimed to strike a decisive blow against the allied armies of Austria.

50,000 Prussian soldiers amassed against a combined army of 79,000 soldiers led once more by Count Pyotr Semyonovich Saltykov of Russia and joined by the Austrian Generalisimo Ernst Gideon von Laudon—widely considered to be one of the greatest strategists of the era.

It is difficult to determine from the order of battle what responsibility Ernst had for the calamity that ensued, when combined with the impetuousness of Frederick II to avenge his defeat at the Battle of Kay, and the loss of his friend, Moritz Franz Kasimir von Wobersnow.

Similar to the Battle of Kay, the disaster which unfolded came as a result of mounting an assault against the carefully prepared defences of a much larger army entrenched in hills, woodland and bridges. The Prussians were famed at this time for their offensive strategies, which often saw their forces overcome more massive armies by utilising a military tactic known as the 'oblique order'. The tactic consisted of presenting a formation of soldiers that appeared to match the enemy formation, but this was an illusion. Unbeknownst to the defender, the attacker would concentrate their men along a single flank designed to strike through with overwhelming numbers.

The success of such an attack was dependent on excellent knowledge of the terrain and an army that was both well-fed and well-disciplined, neither of which applied to the Prussians at the Battle of Kunersdorf.

The consequences for the Prussians were dire as their forces attacked piecemeal, with their attempts to present oblique orders of battle stumbling over steep terrain and massed artillery fire.

By the end of the battle, the Prussian army was routed, suffering casualties of more than 21,000, and the loss of over 170 cannon.

Many Prussian military commanders, officers, and aristocrats were killed or captured during the battle, which led Frederick II to become entirely dependent on his friend and advisor Ernst.

King Frederick II wrote to his old tutor, Count Karl-Wilhelm Finck von Finckenstein on the evening of their defeat, in a letter that survives to this day:

> *This morning, at eleven o'clock, I have attacked the enemy. All my troops have worked wonders but at the cost of many losses. Our men got into confusion. I assembled them three times. In the end, I was in danger of getting captured and had to retreat. My coat is perforated by bullets, two horses of mine have been shot dead. My misfortune is that I am still living. Our defeat is very considerable: to me remains 3,000 men from an army of 48,000 men. At the moment in which I report all this, everyone is on the run; I am no more master of my troops. Thinking of the safety of anybody in Berlin is a good activity. It is a cruel failure that I will not survive. The consequences of the battle will be worse than the battle itself. I do not have any more resources, and frankly confess that I believe that everything is lost. I will not survive the doom of my fatherland. Farewell forever!*

Prussia itself was at the brink of collapse, and without another friend in the world, Frederick II came to rely entirely on Ernst, which perhaps helps us to understand what strange loyalty bound these men. Prussia would survive the devastation of Kunersdorf, thanks in part to the disorganisation of the allies and the exhaustion of their supply lines.

The stalling of the enemy's advances provided Prussia with valuable time to rebuild its defences and, by a mixture of luck and diligence, it managed to survive against the array of enemy nations pitted against it.

By 1762, Ernst had been actively campaigning for over six years. Weakened by the hardships of battle, he fell prey to pneumonia in the winter of that year, at the age of 60. Ernst was forced to relinquish his command during his ensconcement at the monastery of Potsdam, where he battled his illness. After some time in recuperation, he recovered, and was ordered to return immediately to the Palace of Königsberg.

Just one year later, in 1763, the Seven Years' War came to its bloody end. Defying the odds, Prussia achieved victory against Austria, France, and Russia. So tremendous was the prestige bestowed upon Frederick II that he became known as Frederick the Great, while Prussia gained immense power and status.

But the price of victory was not cheap, as Prussia lost almost a third of its population and most of its army. Ernst's reputation had suffered during the war also. He was remembered by the people of Prussia more as a butcher than a commander, with more notable defeats than successes. Upon his return to Königsberg, Ernst became the subject of some controversy and consternation when Frederick II appointed him Minister of War, in recognition of his military service and the generous gift of the Duchy of Livonia.

The office of Minister of War conferred substantial powers to Ernst, who could utilise his new authority to reshape the army as he saw fit. It also afforded him significant judicial powers to dole out military justice. There is little in the official record to indicate that Ernst enacted any modernising military reforms.

The General soon became a fearsome presence at court, dressed in his famously austere attire which consisted of a black frock coat and stockings. Ernst showed little appetite for exploiting his excellent favour with the king, and instead busied himself with increasingly paranoid investigations. He could often be seen loitering in the palace halls at night, or scrutinising the faces of courtiers during the day, searching for signs of treason.

We can surmise several reasons for this change in personality: firstly, his embitterment at his lacklustre performance in the Seven Years' War, paired with the schemes and plots he had faced during his feuds with the House of Saxe-Bergen.

The General revelled in his unofficial role as palace spymaster. He developed a spy ring comprised of former military comrades, who would dole out violent private justices against those he had deemed hostile towards the king. On one occasion, the French philosopher Voltaire remarked upon the notorious manuscripts of the Marquis de Sade with the following quip:

"Let the cruelty of his words be measured against The General's whip."

It would seem that Ernst had cultivated a genuinely international reputation for his sinister and increasingly sadistic activities.

During the 1770s, The General's daughter Talia blossomed into a beautiful young woman, protected under the terms of the agreement between Frederick II and the House of Saxe-Bergen. As she thrived in the Royal Court, Ernst busied himself with intrigue.

In the years that followed the Seven Years' War, Frederick II tried to bring about the political and economic collapse of Poland through a system of subterfuge and espionage. Poland, or as it was known then, the 'Polish-Lithuanian Confederation', was a multi-ethnic state known for its religious tolerance. After decades of prosperity, Poland faced the prospect of decline precipitated by the avarice of her neighbours: Prussia, Austria and Russia. They sought to collapse the country, and eventually achieved their goal in 1795, dividing its lands amongst themselves.

During the 1770s, Ernst was responsible for many plots which caused significant damage to Poland, including ordering the counterfeiting of their currency and staging violent raids against their ports and trade routes. Without allies, Poland succumbed to these assaults time and time again, with each successful mission only encouraging further interventions. In the course of this bold enterprise, Prussia's Royal Court became a place of constant intrigue as the ambassadors and spymasters of Europe came and went.

In peacetime, the king found himself spending most of the year at the Sanssouci or Summer Palace, where he placed himself among a group of elite cultural figures called 'the circle of friends', a society of scholars and philosophers that included the legendary Voltaire.

Access to the circle of friends was tightly controlled by Ernst, who helped Frederick II to resist the church's efforts to disband the group. It would appear that Ernst was not concerned with the personal proclivities of the king or his consorts.

Ernst was forever the king's staunchest defender. As traditional forces corralled to criticise the monarch's libertine behaviour, it was The General who would become the unlikely lightning rod for criticism and accusation. After all, to accuse the king of perversion and decadence is very different from charging his most loyal servant.

Various figures in the church, including formerly loyal servants such as the Chaplain Sigmund Homburg and former Royal Secretary Friedrich von Beust, set their sights on destroying Ernst, and, like him, became spymasters of considerable skill in the art of palace intrigue. Their sponsors were the House of Saxe-Bergen and other noble houses, including several ambitious persons from the House of Hohenzollern from which King Frederick II hailed.

As Talia grew into adolescence, she was not immune to the political games designed to ensure her future marriage to an heir of Prussia, and partial inheritance of the Duchy of Livonia. Despite effectively living as a hostage of the king, Talia nevertheless enjoyed all the freedoms and luxuries a lady of the court might expect.

Talia was also popular at court, with an amiable manner which endeared her to all, from the mightiest government minister to the humblest servant. We can speculate that the enemies of Ernst and the king may have sought to exploit that popularity in a pamphlet that was widely disseminated in Prussia just one year before the arrival of Alexander Mackintosh.

The pamphlet is notable for its striking depiction of The General, which would come to be the enduring image of this controversial figure. It depicts Ernst in his familiar black garb, clutching a riding crop, his face replaced with a grinning skull. Cowering before him, is Talia, her arm raised in terror at his nightmarish visage. The composition is striking for its similarity to the pamphlet disseminated fifty years before by the House of Saxe-Weimar-Eisenach, which had accused Ernst of abusing their daughter Josephine, his first wife.

Many Royal Houses like Saxe-Weimar-Eisenach and Saxe-Bergen conspired to bring about Ernst's end. The years which Alexander Mackintosh spent at court, between 1770 and 1780, were by far the most tumultuous and deadly for The General, and for his enemies.

In 1778, two years before the unveiling of the Immortal Princess, Ernst became the oldest man at court to hold government office. Now 76 years old, his political power was deteriorating fast, along with many of his physical and mental faculties, but his capacity for ruthlessness remained undimmed. Ernst could not count on many allies in his twilight years, as nobles from the Houses of Saxe-Weimar-Eisenach and Saxe-Bergen continued to mount their assaults on his reputation. Despite the collapse of his influence, Ernst retained the title of Minister of War and the protection of his last ally, King Frederick II.

In the years between 1778 and 1780, Alexander Mackintosh was recalled to the palace to produce the Immortal Princess. Several scandals rocked the palace during this period, which may provide clues as to the motives driving the creation of the doll.

On May 12th, 1778, a letter dispatched to Dr Hans Giltenchrist by the master theologian and historian Charles Gottlieb Guichard insisted that Talia was being imprisoned in the palace against her will as a result of her father's mental illness. Charles requested that Hans come to the palace on behalf of the king to investigate The General's state of mind:

> *I fear that this imperious man, consumed by the reign of the Romans, and devoid of any feeling for humanity, enacts his cruel policies against the child without rebuke. I have spoken with our dear friend who requests that we liberate the child discretely, an act which may yet liberate the Roman and our friend from their dishonour.*

In the extract above, we can safely assume that the child is Talia, that the 'imperious man' or 'Roman' is Ernst, and the friend, King Frederick. It should be noted that Charles Gottlieb Guichard and Dr Hans Giltenchrist were members of the circle of friends who regularly visited Frederick II at Sanssouci Palace.

Talia was freed from the chamber in which The General had confined her and accommodated in another wing of the palace. Restrictions were placed upon Ernst which prohibited him from visiting her. Charles would later write to the king to commend the sovereign's 'prudent and moral justice'.

In the winter of that same year, 1779, Charles would be discovered, drowned in a canal near the Sanssouci Palace, dead at just 42 years of age. His discovery by the Captain of the Palace Guard, Erich von Wurzel, the oldest of Ernst's allies, has led to some obvious conjecture.

Regardless of the rumours, Ernst continued to obey his king, assisting him in his affairs at Sanssouci Palace, while Talia remained at the Palace of Königsberg. So grievous was the state of depression that engulfed Ernst when separated from Talia, that a popular legend emerged, supposing that the old man's broken heart led Voltaire himself to suggest a mechanical replacement for Ernst's lost love.

We might suppose that, at the age of 78, The General would have required some rousing from his quarters at the Sanssouci Palace. It is also conceivable that the man standing before him may not have been recognisable to his frail eyes, despite him having met the inventor less than ten years before.

There is no academic evidence to suggest that the meeting which follows actually took place, only an apocryphal story which is scant on detail. According to the account, Frederick II accompanied Ernst into the ballroom of the Sanssouci Place for a meeting with Alexander. There, Ernst announced his plan for Alexander to produce a perfect likeness of Talia, transforming her into an immortal who would remain at his side until his dying day. Alexander is said to have proclaimed that their meeting had come about from divine providence, and that he would create something so beautiful, so extraordinary as to be beyond the realm of the senses.

This remarkable claim stoked Ernst's passions for the project further, and with his backing, Alexander would experience the rebirth of his career, as the dreams of two men manifested themselves in a single creation.

"Thou shalt forge, in her likeness, a model capable of performing five extraordinary deeds, free of the fickle trappings of flesh and bone."

Whether Frederick II ever said the line famously ascribed to him is unknown, but it is remembered to this day.

In 1780, Alexander was 38 years old, and only recently in recovery from illness and debt, so this turnaround in his fortunes was a blessing that he was desperate to cement. Ernst was allowed to leave Sanssouci Palace, and he and Alexander made their return to the Royal Palace at Königsberg.

In the spring mornings, Alexander and Talia could often be seen strolling in the palace grounds, with Ernst shuffling wearily behind them, maintaining a wary vigil. During his absence, Talia had grown into her own, becoming a popular debutante at the Royal Court, with many offers of courtship from the nobles of the land, including the king's own nephew Prince Friedrich Wilhelm. At this time, the various royal houses had filled the palace with their allies, with only the captain of the Palace Guard, Erich von Wurzel, remaining loyal to The General.

Despite the time spent apart, Ernst soon exerted a strange power over Talia once more. As she sang and danced at state occasions and palace parties, she would still, each night, make a predictable retreat to her father's quarters. The visits were recorded by the now aged and near-blind former Royal Secretary to the king, Friedrich von Beust, and shared with Chaplain Sigmund Homburg.

Such was the scope of Alexander's plan that the project became increasingly ambitious, surpassing the original intention of a luxurious private gift, and instead becoming a national project of the arts and sciences. The enormous cost of the incredible automaton, and the sheer scope of its proposed abilities attracted intellectuals, artists, and fortune seekers from around the world. Frederick II had prided himself on being a great patron of the arts, and he basked in the presence of these visitors, this growing circle of friends that occupied Sanssouci Palace, making Alexander the toast of the Royal Court.

It was in the autumn of 1780 that a grand, national celebration would present the Immortal Princess, coinciding with the ascendance of Prussia as the European centre for the arts and sciences.

In the weeks before the unveiling, Alexander and Talia began to court openly, igniting a scandal at the palace. Frederick II had planned for Talia to marry his nephew Prince Friedrich Wilhelm, heir to the Kingdom of Prussia. This marriage would provide a significant dowry, which would compensate the House of Saxe-Bergen for Ernst's bequeathment of the Duchy of Livonia to the crown in 1765.

Palace records provide some insight into the hubris that consumed Alexander, which generated both controversy and envy among the nobles. Ernst himself could do little, as he was engaged in a fight for survival against another bout of pneumonia, evidenced by a letter of correspondence from Dr Hans Giltenchrist, in which he answers the king's call to attend the palace urgently. Such was the state of the old man's health that the Royal Chaplain performed last rites twice in the month of July 1780. Still, The General clung to life.

On the 1st of August, 1780, the most significant technical marvel ever produced was unveiled, and yet, that same morning was marked by tragedy. Talia was reported missing by her servants, and a desperate search of the grounds, led by Captain Wurzel, had yielded no clues whatsoever.

That very same morning, Ernst made a miraculous recovery, recorded as a 'suspicious miracle of God' in the diary of his physician Dr Hans Giltenchrist. Ernst's return to health caused quite a stir among the visiting dignitaries. An ambassador of Bavaria, Auer von Auberg, remarked upon seeing The General marching down the palace halls with full vigour:

"He emerged with the light of the devil in his eyes and blinded us all."

Without any authority or order from the king, Ernst persuaded Captain Erich von Wurzel to confine Alexander to his quarters. The arrest warrant bearing the name of Alexander Mackintosh, now kept in the museum of Kalingrad, is left curiously blank, with no charge or accusation scrawled upon it. Noted academic and modern historian Dr Brendan Cole has suggested that the arrest may have been made simply to delay Alexander from taking any action, rather than to provide a sustained charge against him. Alternatively, Ernst may have suspected that Alexander was responsible for Talia's disappearance. In truth, we will never know the real motives or circumstances behind Ernst's sudden recovery and the deliberate actions he took thereafter, but the consequences were swift.

Frederick II arrived at the Palace of Königsberg only to learn that the great event had fallen into chaos. The king ordered the palace guard to arrest Ernst, which they did with some reluctance, and Alexander was released, with the unveiling delayed until later that evening.

Ernst was summoned to a hastily-prepared court-martial, which was attended by his old rivals, Friedrich von Beust and Sigmund Homburg, as well as several government ministers from the Houses of Saxe-Bergen and Saxe-Weimar-Eisenach.

Frederick II offered his old friend every opportunity to explain his illegal imprisonment of Alexander, which some had feared was the pre-cursor to a palace coup. Ernst did not, or perhaps, could not, justify his actions.

Sigmund Homburg writes in his diary:

> *The General, as he was called, gave the impression of a victor who had reigned supreme in battle, yet we saw no purpose, no intention on his part to explain his arrest of the young fop. Could he have sacrificed his honour and rank for idle jealousy? If so, what contentment could a man derive from visiting such brief captivity upon a rival?*

Many demanded the penalty of death, but Frederick II had seen a friend killed once before, during the notorious Katte affair, and was loath to lose another. Instead, Ernst was unceremoniously stripped of his government offices, military ranks, and honours, while those whom he had come to depend upon, such as former agents and associates, were arrested and imprisoned, including Captain Erich von Wurzel of the Palace Guard.

Sigmund Homburg remarked in his diary that Ernst seemed at peace and sought the return of neither rank nor privilege, but begged only for forgiveness.

Alexander was in a very different state of mind, veering between hysteria and grief as he presented the Immortal Princess to an audience of European royalty while desperately concerned for the fate of the missing Talia.

In attendance was famed artist and poet William Blake, who was commissioned to produce a series of sketches and paintings to commemorate the event. It is these five drawings, each of which depicts one of the 'Five Feats', which provide the only evidence for scholars today to discern what actions the Immortal Princess might have performed.

The five feats included the Immortal Princess extending her hand for a kiss, writing with a quill pen, bowing before the king, performing a dance, and, finally, eating and drinking with the guests. So incredible are these feats of engineering that it is not surprising that the very existence of such an automaton is disputed.

State propaganda of the time declared the unveiling to be a huge success. However, records show that enormous pressure was placed upon the palace guard to mount a thorough search and investigation into Talia's disappearance. It was difficult to celebrate the creation of a new mechanical life when the very muse which had inspired it was missing or dead.

Frederick II returned to Sanssouci Palace with a group of his loyal friends, while Ernst remained in a quasi-state of house arrest at the Palace of Königsberg. Two days later, on the 3rd of August, Ernst was to present another shock for his royal patron when he organised an astonishing escape and burglary.

There is no record to suggest how Ernst managed to escape, but records do reveal that a number of armaments were stolen from the palace guard around that time. Several prisoners were released, including the former captain of the Palace Guard, Erich von Wurzel.

The escape itself was enough to send shockwaves through the kingdom, but the kidnapping of the Immortal Princess from the palace ballroom was an achievement which still confounds scholars to this day.

It would appear that Frederick II was reluctant to order the arrest of his beloved friend, and instead waited until the 8th of August, 1780, before ordering the army to mount a search at Ernst's former residences in the Duchy of Livonia.

Ernst was apprehended at last on November 14th, in a cottage on the outskirts of Holstein-Wutten, a market town in which his mother Marie-Louise, princess of the Duchy of Baden, had given birth to him.

A popular legend tells of a soldier discovering the dead man in his bedchamber, still clutching the automaton, forever unable to release the mechanical effigy of his daughter Talia.

His body was interred at the Palace of Königsberg, where it lay in state for three days before it was buried in an elaborate ceremony, with his military rank and honours reinstated. His grave is located inside Königsberg Cathedral, in the present-day city of Kalingrad, among many historical heroes and villains of Prussian lineage.

Within days, the Immortal Princess was returned to the palace, where it was exhibited in the so-called 'room of curiosities', a space which presented major artworks and creations for visiting dignitaries and guests.

Alexander was left heartbroken, and obsessed still with the Immortal Princess, or more precisely, with its muse, Talia. Before Christmas, he was exiled from the Prussian Royal Court for reasons relating to drunkenness and delusions, none of which, unfortunately, are described in any detail in the palace records.

Captain Erich von Wurzel rejoined the Royal Court, having gained a pardon for his part in aiding the search for Ernst. He was soon appointed Royal Secretary, and it is from his private records that we can see that Alexander wrote three letters to the king in the months of December 1780 and January 1781.

Scholars have long sought the content of these letters, but unfortunately, no record of them remains. Almost a year after these events, in the winter of 1781, Alexander made a foolhardy attempt to smuggle himself into Prussia by posing as a French wine merchant. His arrest report still exists and can be viewed at the Museum of Berlin. It bears the personal stamp of Frederick II, with a note explicitly ordering the prisoner to be escorted back to Scotland.

We can only speculate as to what Alexander might have been planning. However, we can probably assume that he was attempting to gain an audience with the king.

On March 12th, 1782, the Scottish Land Registry bears the record of a man 'of considerable means' by the name of Alexander Mackintosh purchasing the estates of Guildhall Manor in the county of Fife for £25,000—almost $6,000,000 today, accounting for inflation.

Alexander's wealth did not end there, for he spent the rest of that year lobbying the British ambassador to Prussia to press for the return of his famed creation, the Immortal Princess. A report written by the ambassador, Sir John Stepney, 8th Baronet of Llanelli, Carmarthenshire, still exists in the National Archives in London, an extract of which reads as follows:

> *It was with some despondency that I left my meeting with the famed creator of the Immortal Princess, for he was not altogether himself. The man could have become Icarus, ascending skywards in the glory of his triumph, but instead his flight has landed him in the sea, or rather, the bottle. Such torment in so talented a man is indeed a sad sight to behold.*
>
> *He has exclaimed with great purpose that he is on an errand of love, and that a purse of one hundred pounds would be mine if I could secure for him an audience with the King of Prussia!*

It is likely that Alexander would have fallen into obscurity thereafter, were it not for the spectacular sequence of events that was to follow, culminating in a wave of terror so extreme, so notorious, that the legend lives on to this day.

The curse of the Infernal Princess was about to reveal itself.

III

The tragic and mysterious events which occurred between the grand unveiling of the Immortal Princess on August 1st, 1780 and the summer of 1782 would beget the terrifying myth that saw the clockwork automaton earn itself a new name in the annuls of history.

The 'Infernal Princess', as it became known, unleashed an unprecedented reign of terror, which has fascinated devotees of the supernatural and confounded historians for centuries.

With the generous permission of noted automata expert Dr Brendan Cole, we can explore some highlights from his fascinating research, which has uncovered many incidents attributed to the cursed doll. Please note that the author of this essay does not claim that any of the events described hereafter actually occurred. In other words, we are opening a door which leads us from a room of historical record into a nebulous place, filled with conjecture, innuendo, and unattributable fantasy. Dr Brendan Cole, recognised as the world's foremost authority on the subject of antique automata, has declared himself a sceptic, casting doubt on the very existence of the Immortal Princess.

Following the recapture of the Immortal Princess, it was brought back to the fabled Curiosity Room of the Palace of Königsberg. This ornate hall was specially designed to showcase the treasures of the nation for visiting royalty, to inspire awe and wonder among foreign ambassadors, and to deter future enemies.

The wonder of its creation, and the ignominious death of Ernst von Heinrich, had aroused the curiosity of many esteemed persons, who flocked en masse to see the automaton in the spring of 1781. During those early months of the year, Frederick II had conceded much to the House of Saxe-Bergen and her allies as a result of the failed attempt to marry Talia to the heir apparent, Friedrich Wilhelm. The palace was abuzz with new appointments to the government from the enemies of the king, which threatened to unravel the power of the Prussian Monarchy.

By strange fates, the imminent collapse of royal authority was averted when a tragic incident occurred on the 22nd of March, 1781. The new Royal Secretary, Captain Erich von Wurzel, provides an account of a drowning which occurred within the extensive grounds of the palace. The victim was Lady Sophie Saxe-Weimar-Eisenach, an 18-year-old girl who was widely admired for her beauty and skill as a dancer, and who, at that time, had begun a courtship with Friedrich Wilhelm.

Lady Sophie was discovered floating face down in the palace's grand artificial lake by a palace guard called Albrecht, who was immediately arrested and imprisoned by the new Captain of the Palace Guard, Captain Heinrich von Stille. On the 23rd of March, military records show that Albrecht was placed on trial at an army court-martial held in the Chapel Hall at the Palace of Königsberg. After only four hours, Albrecht was found guilty of the charge of murder.

In a striking and widely discredited testimony, Albrecht claimed that Sophie was not alone at the edge of the water, and that she had been fighting with another woman. He could not identify the other woman on account of the distance and the harsh morning sun. He ran towards the women, but upon reaching them, discovered Sophie lying dead in the water, while the other woman had fled, impossibly far into the forest beyond. Perhaps the most chilling aspect of Albrecht's testimony is his description of the other woman, how she moved towards the cover of trees in the manner of a clockwork machine.

This tragic event coincided with several unnerving diary entries written by Dr Hans Giltenchrist, royal physician to the king at that time. The entries describe how the palace servants were so afraid to enter the Palace Curiosity Room, that he asked for the chaplain Sigmund Homburg to perform a blessing. Neither the diary nor the testimony of Albrecht provides specific mention of the Immortal Princess, yet, the clues offer the tantalising prospect that these events may be connected to the famed doll.

One lonely morning later that March, Albrecht was taken to the courtyard of the palace stables to be shot by a firing squad made up of his peers in the palace guard. The death of Lady Sophie had ruined the prospects of House Saxe-Weimar-Eisenach, a firm ally to the powerful House of Saxe-Bergen. Suspicion was rife that the king had reneged on the arranged marriage and was responsible for the young woman's death. In this violent and paranoid time, records reveal that Royal Secretary Captain Erich von Wurzel ordered a doubling of the Palace Guard, including the addition of a cadre of elite death-head hussars, known for their exceptional loyalty to the king.

The officer in charge of the execution was the Captain of the Palace Guard, Heinrich von Stille, a member of the House of Saxe-Bergen with a personal motive to make Albrecht suffer. We may discern this from the letter of satisfaction written by an 18-year-old nobleman, Alexander Saxe-Weimar-Eisenach, who described the execution in some detail to his tutor:

> *Captain Heinrich von Stille is a good man who punished the perverse agent with the divine cruelty that was his due. The murderous animal perished in a fog of gun smoke, but not before the true blade of the Captain's avenging sabre pierced his belly. The villain's howl was so loud as to awaken the angels, and I am thankful that our earnest ally could produce such sweet music for dearest Sophie.*

Another perspective on the execution is presented in an extract from the diary of Duke Hans von Haugwitz, a senior noble in the House of Saxe-Bergen, who noted that: "Even to the very moment of his death, the accused remained troublingly loyal to his account of the other woman, the one who moved so strangely."

On the 13th of April, just three weeks after the death of Lady Sophie, another horrific event would occur, this time involving Royal Secretary and former ally to Ernst, Captain Erich von Wurzel. The previous night, Wurzel was heard speaking to some unknown other for many hours in the Palace Curiosity Room. The next morning, he was nowhere to be found.

No servant or guard had dared interrupt Wurzel, such was the seniority of his position, but alas, the impossibility of identifying the other speaker would terminally hinder the investigation led by Captain Heinrich von Stille.

Stille was no ally of Erich von Wurzel, whose loyalty to the king following the death of Lady Sophie made him a likely target for assassination. One record, which may even provide a motive for which to suspect Heinrich von Stille, consists of an order Wurzel had written to investigate the possibility of disbanding the palace guard. Although the order was never formally issued, if his political rivals had learned of its existence, retribution would likely have been swift.

There is, however, no evidence for this conjecture, and it would appear that Stille led a diligent search for the missing Wurzel, with many soldiers and servants undergoing questioning. No further mention of the search is made, until we discover an entry in the diary of Dr Hans Giltenchrist, written on the 30th of April:

> *So it was that our loyal companion to his Imperial Highness, Captain Erich von Wurzel, was found to be with God. His body was discovered two miles from the palace, in a state of worrisome mutilation, which included the removal of the poor man's tongue. At the request of Captain Heinrich von Stille, I have produced a report based upon my interviews with the soldiers and servants, but there is nought to be gleaned from their testimony. As for the two men who found the corpse, I am at a loss, for what they claim goes beyond all reason, beyond the purview of the rational mind.*

The lack of any further description of what the men saw has preoccupied academics ever since. We can perhaps speculate that their account shared similar sensational traits with that of the executed guard, Albrecht.

Following this second incident, Frederick II made the shock decision to move his residence permanently to Sanssouci Palace, where he would reside with his dwindling circle of friends until passing peacefully in 1784, at the age of 74.

The Palace Guard would remain at the Palace of Königsberg under the command of Minister Erich von Schill, who was responsible for State Security. As a member of House Hohenzollern, his role at the palace was to ensure the smooth transfer of power to Friedrich Wilhelm upon the death of Frederick II.

Erich von Schill had several traits in common with Ernst von Heinrich, including his severe demeanour and his preference for funereal attire. He was also a skilful insider, able to navigate the treacherous relationships and alliances between the Germanic Royal Houses. Under his influence, he successfully brought about a truce between the houses of Hohenzollern, Saxe-Bergen and Saxe-Weimar-Eisenach.

The basis of the truce, which was negotiated in May of that year, is still preserved in the Museum of Potsdam, where it is displayed bearing the wax seals of over thirty nobles. By the terms of the agreement, Friedrich Wilhelm would agree to become engaged to Elisabeth Christine Ulrike of Brunswick-Wolfenbüttel, from the modest House of Brunswick-Berwin. The marriage would ensure that the balance of power between the houses would finally stabilise.

During this time, the palace records reveal that a large number of servants left their positions in the Palace of Königsberg. The region was rife with rumours that the place was cursed, as locals had begun to connect the tragic incidents with the unveiling of the mysterious automaton.

In the course of the negotiations, Duke Hans von Haugwitz of the House of Saxe-Bergen visited Erich von Schill for private discussions. One apocryphal story states that, upon leaving the palace, Hans von Haugwitz requested an opportunity to view the Immortal Princess, remarking that the automaton had become the subject of his dreams.

Erich von Schill obliged and ordered the palace guard to escort Haugwitz to the Curiosity Room. Upon arriving there, the nobleman dismissed the soldiers and remained alone with the automaton for several hours. Later that night, the government minister was shocked to learn that Hans von Haugwitz had not yet left the palace. After hurrying to the room, Schill was shocked to discover the man standing listlessly before the doll, seemingly unaware that more than a minute had passed since he entered the room.

Only two weeks later, on May 28th, 1781, Hans von Haugwitz would become infamous for his role in a scandal which shook the House of Saxe-Bergen to its core. In the early hours of the morning, villagers witnessed a flash of light spreading across the ground floor of Vischering Castle. Within minutes, the entire building was ablaze, with many victims trapped inside, including Hans' six children and his wife Germaine von Haugwitz.

Hundreds gathered to assist the survivors who clambered, choking, from the ruins. Hans von Haugwitz was discovered in his nightshirt, covered in blood, wandering erratically through the fields behind the castle. The confused villagers brought him to Görlitz Sanatorium, a local hospital, for further investigation.

On July 14th, 1988, Dr William Meich of Bristol University led a team of British and German students in conducting an archaeological survey of the ruins of Görlitz Sanatorium, located in present-day Poland, in a territory that formerly comprised the Kingdom of Prussia. The modest ruin was not awarded protected status on account of its poor condition and was set to be demolished to make way for an expanded highway. Students in the study faced the challenging prospect of completing their survey in the two weeks before demolition work was set to commence.

Dr William Meich stated that he did not expect his students to find anything except for roof slates, iron-workings, and other buried architectural fixtures. So, it was with some surprise that the survey uncovered a small iron chest, bearing the seal of the House of Saxe-Bergen.

Inside the chest was a collection of papers, heavily degraded due to the moist conditions underground. Students at Bristol University used computer scanning technology to digitise and reassemble the minuscule fragments which survived.

After two years of analysis, Dr William Meich was able to present six reconstructed notes, which revealed the author to be none other than Hans von Haugwitz. His writings are remarkable for the intimate insight they provide into the mind of Haugwitz, and the devastating obsession which consumed him.

Note I

I am Duke Hans von Haugwitz, and I am an aristocrat of noble birth. Aside from our shared nobility, I am otherwise unlike my father or my mother, my nature deviating much from their own. Now I am just a man, all trace of my nobility wiped clean. I wear the clothes of a pauper, and the orderlies drench me with buckets of ice water, lest I shout, or writhe against my chains.

These words I write are a therapy which assuages the broken mind that brought me here. For the deeds I have committed, I shall perhaps remain here for the rest of my days, yet I know not of what I am guilty, neither have I received word from my wife or children.

I am indeed a man of the House of Saxe-Bergen, a man of honour, born into a family where glory and strength are the epitomes of life. I have called out to my father's ghost from the bars of my cage, yet my scream for restitution brings only the indignity of the water bucket.

This heavy burden I endure is made all the more unbearable for the solitude forced upon me. There are no other prisoners here, and I may receive no visitors. I should have expected my patronage to be worth at least something to all those servants I've advanced through the ranks. Where is Stille? Should he not effect a rescue at once? After all, I saved him from obscurity.

The bucket! The bucket! Damned be to God! Where is my wife? Where are my children?

Note II

In the light of the full moon, I see my father watching me. I see strange shadows on the wall that loom over me like claws, and scramble for a rag of cloth to hide beneath. I remember him telling me, when I was just a frightened boy upon the fields of battle, that honour shall stand a man straight and tall before God, but that wealth or love shall not, for they are the concern of the commoner, while courage and nobility cannot be bought.

Yet, now I must forgo the signet ring of my family to trade with the prison guards for a loaf of mouldy bread.

My destitution would not surprise my father, for he often called me his 'sickly girl' and hid not his contempt for me. He was my opposite—tall and handsome like a prize stallion, adorned with the scars of combat. He was Mars, riding upon the chariot of war, with me, his mere slave, tied behind him, mewling haplessly.

I had a preference for the aesthetic, for I enjoyed the finery of clothes, the taste of wine, and the sensation of a lover's touch. But his approval could be found only through the gasp of a dying man sliding from a sword.

He had no patience for his sickly girl and considered the task of my care and coaching to be futile. If I was woman's stuff, I might as well be left in the care of them and not he. I suppose I was first his greatest humiliation, and now, I am my own.

Ah, but my mother... what an angel she was to me... was she? Mad thoughts rush at me now. Where is Stille? I must see my wife and children! They must fear for me!

Note III

I have drunk from the cup of despair until I can drink no more. It has been many days since I was brought here, and still they tell me nothing. The man who calls himself a doctor is ashamed to introduce himself by name, fearful that my noble status might endanger him. Instead, they ask me, time and time again, what occurred that fateful night, the night of the fire. But I cannot remember, and I shout back at them till the water is thrust back at me!

There must be a royal warrant for my arrest and imprisonment, for I am allowed no advocate to speak on my behalf. Have I been found guilty of treason? Am I the victim of intrigue?

Before, I began to speak of my mother. She was a great inspiration to me, a woman of the sort I might have married, mistress of the arts and sciences, and as free as any woman could be until... how I pitied her marriage to my father. She was a songbird who coveted the aesthetic in life, just as I do, but there she was, cruelly bound to a monster.

Once, my father was so furious that he made my mother faint with fear. I recall so vividly my childish protest, my tiny fist raised at him before he slapped me so hard I flew across the floor. How could I protect her, she whom I had doomed by my entry into the world, forever binding her—who was so much higher than he—by the manacles of God for time immortal? She was a flower that had wilted with time's punishments, and I cannot escape the look of betrayal she gave me when I left home to marry.

I abandoned her, as I too am abandoned in this God-forsaken place. But I will not abandon my wife and children. If Stille does not aid in my escape, I will find a way out myself. Why does he not come? Is he not my servant?

Note IV

The supposed doctor of this madhouse has brought a priest to visit me. This devout servant went by the name of Hans and questioned my acceptance of the Lord. In his eyes, I saw the fear of a man stood before the devil. Is that what I have become? My mind was fraught with wild ideas, and so consumed was I by this, that I cannot recall answering many of the man's questions. Could it be that I've been imprisoned here on a charge of heresy?

He kept asking the same questions, and I did my best to ask my own, but he was steadfast as a stone wall before the shore. I told him that I am devoted to the path of God. I have forever been a loyal servant to the Church and have never strayed from its teachings. I know that the devil lurks in every corner, inciting evil and sorrow in his wake. I tried to impress upon Hans that it was his dark dealings that saw me placed here, and not my own. Hans looked fearful and fidgeted like a crab on the sand, eager to escape my presence.

I screamed at him that I saw the proof of God in everything I'd seen and done, and with that, he bolted like a horse from a burning stable. I tried to grab him, but he threw me off, and the next second, frozen water was thrust upon me.

I write this, soaking still, in the knowledge that my supposed doctor shall read these accounts to try and discern my great secret, but there is none. At night, I wonder which persons have betrayed me at court? Where is my wife? Where is Stille?

Note V

I often lingered like a ghost in the aftermath of the battle, forever trying to curry favour with my father for a proper commission. I believe my father was convinced that, upon the battlefield, I would perish in an instant. As I became a young man, he relinquished some of his prejudice against me, permitting me to follow in the wake of our vast army.

I accompanied our family's militia, which participated in all the grand campaigns against our enemies, but never in the fighting. Instead, we would descend in the aftermath of the battle, capturing enemy officers, finishing off the wounded while recovering our own. My father was shrewd, for a while. He joyously led the charge of men who would fetch his injured enemies, so that they might survive to toil in the fields.

I did my best to gain his admiration, but he would laugh me out of his command tent, even before my inferiors. He especially adored Heinrich von Stille, a bastard of disputed lineage whom he had adopted after the falling of a comrade. He was nought but a commoner to me, with pretensions of familiarity beyond his station, but my father would not discourage him. After all, Stille had a killer's instinct, and he trained with my father on the rapier and sabre from dusk till morning. He would become an expert in the business of killing, just like my father, while I stood and watched them from the window with a dry quill and a blank journal.

As they departed for glory, I was married off to an undeserving wench of lower nobility. There is pity in the hearts of men who accept into their company the lesser beasts of the world, and she carried that look often while in my presence. It wrought great agonies from my heart, which I sought to dispense of, once and for all, and which I did, by some strange coincidence, with my rival and unexpected friend to be, Heinrich von Stille.

Note VI

It has been months since I first came here. The men that have imprisoned me assure me that my departure will be soon be confirmed, but they are liars. They even tell me that a royal advocate has been dispatched to represent me for the crimes of which I am accused, though I still know not what they are.

I also received a note from Captain von Stille, which was carefully inspected by my guard before being given to me, assuring me that the management of my estate is in safe hands. His hands, no doubt? He tells me that he will speak with the warden about improving the conditions of my confinement. I have many questions for him, namely regarding the absence of my wife and children. My concern for them has grown of late; the guards exchange strange looks whenever I ask of them, and I sense that they know a secret which I am fearful of uncovering.

Did I tell you that I also share a secret with Captain von Stille? Let me begin with that fear which I told you I carried in my heart, of forever being the sickly child that was so despised. I've never said this to another soul, and I might suspect that even God is ignorant of this truth. It is, perhaps, even a revelation unto myself. But, as I sit in the squalor of my room, with its stench of piss and humility, I can discern one truth... one true love that has carried me here and shall carry me whence. Despised by my father, resented by my mother, and abandoned by God, I have at last recalled that profound feeling which liberates me from them all.

It came to me in the gardens of a beautiful palace, lush with trees and fruit, where a young man lay in the long grass breathing his last. My eyes fixed upon his, and in his final exhalations, with each second promising to be his last, I could see in his eyes his mother, his father, his brother, his son, and his every love to be. I had become death and truth, and in the eyes of the dead, I had finally found love.

Stille was the man my father had wanted me to be, but compared to me, he was an amateur in the art of destruction. Slaying a man is child's play compared to the boundless prospect of the inferno.

My wife and children were toadstools—simple, ugly ornaments fashioned by peasants, fit only for a blind cotter. How I despised them!

Then came the marvellous night I met the princess! Before my great king, she was unveiled to me—standing there more alive than any who had stood before. She told me that every princess needed her prince, and that my wife and children were the guards to my tomb, forever preventing us from our destined union. How could I refuse a princess? Was it not my destiny to be a prince? A king!

I can remember the fire, the smell of acrid burning and the screams of the little ones whose tiny fists battered the windows for my attention. Could they not see that it was they who had summoned this angel of Death?

My path of the flame is a road to Heaven and love... sweet love! While some of my divine deeds may carry the odour of evil, I shall remain committed to repeating them upon my liberation, for I am forever the servant of my princess... the Immortal Princess.

When one crosses a river of blood, it becomes easier to sail an ocean...

The discovery of these notes sparked enormous interest in the legend of the Immortal Princess, attracting a cottage industry of supernatural study and paranormal exploitation. The notes provided the first real evidence that connected any of the tragedies with the automaton.

The disaster which befell the House of Saxe-Bergen threatened to collapse the uneasy truce negotiated by Erich von Schill. Royal Chaplain Sigmund Homburg expressed the anxiety of that month in a eulogy performed at the funeral of former Royal Secretary, Friedrich von Beust:

> *While the state suffers winter, there is renewal to be had in spring, born from the ground beneath our feet, on a path of light towards the horizon, seemingly unreachable... until we make our long walk towards it.*

We can speculate as to the meaning of these words, but the mood of decay and melancholy impresses upon us the depression which seems to have consumed those left behind in the palace.

Dr Hans Giltenchrist wrote in his diary on the 14th November, 1781:

> *The Palace of Königsberg is becoming a ruin, filled with ruined souls. Despite the best efforts of Minister von Schill, this is not a place that deserves preservation. There is a room in this palace, a heart of darkness, a chamber which I dare not visit or even speak of, and it is the root cause of the evil which engulfs us, yet we have not the power to destroy it.*

In December 1781, the Palace of Königsberg suffered a prolonged snowstorm, during which many servants and guards deserted the building. Such was the state of despair, that Erich von Schill's own wife Theodora fell ill, and was admitted as a patient in the Sanatorium of Westhalt-Bergen.

The fear surrounding the palace culminated in a wave of local protests against the presence of the doll, instigated by the many servants and soldiers who had ceased their service. Pamphlets were distributed depicting the 'cursed creation', naming it the Infernal Princess.

In February 1782, the period of unease would come to an abrupt end with the sudden disappearance of the automaton. Records are scant on the details of what happened, but the research of Dr Brendan Cole gives some insight.

One of those insights relates to Colonel Reich von Hardenburg of the 21st Royal Regiment of Foot, who received orders to leave his barracks in Voitland with a company of one hundred soldiers on the 14th of February.

The order reveals that the men were instructed to march without delay to the Palace of Königsberg, where they arrived two days later.

The great mystery that remains is why, one week later, less than half of that company of men returned to Voitland. None of the returning soldiers would speak of what had happened, and no historical record exists to shed any light on the mystery. The Palace Records come to a sudden end from the date on which the infantry arrived. It would appear from the arrival of persons such as Erich von Schill and Dr Giltenchrist in towns around the country that the palace was hastily abandoned.

Conspicuously, there is no record in written correspondence, diary entries, or the official records of the government to explain why the Palace of Königsberg was abandoned.

What we can discern for a fact, however, is that the Immortal Princess was no longer present, having presumably been removed from the Palace of Königsberg.

The evidence for this comes from an order given to Captain Heinrich von Stille from the office of Frederick II on March 12th to seek out and arrest Minister Erich von Schill, and to uncover the location of 'stolen national treasures'. However, we must note that the automaton is not specifically mentioned.

Curiously, the investigation was marred by an incompetence out of character with the ruthless diligence that Stille was renowned for.

After failing to find either Erich von Schill or the Immortal Princess, Stille would have been displeased to learn that both his target and his hospitalised wife had fled the country to seek asylum in Austria, which was granted on May 6th, 1782.

The Immortal Princess was never recovered, and as Friedrich Wilhelm took over the reins of government, he expressed little interest in pursuing the search. He abandoned it along with the Palace of Königsberg.

In 1784, Friedrich Wilhelm would be crowned king, and though his reign would prove to be tumultuous, never again would the state experience such dark tragedies as those associated with the Immortal Princess.

One might imagine that our tale would end in Prussia, but it does not. Instead, we must return to where it all began—Scotland.

Alexander Mackintosh had acquired a vast fortune in Prussia, and spent much of these spoils purchasing the impressive Forth Estate in Scotland, one of the largest manor houses in Britain. The vast building did not entertain many guests, however, and for the most part, he lived there as an unhappy recluse with a skeleton crew of servants.

He was described as a quiet, melancholic man, curiously at odds with his previous reputation as a libertine. Parish Reverend Malcolm Alexander speaks of his affluent parishioner:

> *The inventor Alexander finally appeared at our Sunday service after many requests from myself and the local elders. I am both fascinated and repulsed by this man who shows a level of genius befitting one of God's finest creations, and a grief-stricken madness that might befit his worst.*

This impression would change drastically on the 11th of August, 1872, on the final day before disaster would befall the man some would call Scotland's greatest inventor.

During the wedding of two parishioners, Alexander burst into the hall and interrupted the ceremony to make a wild pronouncement to the congregation, in an attire altogether unsuitable for the occasion. Again, we must look to the diary of Malcolm Alexander for further elaboration:

> *He was so unlike the man I had first encountered that I did not at first recognise him. All the time I had known him, he had dressed as if in mourning and said almost nothing, yet here he was blasting about like a cannon in extravagant silks and coloured breeches fit only for a visit to a Parisian boudoir. He exclaimed to all who would listen that he had finally found his long lost love and that they would, at last, be reunited. I did not dare question him, and nor would any man who could see the mad glint in his eyes.*

This extract is the last recorded evidence pertaining to the life of Alexander Mackintosh.

On the night of the 12th of August, the grand Forth Estate manor burnt to the ground, leaving no survivors.

Had Alexander Mackintosh become the final victim of the Immortal Princess?

Game Rules

THE OWLMAN

Thousands of years ago, there existed a fiendish civilisation of humans. They worshipped a god that was said to grant wishes in exchange for the lives of children, sacrificed in the burning cauldrons of his shrines.

Nowadays, those ancient cities and temples lie in ruins, inhabited only by the long-dead servants of that god, who exist as mere shadows preying upon unwary visitors.

The Owlman, also known as the 'Mother of Tears', or 'Lord of Tears', is a powerful devil that many consider a god. It resembles a giant owl with a human-like body and long talons. In its prime, the demon was considered a master manipulator, capable of instilling corruption inside the hearts of even the greatest men. Few can resist the devastating lure of The Owlman's power of Charisma, enticing weakened minds to the doom of eternal servitude.

There are those who say that the Owlman has grown tired of his millennia-long slumber, and remark upon the sea of ravens and crows making their way towards his most ancient shrine.

THE OWLMAN

Large Fiend (devil), lawful evil

Armor Class 19 (Natural Armor)

Hit Points 380

Speed 30 ft.

STR	DEX	CON	INT	WIS	CHA
26 (+8)	14 (+2)	24 (+7)	22 (+6)	18 (+4)	24 (+7)

Saving Throws Dex +8, Con +13, Wis +10

Damage Resistance bludgeoning, piercing and slashing from nonmagical attacks not made with silvered weapons

Magic Resistance The Owlman has advantage on saving throws against spells and other magical effects.

Damage Immunities fire, poison

Condition Immunities poisoned

Senses truesight 120 ft.

Languages Infernal, Telepathy 120 ft.

Challenge Rating 20 (25,000 XP)

Actions

Multiattack. The Owlman can make three attacks: two with its diabolical talon and one with its ancient gaze.

Diabolical Talon. Magic Weapon Attack: +14 to hit, reach 10ft., one target. Hit: 2d6 +8 slashing damage and 3d6 fire damage.

Ancient Gaze. 50 feet ranged attack requires line of sight between The Owlman and the target. The targeted creature is struck by a psychic ray of ancient despair forcing them to make a DC 20 Wisdom saving throw. A failed save causes 4d8 psychic damage and the loss of spellcasting actions for d3 rounds, while a successful save results in no damage.

Greater Fear Aura. The Owlman emits an aura of greater fear forcing all hostile creatures within 50 feet of The Owlman to make a DC 21 Wisdom saving throw. On a failed save, the creature becomes frightened, on a successful save the creature is immune to the Greater Fear Aura for 24 hours.

Innate Spellcasting. The Owlman's innate spellcasting ability is Charisma (spell save DC21). The Owlman can innately cast the following spells, requiring no material components:

At will: Dire Charm, detect magic, hold monster
3/day each: **wall of fire** and Corvid Swarm

Shadow Maker. Any intelligent humanoid killed by the Owlman transforms into a shadow, under its control.

Legendary Actions

The Owlman can take 3 legendary actions, choosing from the options below. Only one legendary action option can be used at a time and only at the end of another creature's turn. The Owlman regains spent legendary actions at the start of its turn.

Dire Charm. The Owlman must have a line of sight towards the targeted creature who must be within 50 feet range. The creature must make a DC 21 Wisdom saving throw or become charmed by the Owlman. Unlike Charm, Dire Charm also causes the targeted creature to experience an alignment shift towards lawful evil, along with a desire to protect the Owlman at any cost. The creature must re-roll their save each turn, and should they fail their save three times, the effects will become permanent. Such creatures often become devoted cultists and servants whose lives are spent forever worshipping The Owlman.

Corvid Swarm. The Owlman summons a dense swarm of ravens which produce a 50 feet protective radius causing difficult terrain penalties for any hostile creatures trapped inside. The cloud of birds obscures The Owlman with enough protection that it enjoys three-quarters cover for one minute (10 rounds).

THE MOULD

The Mould is a hideous and unforgiving fungus that lurks in the ceilings and uppermost recesses of old structures, awaiting unwary prey. Without a moment's notice, it will strike with its lightning-fast, whip-like tendrils, sparing few from a horrifying fate.

For it is not just the razor-sharp tendrils, or even the nightmare of being engulfed by this bed of spores that keep men awake late at night, but the Mould Virus. For each one of The Mould that exists was once a human who succumbed to that awful and perverse disease.

Having resisted numerous Ice Ages and natural disasters over countless millennia, The Mould has evolved into a devastating predator. Resilient against most forms of attack, and immune to poisons, its only known vulnerability is to intense fire. But, unless every cell is eradicated from existence, The Mould will return with terrifying effect.

THE MOULD

Large Fungus, true neutral

Armor Class 14 (Natural Armor)

Hit Points 120

Speed 1 ft.

STR	DEX	CON	INT	WIS	CHA
15 (+2)	10 (+0)	12 (+1)	4 (-3)	3 (-4)	2 (-4)

Saving Throws Str +4, Con +3

Vulnerability fire

Damage Immunities poison

Condition Immunities poisoned

Senses tremorsense 60 ft., blindsight 60 ft.

Languages none

Challenge Rating 4 (1100 XP)

Actions

Multiattack. The Mould can make three attacks: two with its whip attack, and fungal entrapment.

Whip Attack. Melee Weapon Attack: +4 to hit, reach 5 ft., one target. Hit: 1d6 damage + Fungus Poison, requiring the hit creatures to make a DC 14 Constitution save, or they will take an additional 2d6 poison damage.

Fungal Entrapment. The Mould concentrates its tentacles to try and ensnare its target. The creature must make a DC 14 Dexterity save or become ensnared, and must reroll their save in the next round to avoid suffering the effects of Fungal Engulf.

Fungal Engulf. Once a creature is engulfed by The Mould, it will inject thousands of spores into any orifice it can find, causing its victim to suffer 3d6 poison damage per round while they remain engulfed. A creature can escape The Mould by breaking free, but to do so must make a successful DC 15 strength save. Should The Mould be incapacitated, then any engulfed players are immediately freed.

Mould Virus. At the end of combat, any creatures who took poison damage from The Mould must make a DC 14 Constitution saving throw at the end of each day to determine whether they have become immune to the virus or not.

A creature can fight off the virus by making two consecutive DC 14 Constitution saves, or by swallowing the Mould Virus antidote. Such antidotes are rare and expensive, but should be available in regions where these monsters exist.

Should the infected creature fail three consecutive saves, then they will succumb to a hideous transformation which turns them into The Mould, whereby they will slither upwards to the nearest vantage point to strike new victims. Once this occurs, the effects are irreversible.

THE INFERNAL PRINCESS (The Immortal Princess)

The Infernal Princess is a famed automaton designed by diabolical minds who soon lived to regret their creation. Intricately constructed in the 18th century by genius engineer Alexander Mackintosh for a Prussian king, this life-sized clockwork doll became forever cursed. Fused with the soul of a tormented young woman, this beautiful but chilling machine corrupts all who come near it.

Trapped for centuries in the cold, hard shell of this exquisite construction, the tortured spirit of the young woman has become jealous and spiteful, craving adoration and unquestioning servitude from the minions under her terrible rule. With each unfortunate creature she claims, comes an ever greater desire to be revered.

She will not be content until all worship The Infernal Princess.

THE INFERNAL PRINCESS

Medium construct, chaotic evil

Armor Class 18 (Natural Armor)

Hit Points 270

Speed 10 ft.

STR	DEX	CON	INT	WIS	CHA
2 (-4)	2 (-4)	22 (+6)	22 (+6)	18 (+4)	16 (+3)

Saving Throws Con +11, Int +11

Damage Resistance fire

Damage Immunities poison, psychic

Condition Immunities charmed, poisoned

Senses truesight 120 ft.

Languages Telepathy 120 ft.

Challenge Rating 14 (11,500 XP)

Actions

Multiattack. The Infernal Princess can make three attacks, one with its Infernal Gaze, and two spellcasting actions.

Infernal Gaze. Range 50 feet, requires line of sight between The Infernal Princess and target creature. The Infernal Princess opens her eyes to emit an invisible ray of pure despair, causing 4d8 +3 Psychic Damage. The creature must also make a DC 18 Wisdom save to avoid becoming frightened.

Infernal Charm. A powerful and evil version of the charm spell forces any hostile creature within the line of sight of The Infernal Princess, along with any hostile creature within 15 feet, to make a DC 18 Wisdom save to resist the effect of Infernal Charm. Should a creature fail to make their save, they will become consumed with a violent desire to murder anyone hostile to the Infernal Princess, and must attack, with the most powerful means at their disposal, any creatures aiming to destroy her.

The effects will last for 24 hours, when the creature must roll a DC 15 Wisdom save to escape the effect for good. Should they fail their save a second time, then they will develop the Infernal Slave Condition described below.

Infernal Slave Condition. Anyone at risk of developing the Infernal Slave Condition should be restrained, or they may vanish forever in servitude to the Infernal Princess. To cure this condition requires a high-level dispel magic scroll performed by a very experienced magic-user.

Without restraint, any creature suffering from the Infernal Slave Condition will abandon their home and comrades to live alongside the Infernal Princess. There, they will act as a guard, agent, and soldier in her perverse version of a royal court, ready to sacrifice their lives at a moment's notice to please her.

Innate Spellcasting. The Infernal Princess's spellcasting ability is Charisma DC 18. The Infernal Princess can innately cast the following spells, requiring no material components.
At will: Command, Compulsion

THE SPIDER MOTHER OF HOIA BACIU

This ancient and monstrous spider has cleverly taken the shape of a woman, or part of a woman, to instil terror in her preferred human quarry. Once the Spider Mother makes its lair in a forest, it is soon overwhelmed by legions of her ghastly spider children.

Scuttling expertly under cover of the dark forest canopy, the Spider Mother of Hoia Baciu ambushes unwary travellers who dare to venture near her nest. With her large pincer fangs, she paralyses her prey before enshrouding them in a silky cocoon to drag back to her lair. There, they remain in a state of wakened hibernation, kept fresh and ready to feed her hungry spawn upon hatching.

THE SPIDER MOTHER OF HOIA BACIU

Medium monstrosity, neutral evil

Armor Class 13 (Natural Armor)

Hit Points 90

Speed 30 ft., spider climb 60ft.

STR	DEX	CON	INT	WIS	CHA
13 (+1)	15 (+2)	12 (+1)	7 (-2)	14 (+2)	7 (-2)

Saving Throws Dex +4, Wis +4

Damage Resistance poison

Vulnerability fire

Damage Immunities poison

Condition Immunities poisoned

Senses darkvision 60 ft., web sense

Languages Telepathy 60 ft.

Challenge Rating 2 (450 XP)

Actions

Multiattack. The Spider Mother of Hoia Baciu can make two attacks, one bite and one Baciu Shriek.

Bite Attack. Melee Weapon Attack: +2 to hit, reach 10 ft., 1d8 piercing damage. Creature must make a DC 13 Constitution save or take 2d8 poison damage and become paralyzed.

Baciu Shriek. Any hostile creatures within 30 ft. must make a DC 13 Wisdom saving throw or become frightened for an hour. Should the creature successfully make a save, they will become immune to the Baciu Shriek for 24 hours.

Web Sense. While in contact with a web, the Spider Mother of Hoia Baciu knows the exact location of any other creature in contact with the same web.

Spider Climb. The creature can climb difficult surfaces, including upside down on ceilings, without needing to make an ability check.

Web Walker. The creature ignores movement restrictions caused by webbing.

Childlings of Hoia Baciu. The Spider Mother of Hoia Baciu can spend an action, once per day to produce a spawn of 1d6 Giant Spiders.

TOOTH

Tooth is a creature of legend, born from the vengeful spirit of a boy whose life was taken by practitioners of the dark arts. These occultists were so disdainful of the boy that they fed his corpse to a group of pigs, but it was there that they made their great mistake.

The magic which had powered their ritual contained remnants which remained with the boy, providing a supernatural resurrection in the form of Tooth.

As an undead pig-man with a mission to destroy all evil-doers, Tooth began by enacting a campaign of revenge against those who murdered him. As a pig god of sorts, Tooth has retained a special connection with the pigs who consumed him, who now follow him wherever he goes, ready to protect him whenever they are summoned.

TOOTH

Undead medium, lawful good

Armor Class **11** (Natural Armor)

Hit Points 78

Speed 30 ft.

STR	DEX	CON	INT	WIS	CHA
17 (+3)	10 (+0)	15 (+2)	10 (+0)	11 (+0)	8 (-1)

Saving Throws Str +3, Con +2

Damage Resistance none

Vulnerability none

Damage Immunities non-silver weapons

Condition Immunities none

Senses darkvision 30 ft.

Languages Common

Challenge Rating 4 (1100 XP)

Actions

Multiattack. Tooth makes three attacks, one with its tusk and two with its hooves.

Tusk. Melee Weapon Attack: +5 to hit, reach 5ft. Hit: 2d6 +3 piercing damage.

Hoof. Melee Weapon Attack +5 to hit, 5ft. Hit: 2d6 +3 bludgeoning damage, the target creature must also make a DC 13 Strength saving throw or is knocked prone.

Boar Brethren. Once per day, Tooth can summon 1d6 wild boars who will fight to the death to protect their master.

Bestial Revenge. Tooth is thrown into a rage when confronted by evil alignment characters and will gain advantage against them in combat.

Primal Relentlessness. (recharges after a Short or Long rest). Tooth is one of the most tenacious creatures in the forest, and to kill one takes a lot of work. Should Tooth use its primal relentlessness ability, then it will take an excess of 14 points of damage below zero, from a single opponent, to kill Tooth, or it will restore itself to one hitpoint.

BLACK SANTA

Black Santa is the evil twin to his red-tunic-wearing counterpart, Santa Claus. Unlike his beloved brother, Black Santa prefers to foment chaos and violence, culminating in a sacred act in which he bites off an appendage of his specially-chosen Christmas victim.

His marked victim is never random, but will be chosen from someone who he tests in the guise of a beggar or someone in need. Whichever creature is least helpful or cruel will become his latest victim, whose atonement can only be achieved with the loss of an appendage.

Black Santa does not seek to kill his victim, but rather to torment them during the night, and to consume the chosen appendage. Once a victim has lost an appendage, they are forever marked, and must leave a gift for Black Santa in the form of flesh each year, or he will return, on the hunt for another appendage.

BLACK SANTA

Medium fiend (devil), lawful evil

Armor Class 15 (Natural Armor)

Hit Points 175

Speed 30 ft.

STR	DEX	CON	INT	WIS	CHA
20 (+5)	17 (+3)	20 (+5)	12 (+1)	12 (+1)	13 (+1)

Saving Throws Str +7, Con +8

Damage Resistance lightning

Vulnerability naughty children

Damage Immunities cold, poison

Condition Immunities poisoned

Senses darkvision 120 ft.

Languages Devil, Common

Challenge Rating 7 (2900 XP)

Actions

Multiattack. Black Santa makes two attacks, one with appendage bite and one with Christmas Battleaxe.

Appendage Bite. Melee Weapon Attack: +7 to hit, reach 5 ft. Hit 2d10 +4 piercing damage.

On a critical hit, Black Santa will successfully sever a randomly determined appendage.

On the roll of a D4 the missing appendage is:
(1-Left Hand, 2-Right Hand, 3-Left Foot and 4-Right Foot).

The missing limb will soon become irreplaceable and cannot be restored by healing, owing to the magical nature of Black Santa's bite. If Black Santa can be incapacitated or persuaded to return the stolen appendage, then the affected creature must seek a high-level healing spell to rejoin the appendage within 24 hours. However, if Black Santa possesses the appendage from his chosen victim, then it will attempt to escape, vanishing in a puff of smoke in 3 rounds.

Christmas Battleaxe. Melee Weapon Attack: +7 to hit, reach 10 ft. Hit 1d8 +5 slashing damage. Black Santa can strike two opponents simultaneously if they are standing within 5 feet of one another.

Merciless Appetite. If the targeted player is incapacitated, Black Santa may expend a round to bite off an appendage as described in the rules for Appendage Bite.

Bad Boys and Girls. Black Santa will always present himself as an NPC to test the morality of creatures. Whichever creature misbehaves the most is the one Black Santa will choose to specially target for the purposes of stealing an appendage.

DOLGAD (The Below)

Dolgad is the ancient moniker given to an extremely rare and almost unknowable entity that strikes terror into the hearts of arcane practitioners and magic users from around the world.

This powerful cosmic demon is peerless at inducing severe insanity, before entrapping its victims' souls within its cloak for all eternity—an infinite abyss of chaos, filled with the demented cacophony of screams from countless victims.

To be trapped forever inside a monster as ancient as the universe is perhaps the most terrifying fate of all.

DOLGAD

Huge fiend (demon), chaotic evil

Armor Class 18 (Natural Armor)

Hit Points 265

Speed 20 ft.

STR	DEX	CON	INT	WIS	CHA
10 (+0)	12 (+1)	15 (+2)	21 (+5)	19 (+4)	22 (+6)

Saving Throws Cha +11, Int +10

Damage Resistance cold, fire, lightning

Vulnerability none

Damage Immunities poison

Condition Immunities poisoned

Senses truesight 120 ft.

Magic Resistance Dolgad has advantage on saving throws against spells and other magical effects.

Languages Abyssal, Telepathy, Common

Challenge Rating 13 (10,000 XP)

Actions

Multi-Attack. Dolgad can make three attacks, one Cosmic Lure and two Soul Grasps.

Soul Grasp. Melee Weapon Attack: +5 to hit, reach 15 ft., one target, Hit: 3d6 necrotic damage. Each hit forces the target to make a DC 18 Dexterity saving throw to resist the effects of becoming restrained. A restrained creature can escape by making a successful DC 18 strength save in their next round.

Cosmic Lure. A creature chosen by Dolgad, within 120 ft., must make a charisma DC 18 save to escape falling into a catatonic state where they cannot fight or move for three rounds. The affected creature can reroll their save each round to escape its effects.

Cosmic Envelop. Any creature that fails to escape becoming restrained by Soul Grasp, takes 3d6 necrotic damage per round until Dolgad is incapacitated or the creature has broken free. Creatures that die from the effects of Cosmic Envelop will remain forever trapped inside Dolgad, doomed to spend eternity with a legion of screaming souls.

Innate Spellcasting. Dolgad has an innate spellcasting ability using Charisma (spell save DC 16). It can innately cast the following spells, requiring only verbal components:

3/day each. Compulsion, Crown of Madness, Command.

THE CURSE OF PINNILEKK

Weapon (dagger), legendary

The Curse of Pinnilekk consists of a very rare weapon, which might initially appear to be a crude stone dagger from the neolithic age. However, upon further inspection, one can discern ancient talismans and symbols which hark to its diabolical cosmic past.

The Curse of Pinnilekk curses anyone who holds the blade without the protection of silver gauntlets. When it is held without such protection, it becomes fused to the flesh and the effects of the legendary curse begin.

So rare is this curse that few who perished by its hands ever knew why, or what it was that had killed them. Only the wisest and most experienced masters of lore can identify the curse and provide any hope for a remedy while there is still time.

The 5 Stages of Death by Pinnilekk

A creature afflicted with the curse must make a DC 20 Constitution save at the end of each day. Success will delay the effects of the curse for 24 hours, but a failed save will cause the effects outlined in Stage I. Each failed save thereafter causes the creature to suffer the effects of the next stage.

Stage 1. The creature cannot drop or prise off the dagger from their hand. They will experience fatigue, with the loss of any strength and dexterity bonuses. In a cruel irony, despite their fatigue, the creature will be unable to enjoy long rests, as they are forever afflicted by strange and terrifying dreams of the sea.

Stage 2. The creature's nails drop off from their fingers and toes, and their pupils become white and cloudy. Bonus modifiers for Charisma, Intelligent and Wisdom can not be used, as the victim becomes obsessed with travelling towards the sea.

Stage 3. A disturbing mutation spreads over the creature whereby their skin becomes stretched and smooth, covering over their nostrils, ears and mouth. In this state, the creature is hideous and will suffer half movement and disadvantage in combat. If they are not restrained, they will attempt to flee, rushing towards the nearest coastline.

Stage 4. The creature is entirely covered in a smooth, glistening skin which has removed defining features that might have once made them recognisable. They can no longer hear or speak, but have an instinctual awareness of the direction towards the sea. If the creature makes it towards the shore, they will burrow a hole in the sand and climb inside to await the sea.

Stage 5. If the creature has not reached the sea, they will have become mad with agony, constantly writhing inside their shiny skin suit. If the creature reaches the sea, they will lie face down in the sand inside their burrow. Once the seawater hits them, they simply dissolve, dissipating into the water, never to be seen again.

If they do not reach the sea, then any failed save beyond Stage 5 will cause the creature to shrivel up into dust, leaving only a dried husk of skin. No creature killed in this way can ever be resurrected, making the Curse of Pinnilekk one of the most dreaded fates known to man.

Curing the Curse

The effects of the Curse of Pinnilekk can be cured with a wish spell or by a remove curse spell if it is cast by a celestial or elemental being of the sea. In either case, the dagger itself cannot ever be destroyed, nor can the curse be removed from it. Once a remedy has successfully cured the affected creature, the dagger must be thrown back into the sea within 24 hours, or the affliction will return.

THE DRONE (Dig For Fire)

The Drone, or a Drone, is a psychic demon that buries itself underground in the material world, where it gestates for many years, until its psychic powers have fully matured.

Like a parasite, it will then slowly take over the minds of nearby life forms to aid it in escaping the earth. Once freed, it will consume those same life forms to provide the necessary sustenance to reproduce.

As a Drone takes many years to mature, these demons favour secluded areas to lay their monstrous larvae, where they may grow undisturbed.

THE DRONE

Medium fiend (demon), chaotic evil

Armor Class 12 (Natural Armor)

Hit Points 145

Speed 20 ft.

STR	DEX	CON	INT	WIS	CHA
7 (-2)	9 (-1)	14 (+2)	18 (+4)	16 (+3)	15 (+2)

Saving Throws Int +7, Wis +6

Damage Resistance cold, fire and lightning

Vulnerablility none

Damage Immunities poison

Condition Immunities poisoned

Senses darkvision 120 ft., tremorsense 120 ft.

Languages Telepathy 300 ft.

Challenge Rating 5 (1800 XP)

Actions

Multiattack. The Drone makes two attacks, with its paralysing bite and twisted ray.

Paralysing Bite. Melee Weapon Attack: +1 to hit, reach 5 ft., one target. Hit: 2d6 piercing damage. Following a successful paralysing bite, the injured creature must make a DC 15 Constitution saving throw against the effects of becoming paralysed.

Twisted Ray. Ranged Psychic Attack: +7 to hit, reach 15 ft., one target. Hit: 3d8 +4 psychic damage.

Human Dominion. The Drone is a parasitic demon that feeds off intelligent humanoids, especially human beings. As a result, the creature can cast dominate person at will against any creature within 300 ft. in addition to its attacks. The target creature must make a DC 12 Wisdom saving throw to resist its effects, which will last for one hour or until The Drone is incapacitated.

TALDUR (And It Walked Into The Sea)

Taldur is the name given to a sea creature that is greatly feared among men for its insidious ability to bring about madness and death under the guise of joy and euphoria.

The creature will find a place to nest, often in a cavern or structure along the coast, and from that place will radiate a strange aura that infects the minds of local villagers and townspeople. Over time, the joy is replaced with listlessness and fatigue.

Eventually, they will become so helpless that Taldur can slowly slither from its hiding place to consume its victims, who lie on the ground, powerless to defend themselves, with smiles on their faces.

Once the tell-tale signs of Taldur become evident, there is little time to rescue the innocent inhabitants of a town from a fate worse than death.

TALDUR

Large aberration, true neutral

Armor Class 15 (Natural Armor)

Hit Points 215

Speed 10 ft., swim 60 ft.

STR	DEX	CON	INT	WIS	CHA
17 (+3)	18 (+4)	15 (+2)	20 (+5)	5 (-3)	8 (-1)

Saving Throws Dex +8, Int +9

Damage Resistance cold

Vulnerability none

Damage Immunities poison

Condition Immunities poisoned

Senses blindsight 60 ft.

Languages Deep Speech

Challenge Rating 10 (5900 XP)

Actions

MultiAttack. The Taldur can make four attacks, three with its tentacles and one with its bite.

Tentacle. Melee Attack: +8 to hit, reach 15 ft. one target. Hit: 2d6 +4 bludgeoning damage, creatures that are hit must make DC 13 Strength saving throw to avoid being knocked prone.

Bite. Melee Attack +7 to hit, reach 5 ft. one target. Hit: 2d10 +3 piercing damage.

Underwater Camouflage. The Taldur has advantage on Dexterity (Stealth) checks made while underwater.

Amphibious. The Taldur can breathe air and water.

Sunlight Sensitivity. While in sunlight, the Taldur has disadvantage on attack rolls, as well as on Wisdom (perception) checks that rely on sight.

Cloud of Ink. The Taldur can surround itself with a 20 ft. radius of ink which extends all around the creature to heavily obscure it. After releasing the ink, the creature can use the dash action as a bonus.

Siren Aura of Euphoria. Creatures within a 300 ft. radius of the Taldur must make a DC 16 Wisdom saving throw or they will experience the effects of the aura. Affected creatures become relaxed and are unable to initiate combat except to defend themselves. Every 24 hours, the affected creatures can reroll their save in an attempt to escape the effect of the aura. If a creature should fail their second save they will succumb to the Siren Europhic Condition.

The Siren Europhic Condition. This deadly condition results in the sufferer becoming so euphoric that they become incapable. They will not eat, drink, or sleep, and are incapable of short or long rests, spellcasting, or moving outside the boundaries of the Aura. The only remedy to this condition is to kidnap the sufferer and drag them outside the area of the aura, or destroy the Taldur.

If abandoned to their fate, a creature will eventually perish from the condition within seven days.

MOM & POP

Mom & Pop is the colloquial name given to a mysterious and horrific entity (or pair of entities), which doom those they afflict to constant torment and betrayal until they perish. It is by the act of murder or inducement towards suicide that these entities procreate. That is to say, those who die become like them. Unless one is haunted by them, they cannot be seen.

Suffice to say that the records show very few people to have ever survived a haunting by Mom & Pop, so few, in fact, that many even doubt whether they exist at all.

What instils so much fear among those who do believe in their existence, is the lack of any moral rationality to these creatures who appear to strike randomly at anyone, anywhere. To make matters worse, they do so initially under the pretence of friendship, in some cases maintaining that pretence for years before turning malevolent.

They are the most dangerous of all tricksters and the least merciful.

MOM & POP

Medium aberration, lawful evil

Armor Class 18 (Natural Armor)

Hit Points 285

Speed 30 ft.

STR	DEX	CON	INT	WIS	CHA
10 (+0)	15 (+2)	20 (+5)	21 (+5)	19 (+4)	24 (+7)

Saving Throws Int +10, Cha +12

Damage Resistance radiant, piercing, slashing, bludgeoning from non-magical weapons

Damage Immunities poison

Condition Immunities poisoned

Senses truesight 120 ft.

Languages Telepathy 120 ft.

Challenge Rating 15 (13000 XP)

ACTIONS

Multiattack. The Mom and Pop aberrations make two attacks with their life-draining touch.

Life Draining Touch. Melee Weapon Attack: +12 to hit, reach 5 ft., one target. Hit: 5d10 +7 psychic damage. Each successful attack will restore 2d6 hit points to Mom and Pop.

Hideous Distortion. The Mom and Pop aberration assumes a terrifying and twisted two-dimensional form, forcing intelligent humanoids who see it to make a DC 18 Wisdom saving throw to resist becoming frightened. In their two-dimensional form, Mom and Pop can squeeze through tiny crevices or gaps, and are considered to be in full coverage, but cannot, in this form, take any attack actions.

One True Friend. Mom & Pop are ancient entities with the strange goal of seeking out and tormenting intelligent humanoids until they can be persuaded to kill themselves.

If they have chosen a player, Mom & Pop will first appear under the guise of a helpful NPC husband and wife, providing wisdom, consolation, and advice to assist the player in their adventure. Yet, only the chosen player can see them, as other creatures are left to wonder if their comrade has gone mad, made an imaginary friend, or is even haunted by ghosts! Of course, Mom & Pop have every intention of betraying the creature they have targeted.

For example, Mom & Pop might at first alert the player in the party to a secret cache of treasure, only to betray them the next day with a suggestion to take a fork in the road which might lead to a hidden nest of giant spiders.

Mom & Pop are relentless, and will torment the unfortunate creature, becoming ever more malevolent, until they can persuade the creature to kill themselves.

Tragic Fate. Creatures who do kill themselves as a result of the torments of Mom & Pop, or are killed by them in battle, cannot become resurrected. Instead, their unfortunate souls are doomed to become an aberration whose first goal will be to torment a victim of the opposite sex. Once paired, they will replicate the path of destruction caused by the Mom & Pop that haunted them.

Protection. The method of defeating Mom & Pop consists of a remove curse spell which first requires the creature to learn the true names of Mom & Pop. They will not reveal them easily, but will never refuse to answer with a riddle.

Once the creature has learned their true names, the remove curse spell can work. Once it is performed in the presence of Mom & Pop, they will be forced to take physical form and can be attacked.

THE BLACK HARE

The Black Hare is a legendary and terrifying monster with the ability to change size at will. Once activated, this monster is widely considered to be one of the most dangerous and cruel assassins in the world.

First appearing to its victim as a curious toy covered in telltale polka-dots and a bowtie, The Black Hare torments its target for days with terrifying lullabies of death and relentless mental torture. Finally, the demon strikes, attacking with the intention of kidnapping its victim.

Those unlucky enough to be spared a horrifying death will find themselves committed to The Black Hare's abyssal lair, becoming the eternal plaything of this malicious entity.

THE BLACK HARE

Medium construct, chaotic evil

Armor Class 19 (Natural Armor)

Hit Points 390

Speed 60 ft.

STR	DEX	CON	INT	WIS	CHA
25 (+7)	22 (+6)	20 (+5)	15 (+2)	18 (+4)	12 (+1)

Saving Throws Str +13, Dex +12

Damage Resistance piercing, slashing, bludgeoning from non-magical weapons

Damage Immunities fire, poison

Condition Immunities poisoned

Senses truesight 120 ft.

Languages Telepathic 120 ft., Abyssal

Challenge Rating 20 (25000 XP)

Actions

Multiattack. The Black Hare can make four attacks, two with its claws, a bite, and a manic stare.

Claws. Melee Weapon Attack: +13 to hit, reach 10 ft., one target. Hit: 2d8 +7 slashing damage.

Bite. Melee Weapon Attack: +13 to hit, reach 5 ft., one target. Hit: 4d6 +7 piercing damage.

Manic Stare: The Black Hare can target a hostile creature within 30 ft with which it has a line of sight, with its manic stare, forcing the creature to make a DC 18 Wisdom saving throw, or it will fall prone with despair, unable to move or attack until they make a successful save in their next round.

Fiendish Kidnapping. The Black Hare is a terrifying construct activated with a single purpose in mind, to kidnap its target and drag them to hell. The monster will prioritise this objective over all others, including its own protection.

To achieve its mission it must first make its target victim fall prey to the manic stare. In the following round, The Black Hare will throw the victim over its shoulder. This will provide other players a single round with which to liberate their companion before The Black Hare escapes.

Once seized by The Black Hare, the restrained creature will fall into a catatonic state and will be unable to resist. Creatures can try to liberate the seized player by successfully grappling them with a DC 20 Strength saving throw.

Creatures kidnapped by The Black Hare will not necessarily die, but will awake without their items or clothes in the abyssal planes as a chained plaything of demons. Subsequent campaigns may allow for players to mount a rescue of their imprisoned comrade, or for the affected player to mount an escape from the depths of the abyss.

The 5 Songs of The Black Hare

The Black Hare does not appear without warning, and its intended target will experience strange sights and sounds over the five days before it arrives.

Day 1. The affected creature discovers an inconspicuous toy resembling The Black Hare. For example, they might see it stand out among the children's toys at a market stall.

Day 2. They will awaken at night to strange lullabies sung in a high-pitched voice, with disturbing lyrics featuring themselves suffering in hell.

Day 3. The Black Hare becomes visible at times in the distance, a figure of about 7 feet tall, but always obscured by trees or walls.

Day 4. On the fourth night, The Black Hare will awaken the player during any short or long rest, appearing only inches from their face to produce its notorious song, which harkens to the creature's demise.

"It's time to come with me now... time to come with me."

Any attempt by the creature to strike The Black Hare will cause it to vanish.

Day 5. On the final day, The Black Hare will strike at a time when the target creature is most vulnerable. It is advisable that in such circumstances the targeted creature should surround themselves with guards and maintain constant vigilance. If they can survive the 24 hours of the final day, then they will have survived The Black Hare, who must leave without its prize.

Legendary Item - The Black Hare is a legendary construct, capable of changing from the size of a child's toy to a 7 foot tall giant.

When it is not activated, The Black Hare is 12 inches tall, resembling a wooden puppet. To activate the item, a player must cast The Black Hare ritual which requires a successful DC 20 Wisdom score. Failure means the ritual cannot be attempted again for another three months.

If successful, the toy construct will unnervingly flicker to life, patiently awaiting the spellcaster to whisper the name of its intended victim.

Should The Black Hare complete its task of dragging a soul into hell, it will once again appear somewhere in the material plane in its toy form. If defeated in combat, it will transform back into its original form, and can be kept by the creature who defeated it.

The Black Hare is considered by those with ancient knowledge to be the most effective and terrifying weapon of assassination ever produced.

THE SIREN OF SILVER FALLS

This entity originated from a woman who lost her child due to the inaction or cruelty of others. Consequently, her evil spirit was reborn to take revenge against those who wronged her. Unfortunately, in her lust for revenge, the Siren of Silver Falls does not stop with those who were at fault, and becomes a vengeful spirit, driven especially to consume the innocent children of others.

She will target them initially with beautiful songs and stories, often befriending them over the course of days until the child becomes convinced that they belong to her. Suddenly, and without warning, she will strike them, or any of her intended victims, with a ghastly attack for which she is well known. Capable of splitting her upper body open, she will create a mouth from the gaping chasm of her wound and swallow her victim whole, or piece by piece.

She is also a capable deceiver, and upon first encounter might try to trick creatures into bringing children to her, claiming that hers are lost.

THE SIREN OF SILVER FALLS

Medium undead, lawful evil

Armor Class 15 (Natural Armor)

Hit Points 151

Speed 30 ft.

STR	DEX	CON	INT	WIS	CHA
14 (+2)	15 (+2)	14 (+2)	12 (+1)	13 (+1)	16 (+3)

Saving Throws Dex +5, Con +5

Damage Resistance necrotic

Vulnerability radiant

Damage Immunities poison

Condition Immunities poisoned

Senses darkvision 60 ft.

Languages Common

Challenge Rating 7 (2900 XP)

Actions

Multiattack. The Siren of Silver Falls makes two attacks, one with its phantom claws and another with its body split attack.

Body Split Attack. Melee Weapon Attack: +5 to hit, reach 5ft., Hit: 1d12 +2 piercing damage. Every creature within 15ft of the Siren of Silver Falls must make a DC 15 Wisdom saving throw or become frightened. Affected creatures can reroll their saves each round. On a successful save, they become immune to the effects for 24 hours.

Phantom Claws. Melee Weapon Attack: +5 to hit, reach 5ft., Hit: Damage 1d6 +2 slashing damage

Call of the Silver Falls. The Siren of Silver Falls produces a unique and beautiful song which has lured many to their deaths. Any intelligent humanoid within 120 ft. may succumb to her song should they fail a DC 15 Wisdom saving throw; in which case they become charmed for an hour.

MAGRET (The Reunion)

Magret is the name given to this cosmological monstrosity, who appears as a fish-like woman wearing a white dress with razor-sharp claws and a scream liable to make a man's head explode.

She first appeared at the vaunted reunion of a prince and princess who had been separated for years. Their meeting went startlingly awry when a spell intended to restore the princess's fair looks went horribly wrong.

The monster she became was consumed by the insidious minds of the ancient gods of the sea, and what remained of the princess was extinguished in an instant. Now, she lurks as a predator in the material world, acting as a spy and assassin for gods beyond human memory.

MAGRET

Medium monstrosity, chaotic evil

Armor Class 15 (Natural Armor)

Hit Points 165

Speed 30 ft., swim 60 ft.

STR	DEX	CON	INT	WIS	CHA
22 (+6)	14 (+2)	16 (+3)	8 (-1)	18 (+4)	6 (-2)

Saving Throws Str +9, Wis +7

Damage Resistance none

Vulnerability none

Damage Immunities none

Condition Immunities none

Senses darkvision 120 ft.

Languages Deep Speech

Challenge Rating 7 (2900 XP)

ACTIONS

Magret makes two attacks, with its claws, or it can make one head rip attack.

Claw. Melee Weapon Attack: +9 to hit, reach 5 ft., one target. Hit: 1d8 +9 slashing damage.

Head Rip. Melee Weapon Attack: +9 to hit, reach 5 ft., one target. Hit: forces the creature to make a DC 18 Strength save (or DC 15 with athletics) to successfully escape the attack, while a fail causes the creature to take 5d6 +9 bludgeoning damage and the target becoming restrained.

A creature can escape being restrained by successfully making a DC 18 Strength saving throw in their next round. For every round the creature remains trapped, they will suffer an additional 5d6 +9 bludgeoning damage.

When the creature reaches zero hit points, Magret will tear off its head and consume it as a bonus action, replenishing 2d10 hit points.

Magret cannot make any other melee weapon attacks while the target creature remains restrained.

Amphibious. Magret can breathe air and water.

Scream of the Sea. Magret produces an ancient scream of cosmological terror, forcing any target creature within 35 feet to make a DC 15 Constitution saving throw. A successful save will cause the creature to take 2d8 thunder damage, but a failed save will result in 4d8 thunder damage, as well as the deafened condition. This ability cannot be used while Magret is engaged in melee combat.

Path of Decay. Magret can often be tracked by the strange trail of decayed plants and wildlife she leaves in her wake. Anyone who touches or stands in the path of decay while it is less than 24 hours old, must make a DC 12 Constitution save or take 1d8 necrotic damage.

THE WOMAN IN WHITE

No one knows for sure what caused the curse of the Woman in White. Was it a betrayed lover who took her own life, or perhaps the spirit of a vengeful woman wronged by men? Her origins remain a mystery, but what is known for a fact is that the Woman in White is a deadly and uncanny apparition whose lairs soon become landmarks to avoid on any map.

Known for her friendly wave and smile, anyone who sees this apparition appear on the top of a lonely hill is advised to avoid eye contact, and not to acknowledge her presence. Those failing to do so will find themselves subject to her malevolent and relentless pursuit.

THE WOMAN IN WHITE

Medium undead, lawful evil

Armor Class 15 (Natural Armor)

Hit Points 135

Speed 30 ft.

STR	DEX	CON	INT	WIS	CHA
18 (+4)	14 (+2)	18 (+4)	13 (+1)	16 (+2)	18 (+4)

Saving Throws Str +7, Con +7

Damage Resistance fire, cold

Vulnerability none

Damage Immunities necrotic, poison

Condition Immunities poisoned

Senses darkvision 120 ft.

Languages none

Challenge Rating 7 (2900 XP)

Actions

Multiattack. The Woman in White makes two melee weapon attacks with her life draining claws.

Life Draining Claws. Weapon Melee Attack: +7 to hit, reach 5 ft., one target. Hit: 3d8 necrotic damage, and the Woman in White restores hit points at a rate of half the damage caused.

Dark Regeneration. The Woman in White regains ten hit points at the start of its round. This ability cannot be used in the next round if the Woman in White suffers radiant damage.

Immortal Birth. The Woman in White is cursed never to perish and will regenerate in its lair within 1d6 +1 days.

Cursed Lair. The Woman in White can appear over a wide radius once she has found her victim, but she has no power beyond a range of 75 miles from the place she is first sighted.

The Curse of the Woman in White

A Woman in White is usually first encountered atop her lair, most often a lonely hill by an abandoned road. There, she will be seen waving cheerfully at some distance, but will not walk when summoned, or speak when spoken to. Any attempts to reach the Woman in White are futile, as creatures who climb the hill never find her waiting there.

If a creature looks at her for too long or tries to communicate with her, they will become marked. A marked creature will notice the Woman in White again and again over the course of days, but each time she will appear to get closer, and every time they are the only ones who can see her.

On the third night, if the creature remains in the lair's area of effect, the Woman in White will appear to the creature in a hideous nightmare during a long rest. At this point, they will awaken to see her standing before them. In the combat that follows, the Woman in White starts with initiative and advantage.

FEAR GORTA (The Bog)

The Fear Gorta is a monster of Irish origin, known to haunt the bogs, swamps and marshlands, usually taking the form of an emaciated old man clutching a metal rod with a burning torch.

The creature will typically approach travellers to beg for food, requesting alms for the poor, and should they be considerate, the Fear Gorta will move on peacefully.

However, if among the party of travellers there is one who insults the Fear Gorta, then they will become marked as prey. The old man may disappear into the mists of the boglands, but he will soon return in a demonic form too terrifying to imagine.

FEAR GORTA

Medium fiend (shapechanger), lawful evil

Armor Class 15 (Natural Armor)

Hit Points 165

Speed 30 ft., burrow 60 ft.

STR	DEX	CON	INT	WIS	CHA
16 (+3)	18 (+4)	16 (+3)	8 (-1)	18 (+4)	6 (-2)

Saving Throws Dex +7, Wis +7

Damage Resistance cold

Vulnerability none

Damage Immunities necrotic, poison

Condition Immunities poisoned

Senses darkvision 120 ft.

Languages Abyssal, Common

Challenge Rating 7 (2900 XP)

Actions

Multiattack. Fear Gorta makes two melee weapon attacks, one with its Grotesque Bite and another with its claw.

Claw Attack. Melee Weapon Attack +6 to hit, reach 5 ft, one target. Hit: 2d6 +3 slashing damage.

Grotesque Bite. Melee Weapon Attack: +6 to hit, reach 10 ft., one target. Hit: 2d8 +3 piercing damage. The targeted creature must make a DC 15 Strength saving throw to resist becoming restrained. The Fear Gorta can swallow a restrained creature in the following round if it makes another successful grotesque bite attack.

While swallowed, the target is blinded and restrained, it has total cover against attacks and other effects outside the Fear Gorta, and it takes 5d6 acid damage at the start of the Fear Gorta's turns. The Fear Gorta can have only one creature swallowed at a time.

THE NIGHTMARE (The Carnival)

The Nightmare is a large jelly creature that often makes its lair inside carnivals and circuses. Once it has infected such a place, it will employ its mind control abilities to take over the minds of entertainers such as clowns, turning them into psychic pawns.

The entertainment and frivolity will continue under the control of The Nightmare, keeping secret the hideous monstrosity lurking just behind the facade of fun. Its pawns will identify those children who had the most fun at the event, and they will then be kidnapped and fed to the monster. Victims are slowly absorbed and dissolved inside his jelly body.

It should be noted that The Nightmare makes its home in places of joy and merriment precisely because happy victims taste the most delicious.

THE NIGHTMARE (The Carnival)

Huge ooze, chaotic evil

Armor Class 18 (Natural Armor)

Hit Points 295

Speed 10 ft.

STR	DEX	CON	INT	WIS	CHA
25 (+6)	18 (+4)	23 (+1)	18 (+4)	20 (+5)	19 (+4)

Saving Throws Str +11, Wis +10

Damage Resistance poison

Vulnerability fire

Damage Immunities acid

Condition Immunities grapple

Senses blindsight 60 ft.

Languages Telepathy

Challenge Rating 17 (18000 XP)

ACTIONS

Multiattack. The Nightmare can make four attacks, three with its large tentacles and a fourth with its giant mouth.

Large Tentacle. Melee Weapon Attack: +11 to hit, 20 ft., one target. Hit: 3d10 +6 acid damage. Any creature which takes damage must make a DC 18 Strength saving throw or become restrained.

Giant Mouth. Melee Weapon Attack: +11 to hit, 5 ft., one target. Hit: 6d6 +6 acid damage. A creature that suffers damage from The Nightmare's giant mouth must make a DC 18 Strength check to resist becoming engulfed. The engulfed creature can't breathe, is restrained, and takes 4d6 +6 acid damage at the start of each of The Nightmare's turns.

An engulfed creature can try to escape by taking an action to make a DC 18 Strength check. On a success, the creature escapes and enters a space of its choice within 5 feet of The Nightmare.

Large Flip. The Nightmare can elect to flip a restrained creature skywards so that it might land inside its giant mouth. The monster must make a large tentacle attack roll as standard, with a successful score resulting in the restrained creature becoming engulfed. A failed attack will see the creature thrown from the tentacle 1d10 +10 feet in a random direction from The Nightmare. If the creature lands on solid ground, they will take 1d10 bludgeoning damage and if they hit a hard object such as a building, they will take 2d10 bludgeoning damage.

Innate Spellcasting. The Nightmare has an innate spellcasting ability using Charisma (spell save DC 18). The Nightmare can innately cast the following spells, requiring no material components:

At will: Dominate Person, Dominate Monster.

Clown Horde. The Nightmare is protected by a bodyguard of D20 +10 mind-controlled clowns, fanatics who are immune to charm or becoming frightened, who will fight to the death to protect their master. Should The Nightmare be incapacitated, the clown's free will and minds will be restored.

Acknowledgements

We would like to thank the following backers, without whom the creation of this book would not have been possible:

A Braunsdorf
A.C. Hasfjord
A.P. Sessler
Adam John Wakeling
Adam Primaeros
Adam Wragg
Alex Joyner
Alexander Zorn
Alistair Bowe
Andre van Mierlo
Andrea Migone
Andrea Zimei
Angela Conner
Ant O'Reilly
Arnaud D'haijère
Arthur Petersen
Bernd Linke
Bill Eikost
Bobby Williams
Brandon Ingalls
Brendan McDonnell
Brett Erik Johnson
Brian Friedman
Brook Hubbard
Bruce Todd
Carlos "Big-Fortuna" Macera
Cato Vandrare
Charles Stiefel
ChipDaleRotteveel
Chris Basler
Chris Douglass
Chris Vick
Christian Schlüter
Christopher Dunnbier
Christopher H. Svara
Christopher Meyer
Cody Van Der Haegen
Colby Swanson
Craig and Rosie
Crystal Taylor
Daniel Ley
Danielle Yagodich
Darren "Deadman" Manion
Darren Lee Simpson
David Hamilton
David Lars Chamberlain
David Massey
David Rains
David Ross
David S
Della-Ann Sewell
Devin Spurrill
Diane Summerisle
DJ Silvae of Decennial Gothica Radio
Doug Roos
Dr.Rev. Matthias666
DrLight
Dylan Stump
Eamonn Daly
Edward Drummond
Elbert D. Wall
Emanuele Pallozzi
Eric Nathaniel M Henson
Eric TC Lee
Evelyn Hall
Everett A Warren
Farron Sutton
Francesc Quilis
Frank Acevedo
Freddie Premo
Garry Peak
Gary
Gary Grice
Gavin Hugh
Geoff McHugh
Giles Harris
Graeme "Synoiz" Donaldson
Greg Kirkpatrick
Greg Orsi
HanoverFiste
Hans Eriksson
Hereward L. M. Proops
Iain Mitchell Leslie
Ian Weiss
Il Principe di Firenze
Ilan Sheady
J.J ten Hoopen
James Wagner
Jason Epstein
Jason Feigles
JC Hawley
Jean-Luc
Jeremiah Rider
Jeremy Terry
Jim Dowell
Joe Biggs
Johann Ingi Albertsson
John Holwick
John Ozment
Jon A. Cohorn
Jon Vangdal Aamaas
Jonathan Cabildo
Jonathan Dolan
Jonathan McLain
Joseph F. Emmerth
Joshua Doohen
Juan Fernandez
Julien Lévêque
Kat Morgan
Keith Robson
Kevin J Thomas
Kevin Lawrence
Kevin M. Williams
Khell
Kira Dinesen
Kristopher Gannon
Kupara Primaeros
Kyle Curry
Landon Adams
Larry DeHaan
Laurie Webb
Leah Rae
Lena Laub
Leon Hitter
Lesley-Ann Kiriyama
Leslie Laurence
Libby
Linnea Pearson
Lisa Gargano
Lisa Sustaita
Logan Maxwell
Luca "Leyart" Galli
Lynne Scanlon
LynnMarie Panzarino
M. Chick
Maeve Swain
MAF
Maisy Kay

MajorEnby
Marc Lalancette
Marcel Osenroth
Marco Mancini
Marcus Luft
Maria Hubble
Mark Strazhari
Markus Rütters
Mary Connell
Mathias
Matt Jackson
Matt Orefice
Matteo Santini (medio)
Matthew Sumner
Megan Matta
Michael A. Bosco
Michael Dean
Michael Di Salvo
Michael McConville
Michael Sullivan
Michal Rudz-ki
Michelle Connealy
Micky & Claire Kay
Mike Shema
Mike Siwy
Mike Whelan
Miranda Murphy
Morrigan Schomburg
Morten Wisting
Natasha R Chisdes
Nick Eldritch
Nick Ford
Nick Williams
Nigel Curl
Norman Canestorp
Obscura Filmfestival
Olivia Gardner
Panagiotis Athanasiou
Paul Bradford
Paul Dulski
Paul Noffsinger
Pete Fitchett
Pete John
Peter 'Fobsee' Roberts
Peter Graham Simpson
Peter Hopkins
Peter L Brown
Peter Ritson
Phil Nicholls
Philip Pagac
Putt
Q Fortier
Ralph J. Bellantoni
Randall S. Lloyd
Raphael Möckli
Rayan J. de Zeeuw
Rhel ná DecVandé
Rhiannon Crothers
Rich Graysonn
Richard J Miller
Richard Pate
Robert Harding
Robert Hood
Rod Meek
Rogulynx
Roisín McCormac
Ronald Tremblay
Ronny Heinz
Ross Hardy (Thineayngel)
Ryan Baumann
Samuel Falkingham
Sarah Morningstar
Scott Bates
Scott Fairgrieve
Sjoerd Klinkenberg
Slayeriste
Sonia Martin
Stephen Jolly
Steve Aucoin
Steve De Roover
Steven Paul Smith
Steven Sullivan
Talal Alyouha And Fatma Ashkanani
Terry Rumbold
The Bevis Foundation
The Carpenters
Therion Bloodsworn
Thomas Kozlowski jr
Thomas Richardson
THUMPA
Tim Easley
Tim Janis
Timothy Boersma
Tobias Gasser
Tony & Tracey Salmon
Toymax
Travis S.
Trevor A. Ramirez
Trevor Harbeard
Unrealistin
Val Martina
Veli-Pekka Muikku
Vincent Franco
Walt Dueck
Whitley's
Will Morton
Winston Kou
Wontolla
Yadin "Ebonweaver" Flammer
Zein Mayassi
Zeke Hanson
Zeke Hubris

Legal Information